James Edwin Thorold Rogers

A Manual of Political Economy

James Edwin Thorold Rogers

A Manual of Political Economy

ISBN/EAN: 9783337077273

Printed in Europe, USA, Canada, Australia, Japan

Cover: Foto ©Paul-Georg Meister /pixelio.de

More available books at **www.hansebooks.com**

Clarendon Press Series

A MANUAL

OF

POLITICAL ECONOMY

FOR SCHOOLS AND COLLEGES

BY

JAMES E. THOROLD ROGERS

*Dans l'isolement, nos besoins surpassent nos facultés.
Dans l'état social, nos facultés surpassent nos besoins.*

BASTIAT.

THIRD EDITION REVISED

WITH INDEX

Oxford

AT THE CLARENDON PRESS

M DCCC LXXVI

[*All rights reserved*]

PREFACE TO THE FIRST EDITION.

THE Delegates of the Clarendon Press, having determined on issuing a series of manuals intended for educational purposes, have entrusted me with the duty of supplying a short treatise on Political Economy. The several topics discussed in this little work have formed the material for certain courses of lectures which I have given during some years in London and Oxford, though they are presented in the following pages in a condensed form, many historical and statistical illustrations being omitted. These illustrations, which should be supplied by the teacher, are of the utmost importance in the study of the science, for just as the historian who is ignorant of the interpretations of political economy is constantly mazed in a medley of unconnected and unintelligible facts, so the economist who disdains the inductions of history is sure to utter fallacies. Much of the merit of Adam Smith's great work is derived from the steady use which this philosopher made of history and statistics, though in his time the former was uncritical, the latter were inexact.

There is I believe reason to differ from some of the views generally entertained by economists on the subjects of Population, Rent, Wages, Profit, and one or two other cognate terms. My reader will be able to judge whether I have succeeded in substantiating the conclusions at which I have arrived on those topics. The ordinary theory of Rent is not historically supported by the facts which it has assumed, and the theory of Population is closely connected with that of Rent.

It is unnecessary that I should comment on the importance of exactly demonstrating all such social laws as the economist attempts to collect. Errors in such inferences are always more mischievous than any other fallacies; most mischievous when the social system of any country is in course of reconstruction, and at a time when the people whose institutions are being remodelled are slow to accept the rule of the great French economist, *Tous les intérêts légitimes sont harmoniques.*

OXFORD, *March* 11, 1868.

PREFACE TO THE THIRD EDITION.

IN the third edition of this book, certain modifications and corrections have been made, partly with the view of bringing out more clearly the inferences at which I have arrived, partly in relation to events which, having occurred since the publication of the second edition, have thrown fresh light on the topics treated here. Thus, for example, the probability of a trade union extending to agricultural labourers was considered to be exceedingly remote in 1869. But the fact has come, and with it those results which might have been foreseen with certainty. Again, it was thought expedient to illustrate the meaning of capital and profit, and to distinguish these terms from others with which they are frequently and mischievously confused. There is no science in which a clear perception of the true definitions which must be given to words is more important than in Political Economy, none certainly in which loose usages have led to more serious fallacies.

In the last, or nearly the last, letter which I received

from my friend the late Mr. J. S. Mill, and dated April, 1870, occurs the following passage: 'I rather think that I differ from you on some important points; but the old generalisations of Political Economy are now found to require so much modification, that our opinions may possibly draw nearer together when duly compared.' I find that the views which I have expressed in this and other works on the subject, are gradually recognised in the United States, and Germany, and I quote the words of the most distinguished economist of modern times in order to show that there is still need of careful inductive reasoning, in order that Political Economy may be free from the charge of onesidedness or dogmatism.

JAMES E. THOROLD ROGERS.

OXFORD, *Jan.* 7, 1876.

CONTENTS.

CHAPTER I.

Introductory. 1—6.

	PAGE
Mutual services the basis of civilisation	1
Particular services only expounded by economists	2
Acts of exchange imply reciprocal benefits	3
Error of believing that one man's gain is another's loss	4
Origin of such an error	5

CHAPTER II.

The Cause of Value. 6—18.

Some articles have no economical value	6
What articles have this value. Labour the cause of value	7
Labour not necessarily disagreeable	8
Expedients by which labour is economised. Tools and implements	9
Co-operation of labour. Division of labour	10
Effects of this division. Dexterity of the workman	12
Variation in rates of wages	13
Unnecessary divisions of labour	14
Development of machinery	15
Equalisation of the price of commodities	15
Division of labour enlarges the market	16
Cost of production the general test of value	17

CHAPTER III.

The Measure of Value. 18—35.

	PAGE
Variation in the values of different articles at different periods	18
No general rise or fall in values possible	20
Difference between value and price	21
A common measure of value necessary	22
Origin of the use of money	22
Money the machinery of trade	24
Errors which have arisen from misinterpreting the functions of money	24
Policy of our forefathers	25
Money, a pledge	26
Why gold and silver are used	27
Variations in the relative value of gold and silver	29
Inconveniences of a double currency	30
Other conditions of a measure of value	31
Coins, the origin of	33
Fraudulent issues of base money	34
Effects of in England in the sixteenth century	34

CHAPTER IV.

The Substitutes for Money. 36—47.

Reasons why people take money	36
But they take it in order to use it	36
Why people hoard	37
Communities use as little money as they possibly can	38
Economies of money. Bills of exchange	38
Deposits with bankers	39
Issues of notes	41
Notes in excess of specie	43
Quantities which a banker can venture on issuing	43
Notes cannot be issued except on gold and silver	44
Effects of a paper currency issued on other values	46

CHAPTER V.

The Distribution of the Price of Products. 47—53.

	PAGE
Many contribute to an object, and each receives a portion of its price	47
But the recipients reducible to three heads	48
Every community must have saved something	49
That which is saved is capital, in whatever form it may be rendered useful	50
Wages, what they are	50
Profit, what it strictly is	51
Rent the residue of the price when wages and profit are satisfied .	52

CHAPTER VI.

Capital. 54—62.

The meaning of capital; its origin 54
The employment of capital 55
Relations of capital and labour 56
Profits of capital 57
Accumulation of capital 58
Errors made by labourers and capitalists 59
Credit not capital, except metaphorically 62

CHAPTER VII.

Labour and Wages. 63—68.

Wages of labour determined by certain causes 63
Adult labour an investment of capital 64
Food of the labourer relevant to his rate of wages . . . 65
Capital invested in labour must be replaced. 66
Labour must be understood in a generic sense 67

CHAPTER VIII.

The Growth of Population. 68—80.

	PAGE
The common theory of population first stated by Malthus	68
Restraints on marriage	69
Customary food of the people	71
The case of the Irish and Belgians	72
Population in the middle ages	73
Alarms of over-population exaggerated	74
Historical circumstances which contributed to the theory of Malthus	75
Instances of excessive supply of labour	77

CHAPTER IX.

Restrictions on Occupation. 80—112.

Artificial restraints attempted in many cases	80
Trade privileges accorded in early times	81
Formation of companies	82
Restrictions in professions	84
Laws regulating wages, origin of	86
Trades-unions originally retaliatory	88
Effect of trades-unions on capital	90
Effect of such unions on rent	91
Trades-unions in the case of articles freely imported	94
On articles produced only at home	95
Effect of unions on unprotected labour	96
Hypothesis of labour being universally protected	97
Trades-unions a phase of Protection	99
The criticism on trades-unions merely economical	100
Remedial schemes. Diminution of persons competing for wages	101
Thrifty habits, and the possession of savings	102
Co-operation in supply, &c.	105
Continental co-operation	106
Plan of M. Schultze Delitzsch	107
Associations of employers and operatives	109
Difficulties in raising the condition of the peasant	111

CONTENTS. xiii

CHAPTER X.

On the Causes which depress the Rate of Wages. 112—132.

	PAGE
Maintenance and training at public cost	113
The use of endowments	114
The nature of education	115
Effects of general education	118
Maintenance of labourers by poor-laws	119
The origin of the custom, religious	120
Sketch of the history of poor-laws	121
Law of settlement	123
Open and close parishes	124
Effect of legal assistance on the labourer	127
Effect of machinery on wages	129

CHAPTER XI.

Profit and Interest. 132—152.

Profit and interest really identical	132
Nature of good-will or connexion	134
Self-acting honesty	135
The Rochdale co-operators	135
The indolence of customers a cause of 'good-will'	138
Money lent is the power of purchasing goods or labour	139
Interest once forbidden	140
Conditions under which loans are made	141
Public and private credit	142
Abundance or scarcity of capital	143
Different rates of interest in land investments and mortgages	145
Discounts, nature of	147
Contrast of discount and interest	149
Variation in the rate of discount, causes of	150

CHAPTER XII.

Rent of Land. 152—168.

	PAGE
Importance of rent in English systems of Political Economy	152
'Natural powers' of the soil	153
Theory that best soils were first cultivated, and that poorer soils were occupied as population increased, not historical	155
Origin of the common theory of rent	157
Agriculture five centuries ago	158
Peculiar position of landowners when the art of agriculture is improved	160
Proper definition of rent	161
Corn-laws and their repeal	162
Rent of business-premises	163
Various rents of corn and meadow land	164
Rents of the middle ages	166
Causes which raise rent	166

CHAPTER XIII.

Various Tenancies of Agricultural Land. 168—185.

Métayer tenancy	169
Once prevailed in England	170
Peasant proprietors	171
Often burdened by debts	172
Disadvantages of small holdings	173
Cottier tenancy	177
Early Irish land system	177
Peculiarities in the Irish social system	178
Scarcity price of land	179
Deplorable condition of Irish under the system	181
Apparent remedy for Irish agrarian disaffection	183
Claim of tenant right	185

CHAPTER XIV.

Demand and Supply. 185—200.

	PAGE
Meaning of the terms	186
Degrees of demand	186
Exhibited in the price of necessaries and conveniences	188
Effects of the corn-laws	192
Demand for cotton in 1862	195
Restrictions on the free transfer of land, and the effect on supply	198

CHAPTER XV.

Trade in Money. 200—215.

The word 'money' ambiguous	201
Money is merchandise	201
But also used to liquidate debts	202
Supplies of gold and silver satisfied as other wants are	203
Inconvertible currencies, their effects	206
Effects of exportation of specie on a note currency	206
Efflux of specie, causes of	207
Foreign exchanges	209
Means by which drains of specie may be arrested	211

CHAPTER XVI.

The Distribution of Capital. 215—223.

Insecurity a hindrance to distribution	216
Effects of loans contracted by government	218
They may or may not raise the rate of interest	219
Productive and unproductive expenditure	220
Theory of Dr. Chalmers	221
Difference between a loan and a tax	222

CHAPTER XVII.

Protection. 223—241.

	PAGE
Free exchange a natural right	223
Curtailments of individual liberty	225
Protection of children, &c. Inventors	225
Protection for reasons of public policy	227
Interference of government with right of letting, devising, settling land	228
'Free trade' in land	229
Protective enactments to manufactures	232
Protection is unnecessary unless a government wishes to divert capital into certain channels	233
Mr. Mill's justification of exceptional protection	235
This opinion examined	235
Protection justified on social grounds by some persons	237
As a means of avoiding dependence on foreigners	238
As a compensation for 'peculiar burdens'	239

CHAPTER XVIII.

Foreign Trade. 242—250.

Natural distribution of materials and products	242
Differences of race and habit	243
Differences of climate	244
Early trade	246
Causes which determine the price of foreign products	248
Profit of foreign trade	249

CHAPTER XIX.

Colonial Trade. 251—261.

British and other colonies	251
The 'colonial system'	252

	PAGE
Value of the British colonies	254
Advantage of the connexion to the colonists	255
The colonies no real outlet for emigration	256
Mr. Gibbon Wakefield's scheme	257
A national scheme of emigration desirable	258
Benefits of colonisation to the world	260
True relations of Great Britain to her colonies	260

CHAPTER XX.

On the Functions of Government. 262—273.

A government intends to do the best for its subjects	262
It is justified not only in protective but in initiative action	263
With popular education	264
With scientific education and scientific research	265
With assistance to the moral progress of a people	266
Sketch of governmental action five centuries ago	267
The conveyance of land more free at that period	270
The effects of primogeniture	271

CHAPTER XXI.

On the General Principles of Taxation. 273—287.

The rules of Adam Smith	273
These rules not strictly logical	274
Taxes the equivalents for a public service	275
Taxation should be equitable	277
What it is that constitutes a man's revenue	278
To what extent he can enjoy it	279
From what resources taxation can be derived	281
Taxes on capital, on legacies	283
Taxes on raw materials	284
On articles imported from abroad, but produced also untaxed at home	285
Taxes on exports, &c.	286

CHAPTER XXII.

Direct and Indirect Taxation. 287—301.

	PAGE
Most of the taxes levied in Great Britain indirect	287
Arguments in favour of indirect taxation	288
Arguments against this system	291
Excises, especially on malt	292
Arguments in favour of direct taxation	293
What constitutes a fair income-tax	294
Poll-taxes	294
Taxes on property	295
House-taxes	296
Taxes on male servants	298
Licence duties	300

CHAPTER XXIII.

Public Debts. 301—318.

Debts before the Revolution	301
Chief part of the public debt contracted for unproductive purposes	302
Grounds on which good faith is obligatory	303
Risks which this good faith ran in the present century	304
Similar risks attend the United States at present	306
The system on which the British debt was funded	311
Disadvantages of this system	312
Advantages of it	313
Extinction of debt. Mr. Price's sinking fund	314
Desirableness of extinguishing debt	315
Security or pledge of public debts	317

A MANUAL

OF

POLITICAL ECONOMY.

CHAPTER I.

Introductory.

A NATION is civilised in proportion to the fulness with which the several persons who compose it render mutual benefits and services, have reciprocal interests, and multiply such benefits, services, and interests. Everything which separates and secludes men from each other, is a hindrance to civilisation; everything which unites them, is a help towards civilisation. This will be plain if we compare the condition of savage with that of settled society. In the former case the social bond is weak, even between the members of a family; weaker still between the members of a tribe. In the latter, there is a continually increasing tendency towards union and association. In the former, there is no place for any right beyond that of the individual; in the latter, society itself possesses and exercises rights for the general benefit. Instances of the former are still very common; but no nation has ever yet been perfectly civilised, still less has the harmony of interests been developed between all nations. Ignorance, vice, wrong-doing, and crime, are still common, even in the best states of society with which experience supplies us; and the intercourse of nations is still hampered by local jealousies, rivalries, distrust, suspicion, and dislike.

Many of the services which individuals render to society are of the highest importance, and are often absolute conditions to the well-being of mankind. No one can over-estimate the benefits which are produced by the practice of justice, truth, integrity, self-restraint. Inferior only to these moral virtues are the mental qualities of culture, refinement, courtesy, and taste. The persons who exhibit these qualities, they whose characters are known for these virtues, are benefactors of mankind. The communities which are thoroughly imbued with these sentiments, whose domestic and foreign policy is guided by morality and good feeling, are of incalculable service to the cause of human progress. It is to the steady growth of such principles, and to such practices, that we must refer all the civilisation by which modern society is characterised. It is in the hope that such principles and practices will be extended, that men can look forward to the civilisation of the world. The fulfilment of these duties is rarely, however, a service for which no equivalent is returned. Few persons have ever conferred any benefits on a civilised society which are equal to those which such a society has conferred on them.

These facts are mentioned in order that they may not seem to be forgotten in a manual which is treating some of the facts of human life from another point of view. It will be found that the inferences of political economy are in complete harmony with the laws or experiences on which morality is founded, and that though the inquiry is narrowed, it is only different in degree from that which discusses the sanctions of duty and right. The subject of a treatise on political economy is, the services which men render to each other; but those services only on which a price can be put, and which are rendered in order that such a price may be put on them—or, to be more exact, that a tantamount service should be given in exchange for them. Hence we must recognise how it is that a person is able to render such a service, what it is which fixes its price, and what are the circumstances under which mutual services of individuals are most easily given and received.

There will be no voluntary exchange of these services unless the exchange affords a benefit to both the parties who enter into it at the time when the exchange is effected. One person may have it in his power, under particular circumstances, to make what is called a 'hard bargain' with another; that is, may exact more for what he renders than would ordinarily be given by any one, or would generally be given by the person with whom he makes his exchange. But at the precise instant at which the exchange is made, the bargain is an advantage to the person who is subjected to 'hard terms.' Of course we must not understand by the power which one man has over another, any force, compulsion, or fraud, but only recognise such arrangements as are free; that is, such as may be accepted or refused at the discretion of the persons negotiating the exchange. The laws of every country prohibit force, and afford remedies against fraud. Unless this were done, society would not hold together. But they have also, from time to time (always indeed ineffectually), tried to prevent or annul contracts which are made under circumstances subsequently unfavourable to one of the parties. Thus most legislatures have sought to restrain usury in the interest of borrowers, to fix prices in the interest of purchasers, to control wages in the interest of employers, and sometimes, but rarely to fix minimum rates of wages, or to find employment, in the interest of labourers.

All these attempts have failed in the long run. The endeavour to lower the rate of interest has in effect raised its rate. Regulations fixing prices have caused great fluctuations in prices; and so, for reasons which we shall see hereafter, have on the whole raised prices. The control of wages has been oppressive, without being effectual; and all attempts to find employment, or to raise wages above the rate at which they would naturally stand, have diminished employment, and so have diminished wages.

If therefore we are to understand the very elements of political economy, we must get rid of the impression, that if the contract be voluntary and the service be mutual, one man's gain is another's loss. So mistaken a view of human society, and of international commerce, has been the cause of infinite evils to mankind. It has introduced into the laws of various countries, regulations intended to grant privileges to certain classes, and to restrict the action of others by way of protection or compensation. It has induced a jealous foreign policy, and put a multitude of restrictions on trade. It has been so inveterate a fallacy, that it affected the judgment of men like Bacon: it still misleads the energies of communities which are otherwise intelligent. The real truth is exactly the reverse; for one man's gain in all acts of free exchange is another man's gain.

It will not be difficult to explain the origin of this error. It arose partly from an ancient mistake about the nature of wealth, partly from the manifest effect of certain bargains.

For many ages an impression prevailed that wealth was money, and that the true policy of a state was to secure as much of the precious metals as possible. If therefore, from this view, a nation or an individual gave money in exchange for goods, it seemed that the giver became poorer, the receiver richer. We have now learnt that, although the exchange of money against goods and services is familiar, the real exchange is between goods and services, goods and goods; and that money only measures values, and enables the recipient to postpone the completion of his part in the exchange. Money seemed to be wealth, because of all values it is the best understood, most easily finds a purchaser, and for a short time at least varies least in value. Besides, the view currently taken was promulgated by governments, and governments do not produce or traffic, but spend.

Again, some transactions between man and man are completed only by gain on one side, loss on another. If one man makes a wager with another, the occurrence of the event on which the wager depends does involve loss and gain. The same reasoning applies to what are called stock exchange transactions. Here, however, it is plain that there is no mutual service, and therefore, in an economical sense, no exchange. The business of a merchant or other intermediary between producers and consumers contains in it some elements of risk or speculation. Occasionally the transactions of a trader are so speculative, that we call them, by analogy, gambling engagements. But the analogy is only partial. The trader, whatever be his personal motives, does a service to society. He may try to obtain a larger advantage than ordinary, either by his being able to anticipate an urgent demand for the article in which he deals, or by his temporary control of the market; but he can effect his end only by satisfying the demands or controlling the necessities of others. He could achieve neither of these conditions unless he offered something which others are willing or anxious to have. He can reach his customer only through the customer's inclination to buy. A speculation in trade is not a wager; but because the man who speculates does incur a risk, and may make a large gain, or suffer a loss in the long run, his acts, by a figure of speech, are grouped with the doings of those who merely make bets with each other. But even such trading transactions are exceptional. In the great majority of cases the trader, like the producer, desires to run as little risk as possible. He knows that the risk of failure is generally understated, the chances of success over-estimated, and that he is quite as likely to be misled by a sanguine temper, as to be justified in predicting the course of the market, in consequence of his intelligence and activity. Most business is managed cautiously.

CHAPTER II.

The Cause of Value.

JUST as there are very important services of which no true economical estimate can be given, so there are objects of great importance which are not appraised, because they are unlimited, and cannot therefore be appropriated. A supply of air is necessary for human life; but air, owing to natural agencies, is universally distributed under ordinary circumstances. So is water in temperate and thinly-peopled regions. Hence these objects have no market value. Air however must be artificially supplied in deep mines and in crowded rooms. In such places air bears a price. An artificial supply of water is needed in densely-peopled towns, and in certain manufactories. Ice has no economical value in polar regions, but is of great importance in tropical climates, and during the summer heat of temperate regions. Solar heat has no economical value in the tropics, but the retention and economy of solar heat is a matter of great interest and the object of great expenditure in colder climates. Thus, in the language of Adam Smith, there are two senses of value—value in use and value in exchange. With the former we have nothing to do; we shall consider the latter only.

All objects and services possessing value in exchange, derive this value from the fact that labour has been expended on them. To this rule there is only one exception, i.e. land in fully settled countries. The natural powers of the soil have their value in the fact that they are limited in extent, and are appropriated. If they are unlimited and unappropriated, as is very much the case in imperfectly occupied countries, they have no more economical value, under ordinary circumstances, than air and water have. The aggregate amount of labour expended on objects and services is called the *cost of production*, and if exchange be free, the value assigned to everything which is susceptible of an economical estimate is generally proportioned to the average cost of production.

Labour then is the cause of value. This labour is either physical or mental, i.e. is either intended to effect some change on natural objects by means of direct muscular exertion, or is busied in devising means by which this muscular exertion may be economised, sustained, made more efficient, or even superseded. Of these two kinds of labour, mental is by far the most important. It is directed towards the invention and improvement of substitutes for mere manual labour,—at first the simplest and rudest; afterwards the most perfect tools. It has aided human labour by animal and mechanical forces, and as its discoveries are accumulated and arranged, it has produced results which we do not wonder at, only because we are so familiar with them. The wealth which the present has inherited from bygone ages is not merely the mass of material objects which have been transmitted from generation to generation, and the permanent improvements which have been induced upon the surface of the soil; but comprises the aggregate of experience, skill, and knowledge, which mankind possesses and employs in order to make the fullest use of all the powers and forces in nature.

Not every kind of muscular and mental labour is susceptible of an economical estimate. Nobody works harder than men do who row in a race, shoot all day long, or engage themselves in hunting or travelling. So again, they who busy themselves in abstruse mathematical calculations, or study astronomical phenomena, undergo severe mental toil. But unless these labours are undertaken with some purpose which lies beyond the labour itself, and which can be brought to market, they are not such labour as the economist appreciates. To have any significance they must be priced and exchanged.

Nor does it follow, on the other hand, that labour, in order to have any economical meaning, should be onerous or disagreeable. Labour is no doubt generally avoided;

and most labour undertaken for ulterior ends and for some material advantage is more or less involuntary. But it need not be so. Turner was passionately attached to painting; Beethoven was equally devoted to music. Neither can be charged with indifference to the material advantages which ensued from practising these arts, though it is probable that had the former sold none of his pictures, the latter never disposed of the copyright in his music, each would have followed the pursuit in which he took so much delight.

As however in all kinds of such labour as the economist discusses, the end is preferred to the means, the product to the process; and as the end is followed, and the product effected, in order that they may be exchanged against other ends and other products, it is the interest of every one who labours to achieve the end and complete the product with the least possible expenditure of labour. In this way it is manifest that the exchange will be effected on the best terms, i.e. for most money or goods. If by some process, for example, a farmer is able to produce ten quarters of wheat at the cost of ten pounds, and by adopting some other process he can produce the same quantity at the cost of eight pounds; he will, if he be intelligent and industrious—qualities which we must postulate—choose the latter in preference to the former process.

This disposition to produce the greatest possible result with the least possible expenditure of force, leads individuals, and ultimately societies, in so far as they act together, to adopt several expedients by which labour is lessened and production is increased. These expedients are traceable in the history of civilisation. First then by

Tools and implements. The savage who lives by hunting is urged, as much by the love of ease as by necessity, to economise his labour and improve the weapons which he uses in the chase. Rude as his materials are, they are singularly efficient in practised hands. The lasso of the Guacho, the trap of the Red Indian, the harpoon of the Esquimaux, the lance of the Australian, are wielded with the same skill and precision as, for instance, the blow-pipe of the glass-blower. The use of these weapons is nearly all that these savages know; but what they know they must know well in order to live. So again ethnological researches seem to show that the first tools used in agriculture were rude both in their material and their construction, and that they were gradually improved. In our own experience, we know how mechanical science has developed that exact and precise machinery by which such marvellous results are arrived at in modern history.

Co-operation of Labour. United labour, even though the labourers perform just the same operation, is more effectual than the separated labour of each individual. Two men hunting together will bring down more game than they would if they hunted apart. Two or more horses in draught will draw a heavier load than would be done if each horse had a cart to himself. Two greyhounds will run down more hares, if they course in unison, than if they are coursed separately. Organisation and combination, even if they be of the simplest character, have a great economical significance.

Division of Labour. Much more striking, however, are the effects of the division of labour, or as Mr. Gibbon Wakefield has called it, with greater precision, division of employments. By this expression is meant the parcelling out the several functions which the contributors to any produce perform, among various individuals, each of whom has his own work to do in effecting the production in question.

The number of persons who contribute towards producing any common article—and as a rule the commoner it is the more numerous are the persons who contribute—is found on examination to be very great. A yard of calico represents the labour of very many persons. The cotton from which it is manufactured was obtained by the joint labours of one set of persons; the carriage of it from a foreign country required another set; the transmission of it to the manufacturer a third organisation; the process of manufacturing the cloth a fourth; its distribution by sale a fifth. The fourth in this series is subdivided, for the business of spinning is generally different from that of weaving. To these may be added the different persons who manufacture the machinery by which the process is effected. It will be plain, if all the kinds of labour which aid directly and indirectly in the production of a yard of calico were discussed, and its part assigned to each kind, that the series is almost geometrical, in the same way as the ancestors of any man amount in a few generations to many hundreds. And it is plain also that this division of labour is the result of certain social causes; for in a country like India the same person grows, gathers, cleanses and spins the cotton-wool, and afterwards weaves it into cloth.

The same tendency to the division of labour exists in other manufactures. Adam Smith illustrated the principle by commenting on the number of persons engaged in so trifling a manufacture as that of pin-making. The same rule holds good with watch-making, the manufacture of playing-cards, of paper, and of an infinite amount of other articles.

The cause which has brought about this appropriation of labour to special functions is that to which allusion has already been made, viz. the desire to obtain the largest possible produce at the least possible cost. This desire is itself powerfully stimulated by competition; for producers find that their rivals will carry off business unless they accommodate themselves to the state of the market. Hence everything which checks competition, checks the division of labour; everything which enlarges the market, induces and aids it.

We have yet to see how it is that the division of labour lowers the cost of production, cheapens goods, and therefore enlarges the market.

First, it makes the workman more dexterous. A man who continually does one thing acquires great readiness in doing it, or, as we commonly say, 'gets a knack of it.' Any person who watches a practised hand, can see how rapidly he executes the work he has to do. The number of nails which a nailer can make in a day is far in excess of that which could be fabricated by any general smith, however skilful and intelligent he may be. In playing music, no excellence of ear, no taste or feeling, will avail, unless the player has diligently practised on his instrument. According to some persons, genius itself is 'a great capacity for taking trouble.' It is very difficult to distinguish between natural and acquired capacity. Sydney Smith used to say, that any person could be witty or brilliant in conversation, if he took pains to make himself competent. Great orators have generally acquired their command over language, their skill in debate and retort, by long and diligent study. It is not rare for an accountant to run up three columns of figures simultaneously, and thus reckon a product almost at a glance. When, however, the mind attentively watches, and the hand performs one act only, the ease and quickness with which the result is achieved are even more remarkable. But any economy of time and labour diminishes the cost of production, makes the article cheaper, and enables a larger number of persons to use or enjoy the product.

Next, it becomes possible to vary the wages of the different contributors to the product in proportion to their skill and capacity. If one person began and completed the manufacture, he must be paid for the easiest and simplest work at as high a rate as he is paid for the most difficult. For example, the various workmen in a glass-house receive wages ranging from 5*l.* to 5*s.* a week. If one person mixed the materials and smelted them, blew the glass, annealed it, squared it, and packed it, and besides performed the multitude of minor and easy operations which are subsidiary to the manufacture, the whole service must be paid for at one, and that the highest rate. In the infancy of manufactures such an accumulation of functions is necessary, and the cost of the article is therefore high. But competition for the sale of manufactured articles soon leads to the discovery that different rates of wages may be paid to different agents in the joint labour of production, and that an economy of a very important kind can be effected by these means.

The division of labour tends continually to the multiplication of intermediaries to the process by which the material is fashioned into a saleable commodity, and the commodity is put within reach of the consumer. If these agents are not interposed arbitrarily, but are present because they facilitate operations, they each and all perform a service with which society could not dispense to its advantage. The case of course is different, if by any law or compact more persons are engaged in any occupation than necessity and convenience demand. Thus for example, at different periods in economical history, police regulations have been laid on the manufacture and trade in cloth, and payments have been made for the service which the police is supposed to have rendered. But as the purchasers of cloth are as a rule perfectly competent to judge of its texture, quality, and measure, the interposition of such an official service is needless and wasteful. So again the etiquette of certain professional functions prescribes that a service should be divided. It is a rule in the practice of English law, that clients should not consult a barrister directly, but must employ the intermediary service of an attorney. If the custom were an economy (and in such a case the rule is needless and superfluous), no objection could be taken to it, since it would be an illustration of the division of labour, and a gain. If it be a mere arrangement, which is intended to secure wages to two persons where the service of one is sufficient, it is a loss. So again, if it be the custom in building that there should be an unnecessary number of overlookers or foremen, the apparent division of labour is only an arbitrary increase of cost. In short, the rule by which the multiplication of intermediaries in any transaction can be tested, and its limit determined, is contained in the answer to a question, Does the increase diminish the charges put upon the consumer, or purchaser of the commodity? If it does, it fulfils the economical conditions which attend the natural division of labour. If it does not, the service is apparent, not real, and the natural course of production and exchange is obstructed.

The division of labour again tends to the development of machinery. Animal is used instead of human labour, because it is cheaper; machinery instead of both, because it is cheaper still. But though these results are in the end obtained by machinery, the outlay necessary for its adoption is large. A machine is a very costly affair. Some, which aid in the manufacture of the cheapest articles, are exceedingly expensive: they cannot therefore be obtained except the manufacture is extensive, the demand large, and the market wide. But these circumstances are the conditions under which labour is most fully subdivided. And thus as the division of labour is the stimulant to the adoption of machinery, so the use of machinery tends still further to subdivide labour.

Again, the conditions which bring about the division of labour tend towards equalizing the price of commodities. The producer and consumer are equally interested in effecting as nearly as possible a uniformity of price. But when the process of production is interrupted or discontinuous, prices fluctuate greatly. It is clear, however, that such processes of production as are effected by divided labour must be continuous, i.e. the demand and supply of the articles in question must be steady and anticipated. No one would organise a body of workmen, and assign each his proper place in any manufacture, except he understood that there was a market, and a sure market, for his goods. He may indeed, in the competition of manufacture, temporarily overstock the market, i.e. produce in excess of the demand. But on an average, all manufacturers carrying on the same business will not commit this error.

Furthermore, as the cheapness of articles is relative to the extent to which labour is organised for the purpose of production, it will be seen that the greater is the width of the market, the better is the natural division of labour carried out. When therefore unwise or jealous legislation, temporary and personal interests narrow the market, they check or restrain the process by which labour is divided and society benefited. This mistaken policy, under various forms, has done much to hinder the true progress of mankind. Nations can and may render mutual services, confer mutual benefits. The superfluities of one country are the necessaries or luxuries of another. The interchange of this overplus is the foundation of international commerce, just as the wants of the country are supplied by the towns, those of the towns by the country. And as this friendly rivalry in the bestowal of reciprocal advantage is a bond between nations, as well as a profit to both parties entering into trade; so the denial or prevention of such an intercourse is the source of numberless evils. Nations gain by mutual trade, lose by isolation. A community is not profited, does not grow in wealth by such artificial regulations as hinder or prevent commercial intercourse. Political economy, as Adam Smith saw, and was the first to demonstrate, does not consider the wealth of one people, but the wealth of nations.

When therefore it is said that labour is the cause of value, and that prices are estimated on the whole by the cost of production, we must understand that the object on which labour is expended is in demand, and that the labour devoted to the end is judiciously and economically applied. Communities as well as individuals may waste their labour; their efforts may be misdirected; their energies may be perverted. As we continue this inquiry, we shall unfortunately have occasion to see that such consequences are not rare, and that, as a rule, these errors are the effect of unwise laws and regulations. But when competition is healthy, and trade is free, such errors are soon corrected.

Taking this formula, then, that the value of all objects and services in demand is due to the cost of production, we shall be easily able to interpret the most familiar economical problems, and find a clue to those which are more difficult.

The reason why a diamond of five carats weight is worth, according to Mr. Emanuel, upwards of 300*l.*, is due to the fact that on an average, and at the present time, an amount of labour equivalent to this sum is expended on the discovery of such a gem. The reason why, on an average, a quarter of wheat is worth from 2*l.* 10*s.* to 3*l.* is because it costs as much labour to get this amount of gold as it does to procure a quarter of wheat. The reason why the average income of a physician is, say 500*l.*, is because it costs a capital sum in the first instance, a continuous outlay in the second, and a replacement of the capital expended in the third, in order to provide and secure the professional services of such a personage; and these sums together make up the fund on which (just as in the case of interest on money lent) the 500*l.* in question is paid by way of compensation. There are indeed two elements in price which disturb or qualify these interpretations of relative values; these are, first, the cost of carrying the article from the place in which it is produced to the place in which it is bought or sold; and next, the rent of land, the origin and significance of which will be treated in a subsequent chapter. The cost however of carriage is part of the cost of production; for everything which is produced is, when economically considered, produced for sale, and production for sale implies a demand and a market.

CHAPTER III.

The Measure of Value.

As the value of every object or service in demand depends on the cost of producing or supplying it, this value either rises and falls according to the easiness or difficulty with which it may be obtained; and as values are relative to other values, the value of any one article may and does vary as the circumstances under which it is produced vary. Thus for example, a little after the middle of the thirteenth century the value of gold to silver was ten to one; at the conclusion of the same century it stood at twelve-and-a-half to one; in the middle of the next century at thirteen-and-three-quarters to one. At present it is at about fifteen-and-a-half to one, weight for weight. There is every reason to believe that this rise in the value of gold was due to the fact that at about the end of the thirteenth century gold currencies became common in Italy and elsewhere; that therefore existing stocks of this metal were absorbed by the demand for gold coins; and that consequently greater pains and more labour were devoted to the extraction of gold from its ores, or, which is in effect the same thing, poorer mines were worked. So again, the value of iron during the thirteenth and fourteenth centuries was about two-and-a-half times higher than that of lead. At the present time, however, lead, weight for weight, is worth about four times as much as iron. This change in values has been induced by the fact, that although the cost of producing lead has been greatly diminished since the period referred to, the cost of producing iron has been still more diminished. On the other hand, very little variation can be detected in the relative values of objects which are obtained at nearly equal cost under all circumstances. Thus there can be no doubt that the crops of wheat, barley, and oats, produced in England at the present day, are many times more in quantity than the produce of England was five hundred years ago. But though the quantity of each has increased, the relative cost of producing each has not materially varied; for it has been found, from the evidence of prices, that while in the earliest period for which evidence has been collected, i.e. from 1260 to 1400, the relative values of wheat, barley, and oats, were respectively 100, 73.14, and 42.05; the same articles have during the ten years 1856–1865 stood in the proportion of 100, 70, and 45.95. This discrepancy, slight as it is, may be accounted for by the large importations of foreign barley; perhaps by the incidence of the malt-tax on the one hand, and the increased use of oats for feeding horses and fattening cattle on the other. But perhaps the most striking illustration of variation in values is to be found in the rent of land. Five hundred years ago, good arable land, naturally drained and in the neighbourhood of a town, was let at the rate of sixpence an acre annual rent. At the present time the same plots of land are let at 3*l*. the acre. The relative value of this land, therefore, as compared with wheat, has risen, in this period of time, by nearly fourteen times.

Values therefore are relative to each other. It will be seen in consequence that there can be no universal rise in values. If everything were said to be worth more than it had been, all that such an expression would imply is, that it costs more trouble to produce or procure everything, and though labour would be more heavily taxed to get what it needs or what it exchanges, as everybody would have to work harder, no one could be better or worse off in comparison. Thus five hundred years ago, every commodity which could be procured cost vastly more labour and trouble to get than it does now. The labour of the agriculturist produces, it is probable, six, perhaps eight times as much as it did in those days. So the rapidity with which clothing is manufactured, the ease with which metals are smelted and refined, the economy with which merchandise is transported, are at the present day, when compared with the past, incomparably greater. But unless the process by which any one of these conveniences or necessaries can be obtained has been rendered easier or more rapid, the relative values of food, clothing, metals, and sea-carriage remain the same. Similarly, if there can be no general rise in values, there can be no general fall in values. General prices may rise and fall; for price is the measure of an article by one standard, value is the measure of any one object by all other objects. It will be remembered too, that the value of an object is not determined by the use it can be put to, or the importance which its possessor assigns to it, or even to the desire which another has for it, but that it resides in the power of exchange which the owner has by virtue of possessing it. If a merchant wishes to trade with savages, it would be of no use for him to export such merchandise as is fitted for civilised societies only. There is great use, it may be, in such merchandise, but under the circumstances there is no market for it. If, again, a merchant were to import food into a country suffering grievously from famine, no trade can ensue, unless the starving people had something to offer in exchange, though the desire which such persons would entertain would be urgent and vehement. In short, it is necessary, in order to give value to any object, that it should be, as is technically said, in *demand ;* and this demand must be *effectual*, that is, must be accompanied with the power of proffering some other object in exchange.

Having seen, then, what it is which constitutes value, we may now be able to determine what constitutes price. The price of an article, as has been said, is its estimate in some one uniform measure. If this measure did not itself vary in value, i.e. if the cost of producing it was always one and the same, and any increase in its quantity was absolutely relative to an extension of the area over which it was used, a general rise and fall in prices would be as impossible as a general rise and fall in values. But as the value of one thing may rise or fall in relation to other things, so the value of the measure itself may rise and fall in relation to all other things. This variation we know to have occurred in the case of those objects, gold, silver, and copper, which have formed the measure of value among all civilised nations.

A little reflection will shew that some common measure of value must needs be adopted in all societies whose condition is superior to mere barbarism. Society, as we have seen, exists by the interchange of services; and that community makes but little progress in which each man is able, or rather is constrained, to supply all his own wants by his own skill or labour. But the fact, that such an interdependence characterises civilised society, makes it necessary also that some of those who work at special objects of utility should be far less numerous than others. Thus for example, the number of bakers in any community is far larger than that of shoemakers; that of shoemakers again than that of wheelwrights; that of wheelwrights than that of engineers, and so on; while there are some occupations which are fully served by two or three persons in a vast community. Now where dealings are transacted on a large scale, it is not difficult for commodities to be exchanged against commodities; as indeed is the case in the trade between two countries. Here as a rule, the actual transfer of gold and silver is rare, goods being exchanged against goods. But the case is quite different when the transactions are small. Here the exchange of commodities is impossible, or at least inconvenient; and the persons who deal together are obliged to adopt some common object of value, which each is willing to take, because he knows that he can easily get rid of it in exchange for whatever he wants or may want. This object is money. Money, then, is a means by which two persons who do not deal together mutually as producers and consumers, are able to enter into transactions.

THE MEASURE OF VALUE.

The baker does not want shoes, and so takes money from the shoemaker; he does want wine, but the wine-merchant does not want bread. He therefore gives the wine-merchant the money which he takes from the shoemaker; and so the same money is made to represent an endless series of exchanges, each seller receiving the money in order to buy what he needs of those who sell what he wants. Money, then, is essential to the subdivision of labour and services, and the organisation of society.

Even, however, if money were not a physical object, it would still be necessary as a symbol or calculus. We need some common measure of value, as we need measures of length and capacity, even though we never transfer that which is designated by the name *money*. The merchants who trade between different countries, even though they exchange goods against goods, must needs estimate what they sell and what they buy by some common measure. A British merchant trading to France does not reckon so many hogsheads of wine against so many pounds of cotton yarn, or so many tons of iron, but he measures what he buys and what he sells by money. So necessary is this process to trade, that we are told of nations who have no money, properly so called, but who have been constrained to invent a fictitious measure in order to express values.

In short, the functions of money in the act of exchange present a close analogy to the functions of language in relation to thought. As there may be a rude barter, so there may be a rude language of signs. But there is no ready and extensive communication of thought except by articulate speech; and similarly there can be no real and effectual trade except by the use of a common measure.

Money, however, is only a means to an end—the machinery, namely, of trade. For reasons which we shall see shortly, it is a very costly machinery, which society is always striving to economise. And for the same or similar reasons everybody who takes money wishes to get rid of it as soon as he can, because as long as he holds it it is to him wholly unproductive. Knowing that it is, by its very nature, that which is most easily got rid of, and is always in demand, he will always retain a small portion against emergencies ; and if he thinks these emergencies are very imminent, he keeps a larger quantity by him. Sometimes, too, though this practice is giving way, he hoards it ; but in general, he tries to get rid of its actual possession as soon as he can. If he does not purchase goods with it with a view to a profit on the purchase, he lends it to others.

It is because everybody wishes to get money, and everybody is willing to receive money in preference to that which money will buy, that many persons, and even nations, have believed that money is the only wealth. It is undoubtedly that part of wealth which is most easily accepted in exchange, because when the seller of a commodity gets money in exchange for goods, the money is worth to him more than the goods, the difference between the two being his profit on the transaction. But though he takes the money, it is far from his thoughts to contemplate retaining it, he takes it to get rid of it, for he loses profit as long as he retains it.

The forgetfulness or ignorance of the true use of money, that, namely, of its being an instrument of exchange, has been the cause of an infinite variety of economical and political errors. For many centuries the policy of our laws and of our trade was professedly the retention of as much money as possible. It is an instance of the difficulty there is in generalising correctly, that the act of hoarding, which no reasonable trader would practise for himself, was held to be the greatest wisdom in the commerce of the state. Had the legislature confined itself simply to putting stringent regulations on the exportation of money, no great harm would have been done, because these regulations were always and necessarily inoperative. The most efficient police is unable to prevent smuggling, is hardly able to check it, even when goods are bulky and cheap; how much more difficult would it be, then, for a rude police to prevent the efflux of that which is of great value, and which lies in small compass!

But the acts of the legislature took a different turn. They strove to encourage exports, and discourage imports, because exportation increased the money of the country, importation diminished it. Hence, protective regulations were adopted, and a host of laws, instituted originally from mistaken notions of the public good, became, in course of time, the strongholds of ignorance, indolence, and selfishness. We have got rid of these arrangements only in our own day; and no other nation has made nearly so much progress in the true theory of public wealth as we have. At present we have reversed the policy of our forefathers. Their rule was, as has been said, to discourage imports, and encourage exports; ours is to encourage imports, and to let exports find their own market for themselves. In other words, we are always willing to buy, because we know that when nations wish, as all nations do wish, to sell, they must also buy, and that if they are resolved to put hindrances on·

their own power of buying, they must sell their own goods at cheaper rates, if indeed they want to sell them at all.

Money, then, is an essential part of the machinery of trade. It forms a measure of value even when commodities are exchanged; it is the most convenient, intelligible, and available *pledge* which a seller of goods can obtain, for it is that which he can make use of at his discretion when he needs, in his turn, to effect a purchase of any goods which he may desire. To receive money in exchange for goods, is to receive that commodity which, more than any other, will give its possessor command over the general market.

This money is generally, but not invariably, one or both of those metals which are called *precious*, for a reason which we shall presently see. Sometimes the standard is copper, as it was in ancient Rome and in mediæval Sweden. Sometimes it is gold, as in Great Britain and the United States. It has most frequently been silver. Occasionally, as in France, it is either gold or silver, at the discretion of the purchaser. It is said that other articles besides the metals are employed as a measure of value. Thus we are told that rock-salt is used in Abyssinia, hides in South America. The travels of Mr. Speke seem to imply that pieces of cotton cloth answer the purpose of a currency in Eastern Africa. For many ages a small univalve shell, the cowrie, has been a form of currency in Bengal, though its use is now dying out.

But civilised communities invariably employ one or both of the two precious metals, gold and silver. Here, however, we must distinguish gold and silver as used in the arts, and as used for the purpose of trade or exchange. In the former case they are strictly merchandise, in the latter, as we have seen, they are a kind of machinery by which exchanges are adjusted. It has been said by an eminent economist, that the value of gold and silver is determined by their use in the arts. This statement, however, is not quite correct. Their use in the arts is an index of their value, but not the sole cause of that value. If the employment of gold and silver as a measure of value should cease, the liberation of existing stocks would be followed by a great fall in their value, and they would forthwith become of less value in the arts. Their value is as much due to the demand which exists for their use as currency, as it is to the demands of the arts. It has been observed above, that the rise in the value of gold, a fact fully ascertained from the rate of exchange after the beginning of the fourteenth century, was due to the general use of gold as a currency.

The causes which have determined civilised communities to use gold and silver as the material of money are as follows. First, in the natural course of things, they are produced in nearly equal quantities by nearly equal labour, or at nearly equal cost. Over a long period of time, the labour necessary to produce equal quantities may vary, and has varied considerably. But over short periods of time, no great variation ensues, and for several reasons. In the first place, the stocks of gold and silver possessed by civilised communities are so large, that very considerable additions are, comparatively speaking, small by the side of the quantity existent or in circulation, and the quantity annually required for employment and use. In the next place, the precious metals are generally found in districts which are otherwise unfitted for the supply of the necessaries of life; among barren rocks and mountains, to which food must be transported, in which, therefore, living is dear, and the cost of production great. In the next, after the few prizes in the shape of metallic masses of gold and superficial ores of silver are secured, gold must be obtained from very hard rocks by very expensive machinery; and silver is ordinarily found in slender and deep veins, in alloys from which it is extracted with difficulty, and in small percentages to the weight of the ore.

Now if large quantities of gold and silver could be found within easy reach of abundant labour and food, and could be collected without any great amount of labour, the first finders and miners would be enriched, and by degrees the possessors of the old stocks of gold and silver would be impoverished. But no such thing has ever happened. It is said that at the close of the Roman Republic, the vast mass of gold which Julius Cæsar brought into the Roman treasury, reduced its value by twenty-five per cent. It is certain that the occupation of the New World by the Spanish conquerors of Mexico and Peru reduced the value of silver so considerably, that it was not worth half as much at the close of the sixteenth century as it was up to the first half of the same period. But in both these cases, the fact did not ensue from those ordinary economical conditions which affect and determine production. Both these phænomena were the results of violence. Julius Cæsar was bringing with him the plunder of the Gauls, the masses of native gold which this people had roughly fashioned into articles of personal adornment, and which, it seems, they procured in abundance. The Spanish colonists of the New World exhausted the population by compulsory labour in the mines. If, then, by some similar action, or by some exceptional circumstance, it were possible to add largely and suddenly to the stocks of the precious metals, serious results would ensue to many persons, and the fitness of gold and silver as measures of value would be impaired.

Again, if both gold and silver are used simultaneously as a currency, the proportionate amount of labour required to produce each cannot, without great public inconvenience, be disturbed. In the rough, it may be said that the cost of producing a pound Troy of gold is fifteen-and-a-half times as great as that of producing a pound Troy of silver, and that therefore, a pound of gold is worth about fifteen-and-a-half pounds of silver. Now it is of course impossible that the production of any two commodities should always represent the same proportionate cost, or that variations in the annual quantity of silver or gold brought to market should not occur. But here again, though there are always oscillations in price, the oscillations are very slight, partly because the excess in production for one year or one period is compensated by a defect in another year or period; and so the average cost of producing these objects rectifies occasional irregularities; partly because, as was observed before, the existing stocks are so vast, that even a considerable addition in any one year or period produces very little effect on the aggregate in existence.

Still this change in the relative values of gold and silver has been witnessed. The proportion between the two has been stated above (p. 18) at different periods of European history, and an explanation of the cause has been given. These, however, were great changes in the relative value of the two metals. A slighter variation with its economical effects have been manifested on a large scale, and in a very significant manner in France, during the years 1850-1865. In that country there is a double currency, i. e. any debtor may proffer the amount of his debt in gold or silver at his discretion. On March 28th, 1803 (7 Germinal, year 11), the French republic fixed the proportion of gold to silver at fifteen-and-a-half to one. High as this proportion is, the gold was undervalued; silver was the cheapest currency in which a debtor could pay his obligations, and consequently gold almost disappeared from circulation. Since the discoveries of gold in Australia and California, the relation has been reversed, silver is now undervalued, and has rapidly flowed out of France. The adoption of a gold currency by Germany and other states of Northern Europe will probably induce a new relation between gold and silver in France, Belgium, and Italy.

It may be stated here, that the inconveniences of a double currency are, (1) Any marked change in the relations of the two metals induces an efflux of the one, and an influx of the other, as the case may be, and tends to bring about certain complications in foreign trade; (2) It is difficult to use the undervalued metal as a bank reserve, because it is drawn out of the banks for exportation; (3) It tends to cripple the use of gold for large, and of silver for small payments, compelling the public to use a heavy and cumbrous currency under one set of circumstances, or to have great difficulty in getting 'change' under another set.

In this country we have apparently a double, or rather triple currency. But the inconvenience of the French system is obviated by two regulations: (1) Silver is con-

THE MEASURE OF VALUE.

siderably overvalued, copper or bronze money much more so; (2) But a debtor is not allowed to proffer more than forty shillings in silver, or twelve pence in copper, unless of course his creditor is willing to take more of either. The result is, that the silver and copper currency never leave the country, and are confined to the true purpose for which they are issued—the supply of small money. Were silver not only overvalued, but allowed to be a 'legal tender' to any amount, all the gold currency would rapidly disappear.

A second condition, which must belong to any measure of value, is, that it must be indestructible under the ordinary conditions of the atmosphere. If an article is depreciated by time or decay, it ceases to be a satisfactory measure of other values. Now of all natural objects certain metals are the least destructible, and among these especially gold and silver, which do not rust, corrode, or decay.

A third is, that the material of which this measure is made must be susceptible of such easy division or reunion, that a number of small pieces shall be worth no more, and no less, than an aggregate piece of equal weight. The quality being understood, the value of the measure will be determined by the weight only, and not by the size of the pieces which make up the weight. Precious stones are very valuable; they are highly indestructible. They are produced, certain conditions fulfilled, in nearly equal quantities, by nearly equal labour. But they are valued, not by their weight only, but by their size, because though they may be divided, they cannot be united. Hence they are wholly unfit for the purposes of a currency.

These conditions are fulfilled by no other object except gold and silver. Hence the selection of one or both of these metals as a measure of value is universal among civilised communities.

Still, in order to become available for currency, and as a measure of value, gold and silver must be subjected to some further manipulation. These metals are rarely found in a state of purity, but have to be extracted from their ores by various refining processes. Furthermore, it is easy to adulterate them; and it is difficult, except great trouble is taken, and considerable skill employed, to detect adulteration. But it is plainly essential to a measure of value that it should be rapidly and easily estimated. If one had to test the value of lumps of metal whenever they were received, and to guard against adulteration whenever it is practised, it is hardly possible to conceive that the mass of mankind would use these metals at all as a currency.

Gold is very heavy, and silver is very bright. But a mixture of gold, silver, and copper will deceive the eye, and be very likely undetected, unless the possessor of it be skilful enough to compare its bigness with its density. The story of Archimedes and the crown is well known. So silver will bear a great deal of alloy without losing its brightness, or at any rate will retain it sufficiently long for purposes of fraud.

It is therefore a very early and necessary act of police for a government to take on itself the duty of certifying the fineness or purity of the masses of metal which circulate in a community. It is proper that a government should always do its best to protect its subjects from any systematic adulteration or fraud. Governments indeed

THE MEASURE OF VALUE.

are frequently incompetent for such ends, and in a great many cases the community is a competent judge of the goodness or badness of the various articles which it purchases in the market. But the adulteration of such gold and silver as is used for the general purposes of exchange is a much more serious matter. It needs imperatively the superintendence of a public police; so that imperfectly civilised, despotic, and even barbarous governments recognise the necessity of securing the purity or standard of their currencies; generally by prohibiting any private person from issuing or certifying these metals, and by assuming the right or duty themselves.

The earliest form which this certificate takes is that of affixing a stamp to masses of metal. This is the practice in China, where many very familiar inventions have been made, as it seems, at an early date, but have been strangely undeveloped. Here, however, owing to the weakness of the government, the issue is not the act of the administration, but of well-known mercantile houses, who cast the silver, nearly pure, into rude masses, something like a shoe, and punch their symbol or trade-mark into the ingot. These ingots are called *sycee*.

When a government takes this duty in hand, it generally accommodates its subjects by issuing small pieces of stamped metal called *coins*. These coins generally possess a certain weight; but they must have, in order to be current, a certain and invariable fineness. It is an inconvenience, if the government diminishes or enlarges the weight of the pieces; but the inconvenience is comparatively trifling, since payments may be, as they were up to comparatively modern times, made by weight. Such a process, as is well known, was common in rude ages; and there is reason to believe that payments by weight were general in England up to the time when Elizabeth, shortly after her accession, reformed the currency.

But the case is very serious when the government, which has taken the coinage of money into its hands in order to prevent fraudulent adulteration, commits the crime or fraud itself, and issues money below the standard of fineness. When such base money gets into circulation, all confidence and nearly all home trade are at an end. The effects are as disastrous on the credit of a country as the invasion and success of a hostile army are. Afraid of losing, men will not sell; for some person, in the long run, must sustain the loss of bad money, if indeed the value of money is ultimately determined by the cost of getting the metal it contains. Those who have good money, hoard or export it; for the facts which we see characterise a double currency, when one of the two metals is undervalued, affect the double currency of good and bad money in an exaggerated form. Prices rise, and all the appearance of a general dearth ensues. The country in which such a fraudulent policy is adopted, may permanently or for a long time retrograde in civilisation and opulence.

Only two English monarchs have issued base money. These were Henry VIII and Edward VI, though in the last case it was more properly the act of the Protector Somerset. If we can trust Edward's diary, it was an object of great anxiety to the young king. It took a century at least to do away with the ill effects of this financial expedient. In France the practice was carried to great lengths; and it seems probable that the backward state of that country during many centuries is, concurrently with other causes, to be assigned to the practice of tampering with the currency, and thereby inducing general distrust. It should be observed, that though all classes suffer when any such political crime is committed, the poorer classes suffer the most, and recover from the effects of the crisis most slowly. The merchant who deals with foreign countries is more likely to make a gain than a loss, for he certainly reckons the debased coin at no more than its actual worth, and he has great opportunities for reckoning it at less. The landlord is not likely to suffer much, for his rent accommodates itself to prices. The farmer is not likely to suffer, for he sells his articles, objects of the highest and most urgent necessity, at the full price which he can exact from the wants of his customers. The manufacturer will not employ his capital at a loss, or, at any rate, he can recompense himself by enhanced prices. The retail trader may suffer by the fact that his customers are likely to be fewer. But the labourer is sure to suffer; for, first, he is obliged to offer his labour for what it will fetch at the moment, and he has generally no power to wait till the market improves; and, next, custom determines the price of labour more than it does that of any other article which is offered for sale. We shall have occasion hereafter to give abundant proofs of these positions. It may be added, that the last issue of base money, and the last refusal to redeem such money at its nominal value, was the act of a petty German prince some forty years ago.

CHAPTER IV.

On the Substitutes for Money.

WHEN a man sells his goods or his work, he really means to get other useful articles in exchange. If he takes, as he almost always does, money, he does so because, as we have seen, he can always get as much or nearly as much for money, at some future time, as he would get for it when he took it. During the time that he holds his money, it is of no use to him, that is, it brings him no revenue, no advantage beyond the command which he has over such articles as he wants, by the fact of his possessing it.

Everybody however who has property, wishes to get some use or advantage out of it if he can. He does not want it to be idle. If he buys land, he expects rent; if he gives labour, he expects wages; if he lends, he expects interest. No reasonable person would care to have his land untilled, his labour unemployed, his capital unproductive. And as he does not wish other parts of his property to be useless, so he does not wish his money, i.e. such part of his property as is represented by the precious metals, to be of no service to him. No rational man now-a-days would turn all his property into gold and silver, shut it up in a box, and take it piece by piece out, as he wanted to purchase what he needs for his daily life. He must, to be sure, have some ready money, but he only keeps as much of this as he needs.

Now it is from the confusion between the convenience

of having ready money, and from the fact that money is, for any other purpose than the supply of what one wants, wholly useless, that people have failed to see the real functions which money fulfils. If a man were alone on an island, or indeed if there were few persons on such an island, and they had no communication with any other country, the most abundant supply of the precious metals would be of no earthly use at all as money. It is only when labour is divided, and men rely on each other for the supply of the necessaries or conveniences of life, that money has any use.

A man hoards because he fears for the future. He knows that he can sell gold and silver more easily than he can anything else, particularly if he has it in such a form as that the least possible trouble is given to those who buy it, as far as regards their giving a judgment on its weight and quality. So if governments are rapacious, or credit is low, or the future is uncertain, men hoard money, because they know that what they hoard gives them a fuller and surer command over the market than anything else can. But if on the other hand government is conducted with a view to the public good, and credit is high, and there is no fear for the future of society, men do not think of hoarding, because hoarding money means losing a profit on a part of one's property. Money, in short, is to an individual that part of his possessions which gives him the greatest power over other objects, but which as long as he retains it yields him no return. To a community it is the machinery of trade, necessarily expensive, because it must be a great value in small compass, but still it is only machinery.

Now we have seen, in the outset of the inquiry into the

causes which bring about public wealth, that one of the most powerful of these causes is the disposition which people have to get the greatest possible results with the least possible labour. This motive influences societies of men as well as individuals, and if it be unchecked, it leads men, first to select that kind of labour which they can do best, and next to make the work they do as easy and as little costly as possible. And as they economise to the fullest possible extent the machinery of production, so they economise as far as they can the machinery of exchange.

To effect this result, they ordinarily, though perhaps without reflecting that they do so, use as little money as they possibly can. They buy and sell in foreign countries, but they contrive either directly or indirectly to make what they sell pay for what they buy. Occasionally they are obliged, for causes which we shall investigate hereafter, to buy with money; but in the vast majority of instances no money is used to liquidate debts on either side. The foreign trade of this country is now (1875) estimated at more than £500,000,000 annually, taking exports and imports together; but the specie which constitutes the machinery of this enormous trade, cannot be more than the sum which is retained by the Bank of England as bullion, i.e. less on an average than a fortieth part of this sum; and great part of this is used to support the notes which circulate within the country. Now let us see how this economy is effected.

In the first place, then, and for many ages, the cost and risk of transporting money from one country to another has been obviated by the use of certain instruments called Bills of Exchange. An Englishman has bought goods in France; a Frenchman has bought goods in England. If the transactions were single and independent, the Englishman would need to transport money to France, the Frenchman to transport money to England, and each must incur the cost of carriage and the risks of the transit, to say nothing of losing all use of the money during the process of transfer. Now it is clear that in these cases, it is possible to adopt some mechanism, by which these risks and losses may be obviated, and that persons will be found who will take upon themselves the office of intermediaries between these merchants. And the machinery for effecting this result is very simple: the Frenchman calls on the Englishman to acknowledge his debt by accepting a demand which the Frenchman makes on him for goods sold; and similarly the Englishman makes his claim on the Frenchman. If, thereupon, some one can be found who will undertake to exchange the acknowledgment of the first debt against the acknowledgment of the second, the debts may be made to act as a set-off against each other; and provided all the bills on England equal all the bills on France, the debts may be balanced without the transmission of any money at all. Even if they do not balance between two countries, there is sure to be found some third country whose transactions will supply the means for bringing about this reciprocal extinguishment of obligations; for no country can, by the very conditions of trade, import that which its exports will not pay for.

This negotiation of bills of exchange is one of the earliest functions of a bank, and one which is always a principal aim in the establishment of a bank. But a bank has also other functions hardly less important in the economy of the precious metals. Gold and silver wear, and are liable to loss. The property which, as we have seen, gives a peculiar fitness to these articles as money, that of easy division and reunion, has its disadvantages. For example, it is difficult to identify money which has been stolen or fraudulently kept from its owner; and if the money has been melted, it becomes impossible to identify it at all. Now if some person can be found who may be trusted, and this person will take money and give in place of it either a power to withdraw the money at discretion by orders on him, or will give such a document to the depositor as entitles him to demand his money, the loss and risk will be obviated.

But this is not all. When the possessor of a sum of money puts that money into the hands of a banker, he does not stipulate to receive again the very coins which he had deposited, but their equivalents. In other words, he makes over his money to the banker, and takes in its place a security, which is worth all his money, and has some conveniences which his money has not. The banker lends this money, for he knows that all the money that he keeps is of no profit to him. He sells his obligations for money; he buys obligations with money; and an enormous mass of obligations is built up on a very small foundation of actual money. It is probable that the London banks do not possess altogether as much as £30,000,000 in gold; but by means of this machinery of banking, more than double the amount of all this gold passes hands under the form of drafts on bankers every week in one particular room in the city of London. No mechanism can be apparently more perfect; for the excellence of mechanism consists in the number and exactness of the operations it performs, in the ease with which these operations are effected, and, (to use a metaphor from mechanics,) in the reduction of the necessary friction to the least possible quantity.

A small sum of money can therefore be made to represent an enormous amount of property, and by means of these substitutions to effect a prodigious number of exchanges; and unless there were a universal panic, and thereupon those facts recurred, which induce individuals to hoard gold or silver, the creation of these obligations on paper will be developed to the fullest extent, since no one, as we have seen, ordinarily retains more gold or silver than he finds necessary or convenient, a single day longer than he can possibly help.

There are yet other economies. Bankers who receive deposits from persons wishing to put their money in a safe place, gave, from the earliest times in which the trade of a banker has been carried on, acknowledgments of receipt. These acknowledgments can be transferred from hand to hand, and such an obligation may have passed through the hands of a very large number of persons, between the time at which it was first given to the depositor, and at last presented in the form of a demand on the banker. 'But why should I not,' the banker begins to argue, 'issue these pieces of paper, which may be so profitable to me, and are so convenient to the public, upon the security of my own property, as well as issue them in acknowledgment of money received? Why should I not, instead of declaring in such an instrument my indebtedness to A. B., declare my indebtedness to any person who presents the piece of paper?' This easy change from a note of receipt to be paid on demand to the depositor or his assignee, to a general note addressed to the bearer, is the origin of the bank-note.

Now if the banker kept exactly as much metallic money in his possession as he had acknowledged in the notes which he has issued, he would get no profit on his business, except in one way—that of making a charge for supplying a great convenience. A bank-note is a great convenience : with proper precautions, its use involves no risk of violence or fraud. If it be lost or stolen, it can be traced. Intrinsically valueless, its practical utility consists in the power which its possessor has of obtaining that which it represents whenever he thinks proper to make a demand. If persons know that they have the power over a sum of money, and that they can exercise this power at their discretion, the power is as effectual as the possession. A large sum of money can therefore be, to all intents and purposes, conveniently carried, counted, and secured, by means of notes issued by a thoroughly trustworthy bank. So great therefore are the conveniences implied in the use of notes, that if the banker reaped no profit by their issue, and therefore could not afford to offer them for exactly the same amount of the precious metals which they represent, the public would be willing to, pay a premium for them. And this, in fact, was the practice with the old banks of deposit, such as those of Venice, Genoa, and Amsterdam. These banks professed to cover all the paper which they issued by the gold and silver which they retained. They broke their pledges indeed, and they all became finally insolvent, for in those days public morality was hardly understood. But they were trusted in the better times of their history. Now it is plain, had they exactly and invariably fulfilled the pledges which they gave, that they could not have paid the expenses of their establishment, unless they made a profit, or set a premium on their notes.

But a banker very soon finds out that the notes which he issues may be considerably in excess of the gold and silver which he holds, and that he may employ a portion of his property in some form from which he may get a profit, in place of keeping it in that form in which, as we have seen, it is quite unproductive. If he issues notes upon no property at all, the issue is fraudulent, and ought to be criminal, for not only has he committed an act of bankruptcy, but he has done it in such a way as makes a loss fall on persons who have had no dealings with him and have no privity of information as to his trade. It is probably because the issue of notes at the discretion of a banker does not and cannot involve the power on the other hand of exacting adequate security on the note thus issued, and because an unsecured and therefore fraudulent note has worse effects than any other bad debt, that the government of this country has restrained the issue of notes by private bankers, and for the future has prohibited them.

The amount of notes which a banker may issue, in excess of the gold and silver which he retains in his hands, is not, and cannot be, a fixed quantity. The public which takes notes, or (which in effect comes to the same thing) lends a bank deposits on which the banker may trade, takes the note because it is more convenient than gold or silver; makes the deposit, partly because it is safer to put money into a banker's hands than to keep it oneself, partly because it is convenient to have an account with a banker, and thereby to check receipts and payments, partly because bankers are in the habit of encouraging depositors, by offering them a share in the gain which the lender obtains from the borrower. But these conveniences and advantages are all contingent on the fulfilment of two conditions. First, the deposit must be in all human probability safe; next, the depositor must be able to recover his deposit at pleasure, and know (in case he leaves his money at notice), that when the period of the notice has elapsed, he shall certainly recover his deposit. Failing these securities, no one would, if he were in his senses, take a note or make a deposit. No commercial undertaking needs so high a reputation and so unsmirched a credit as that of banking. At any sacrifice the banker must be solvent.

We see then that the banker is obliged to take into account several circumstances which seem to contradict each other before he can carry on his business successfully. In the first place, he must discover the minimum to which he can, consistently with safety, reduce his stock of metallic money or, what is the same thing, his power of drawing money. If he holds more of this money or keeps more of this power in his hands than seem to be necessary, he loses a certain part of his profits. If he holds less, he runs the risk of commercial ruin, of destroying his reputation, or at least of sacrificing his property by a forced or unfavourable sale, in order to save his reputation. There are, of course, occasions on which the banker finds it necessary, if he has common prudence, to fortify himself by enlarging these reserves against contingencies, but he will never at any time suffer the amount of his reserve to go below what experience points out to him is necessary for the protection of his commercial reputation; and he will of course take care that all the property which he possesses in his bank shall be of such a character as can be converted into specie with the least possible delay and loss.

We must not forget that money, i.e. coined gold or silver, or both, is the measure of value, and that it has been chosen for this end because it has certain properties. Hence, though persons will, for certain purposes and for a certain time, take the representative of money, they will do so only because they are thoroughly convinced that they can claim the money which the symbol represents whenever they please, and on the instant at which they claim it. There must be no risk or delay, else the representative of money falls inevitably in market value below that which it professes to guarantee. Hence it will be seen that any attempt to base an issue of notes on anything besides money, or that which can instantly be turned into money, is sure to be a failure, however valuable the security may be, and is sure to bring discredit on the note. The history of banking is full of examples of the consequences which ensue from issuing notes based on securities or property, or, in short, on anything but the precious metals. In our own country an attempt was made, in 1696, to issue notes on the security of land. It was a failure, fortunately at an early stage in its proceedings. In France, in 1718, Law attempted to circulate paper on the security of stocks. The plan broke down, and induced widespread ruin. In France again, at the Revolution, an attempt was made to issue paper on the security of the public lands. But the government found out very soon, that a security which is of first class character for the purpose of a mortgage, is wholly worthless as a basis for a currency. Similar though far less serious consequences ensued from the fact, that during the greater part of the continental war this country had an inconvertible paper currency, that is, bank-notes which the holder could not at his pleasure turn into gold at the counter of the bank which issued them, though these notes were based on gold. Just the same results would ensue if an attempt were made to found a paper currency on the public funds. In short, what the holder of a note requires is that he shall be able to change this into—not public securities, or land, or goods, or anything of the kind, but simply into—gold or silver. The power of converting goods into cash diminishes as the amount of available cash diminishes, but in a progressively greater degree. The rule applies still more strongly to the conversion of public securities into cash, because these represent, not goods, but the future earnings of the community.

We now see why it is that persons will take pieces of paper (which have absolutely no economical value, since the pieces have no appreciable worth, and can be produced at discretion, at no appreciable cost) in lieu of these costly products, gold and silver. We can also see under what circumstances they will not take them at all. Between these two extremes of complete confidence and entire distrust, there are many degrees. But that which determines the value at any one time of a paper currency which does not command complete confidence, is the answer which the person who holds it can give to the question. At what time and in what degree of fulness will the persons who issue this paper redeem the pledge which the paper represents? It is plain that the power of answering the question is far more in the hands of astute men of business whose attention is constantly directed to these things, and whose acuteness is aided by experience, than it is in the hands of the general public. A discredited paper currency therefore, as long as it is not absolutely worthless, when it is of course the same to everybody, is always a great public injury, for it helps the strong, and it weakens the weak. It is also a complete reversal of the true function of government; for governments are, in general, the only personages who can commit the crime of issuing bad paper. The business of government is to protect the weak against the strong. But such a paper currency as has been alluded to helps the strong against the weak. This evil is the more urgent when, as is the case with many foreign governments, the paper money is of small denominations. When the lowest note means a considerable sum, the struggle is between persons who do not sacrifice much, or do not gain much. But when the notes are so small that they come into the hands of the poor who live by day wages, the capitalist has every power, and therefore every temptation, to employ every advantage against the labourer.

CHAPTER V.

The Distribution of the Price of Products.

IF we were to take the simplest or commonest thing, we should find on inquiry that a vast number of persons have contributed to the production of it. For example, a loaf of bread represents a great variety of labour. The seed from which the corn was grown was originally saved and sown, the farmer necessarily subsisting from other sources during the period in which the wheat was growing. Various kinds of agricultural labour precede and accompany the crop, from the time it sprouted till it is threshed; and several of these operations are aided by expensive and elaborate machinery. The sale of the corn is the business sometimes of many intermediaries. To grind it into flour, it is necessary that another set of labourers should quarry the stones, build the mill, dig the coal, spin and weave the cloth. A further class of labourers supplies the means for baking the bread, and for selling the article when it is ready for consumption. It is impossible to calculate the number of persons who have contributed to so simple and familiar an object.

It would be nearly as impossible to distinguish the portion which each of these contributories receives from the price of the article when it is sold. It is certain that some portion of the price does go to each person who assists in the production, and that the portions, if they could be determined exactly, would fill up the aggregate price in quantities like those which chemical analysis discovers in exceedingly complex substances.

But though we may not be able to count all the agents, and assign his portion in the distribution of the price to each, we can distinguish two broad classifications, under one of which every person who aids in the result will inevitably come; and a third, which, when the other two are satisfied, absorbs the remainder. We shall find, too, that the circumstances fixing the share which each of these claimants can appropriate, can be interpreted by a few broad but invariable laws. These two classifications are profit and wages; the third, which represents the residuum, is rent.

The analysis of the process by which value is imparted to physical objects cannot be continued to its first beginnings. The phenomena of human society, as interpreted by the conditions of human life, cannot by any experience be carried further back than to the existence of adult men and women. Man has a long and very helpless infancy, during which he must be maintained by the labour of others. He must have cost something in order to have grown up, and to have been able to supply himself with the coarsest and commonest necessaries of life. He must receive from the toil of others that subsistence which, continued during his infancy, will enable him to take his place, when he is strong enough; in order to fulfil the same duties towards his descendants which have been done for him by his progenitors. If the labourer has children, he must save some of his means in order to sustain them. We cannot conceive a state of society in which nothing is saved, but everything is consumed by those who work. Such a state of society, as far as our experience can aid us, could have no beginning. If by some process, of whose possibility we have as yet no scientific evidence, such a society were suddenly constructed, or abnormally developed, but which, when fairly set on foot, would not or could not save to sustain its offspring, the society would come to an end in a generation.

These facts are alluded to in order to point out that, economically considered, the existence of mankind is conditioned by some sort of saving, even though this saving be employed in the maintenance of children, or in the supply of rude aids to manual or other muscular labour. The veriest savage feeds his children, and manufactures tools and weapons; that is, he employs labour on other objects than his own subsistence. He saves something, small though it be; and in this saving we see the germ of that which constitutes the wealth of nations—the accumulation of capital.

Capital is, in the first and most important sense, that part of a man's food, or his power of procuring food, which he does not consume on his own necessities or pleasures, but accumulates in order to be able to continue his labour for the time during which he cannot get any product for that labour, or in order to shorten or economise his labour, or in order to provide for a succession of labourers after he has played his part. All these conditions must be fulfilled, and fulfilled simultaneously. He must make these accumulations, for he has impulses (how originated or encouraged we need not inquire) which lead him to provide for his offspring, to foresee the contingency of want, and to shorten or otherwise aid the labour which he gives. The accumulations of capital in highly organised and civilised states are only expansions of these motives or impulses, and may be fairly taken to be constitutive elements in human nature.

It is important to refer to these facts, because it is the practice of economists to limit the use of the word 'capital' in a loose way to those forms of saving which are exhibited in a tangible form, or at least in a form which is easily alienable. These thinkers are apt, while they acknowledge the place which accumulated or saved labour takes in goods, in machines, in cattle and other live stock, in improved land, and the like, to ignore it when expended on maintaining or instructing man. Now, whatever may be the moral or economical objections to the institution of slavery, the mere existence of such a practice is plain proof that capital can be accumulated in the production of labour; for, with one exception, there is no market value to that which has had no labour expended on it. That exception, as we have seen before, is the natural properties of land, in so far as they are exhibited in the form of rent.

Whatever is needed to sustain labour during the time that it is engaged in such functions as lead to something which may be bought or sold, is wages. Labour may be a service of the body or of the mind. But whatever the service may be (and we take for granted that it is required when it is offered or given), the remuneration is wages. The demand may be foolish, mischievous, immoral; it may be in the highest interests of society that the service should be discouraged; it may be necessary to control or forbid both demand and service: but as long as the demand exists, it is the offer of wages; as long as the service is proffered, it is the demand of wages. We shall see in course of time how important it is to extend the term *wages* to the remuneration of all kinds of labour, whether they be high or low; to the greatest benefit which, under economical conditions, man can do to man, as well to the meanest service; to the function of the statesman, and to bird-scaring of the peasant-boy.

If the capital necessary to production, and engaged in it, is wasted or worn out in the process, it must be replaced. As it represents the saving of past labour, accumulated with a view to sustain or shorten labour, its possession must present certain advantages to the person who has saved it and intends to employ it, either for his own purposes, or to transfer or lend it to another in order that the borrower or receiver may carry out his purposes. If no advantage ensued from this accumulation, no man would save for himself; if no advantage could be secured by the transfer to another, no one would lend. This advantage is called *profit*, a word which, like many other terms used in Political Economy, is very loosely applied. Profit is most obviously recognised when a man possessed of capital lends it to another on certain terms, these being that the capital shall at a given date be restored, with the addition of a certain amount of what is called *interest*. But profit is just as fully realized in such cases as those in which a man makes his own use of his own savings, and consumes all the product of his labour in the supply of his own wants and the improvement of his property.

Profit then must be secured, and wages must be paid, out of the gross value or price of the article or service tendered to society. These must be satisfied first. When they are paid as fully as they can be, that is, when they have appropriated as much as the laws which govern their remuneration will permit, the remainder of the price is appropriated by the owner of the soil, under the name of rent. In fully settled countries, there is hardly any object or service sold which does not pay rent; for a *locus standi* is needed for carrying on all industrial occupations; and as the soil is appropriated, and the licence to use it is conceded on paying the owner such a price as may be agreed on, rent inevitably issues from all objects or services which require the use of a part of the surface of the soil for their manufacture or development. We see, to be sure, the place which rent occupies most fully

v.] DISTRIBUTION OF THE PRICE OF PRODUCTS. 53

in those cases in which it forms a dominant element, as in land used for agricultural purposes, but it is none the less a condition of the exercise of other industries.

It may happen that the satisfaction of profit, wages, and rent are combined in the same person. The most obvious illustration of such a state of things, is that in which a peasant cultivates his own land, with his own capital, a condition common in almost all countries except our own. In this country, however, one person often owns the land, another the house built on it, a third some part of the capital required for the industry which is carried on in the premises, a fourth the remaining capital, a fifth great part of the labour given to exercising the industry. The first of these persons is paid by a ground-rent; the second by what is called a rent, but really is profit on capital laid out in erecting the premises; the third is remunerated by interest or discount, according as he lends money to be paid at some future date or gives the present value of a security to be paid also at some future date; the fourth gets his portion, partly because he secures profit on his part of the capital, partly because he earns the wages of superintendence, and of some other kinds of labour; while the fifth receives the wages of labour only. But however much these persons may be multiplied, however variously they may be associated, it will be found that they can all be referred to these three heads, and that they receive profit for capital, wages for labour, rent for land.

CHAPTER VI.

Capital.

LIKE many other words used in Political Economy, Capital has been taken from common and familiar language. The original meaning of the term is 'a sum lent, on which interest is paid, and which is therefore contrasted with interest.' Hence it has come to mean 'the source of profit,' and should be distinguished, first, as the aggregate saving of a community; next, as the stock which each individual possesses, and which he offers for sale or exchange. In the latter sense, it makes no practical difference whether the individual be a numerical unit, or an aggregate unit, as a partnership, company, or corporation of traffickers.

Origin of Capital. All capital has been saved. As nations advance in civilisation, as societies become more organised, and a larger number of persons are able to subsist on a narrower area of the earth's surface, wealth is more and more accumulated. The impulse to save becomes keener, partly in proportion to the facility with which such savings may be invested with a view to profit, partly as persons desire to improve their condition and multiply their conveniences. The general growth of wealth in any country is relative to the security afforded to property; the growth of productive wealth, to the multiplication of the means of employing accumulations, and to the facility with which the advantages of trade are attainable. Hence, when the profitable investment of saving is discouraged or diminished, capital is less eagerly accumulated; and, on the other hand, when the customs of society favour such investments, capital is increasingly aggregated. The origin of capital is therefore to be found in the necessities of human life; its development and employment, in the assistance which society renders to the individual.

Employment of Capital. This is threefold, first, the direct maintenance of labour; next, the cost of producing the labourer, and thirdly, the supply of those means by which he becomes capable of using his energies with greater precision, with greater fulness, or in multiplied degree. These employments of capital consist in the education of labour for such services as society may demand; in the substitution of animal or mechanical forces for the direct use of human exertion; and in the improvement of natural agents. The education of labour is one of the most important investments of capital, conducted generally of course by those whose moral instincts or natural affections lead them to bring up persons who shall supply the waste of human life and strength. So, again, the progress of human society and the increase of opulence are connected with the use of animal forces, and with the discoveries of mechanical science. And similarly, capital is invested productively in the enclosure, drainage, and other improvements of land, and in the supply of means by which produce may be distributed; that is, in the construction of roads, railways, shipping, docks, harbours, and the like. In the estimate of public wealth, every investment of capital which is destined to be used productively, and is so used, must be included, whether it be represented in the skill of the labourer, the goods, tools, and money of the capitalist, the improvement of the natural capacities of the soil, or any other object from which profit is derived, besides accumulations of unremunerative wealth, as plate, pictures, &c. But the rent of land, the interest on public debts, and the reserves which are held against emergencies, are not part of the capital of a country. Rent in the sense of a licence to use the natural capacity of the soil does not differ from the interest on public debt, except in the fact that it arises from natural causes, or has been allowed to be appropriated; while the dividends on stock are so much annually deducted from the profits of capital invested in various directions. A reserve is, by the meaning of the term, property or wealth which may be made serviceable, but is now withheld from production. It is equally unscientific to treat rents and dividends as part of public wealth, and to deny the name of wealth to those immaterial properties which bestow on objects or persons the faculty of fulfilling purposes, or effecting services which are in demand. Wealth then is greater than capital, and includes it.

Capital and Labour. These two elements, reciprocally necessary to each other's existence, are always in harmony except by error or mismanagement. It is true that the remuneration which the labour takes under the name of wages, is naturally determined by the competition of labourers; the profit which the capitalist appropriates is equally determined by the competition of capital. But there is one cause which gives the possessor of capital a great advantage over the labourer, the comparative ease with which his capital may be transferred from one object to another, from one centre of industry to another, from one country to another, when compared with the facilities with which labour can seek a better market. In order to sustain or succour this weakness of labour, combinations have, as we know, been entered into among labourers, which seek to fix the price, and regulate the process of labour. These practices are an interference with the natural reciprocity of labour and capital, and it may be doubted whether labour has been really benefited by the expedient. The true processes by which the problem of the remuneration of labour can be interpreted, are the development of those means by which labour can seek its own market, and the union of capital and labour in the same persons, under the system of co-operation, and on which I shall speak below (Chap. IX.).

Profits of Capital. Profit is used popularly, and even by economists, in a somewhat loose way, and the usage tends to confuse the relations between capital and labour. The real rate of profit is the average rate of interest, and whatever advantage the employment of capital can bestow on its possessor beyond this rate is not due to profit, but, as we shall see, to some other cause. Interest on advances supposes that the principal sum or value is permanent, and not liable to any diminution. When, therefore, the person who is engaged in the employment of capital has satisfied this portion of his return on capital, he requires that the wear and loss of capital should be replaced. This constitutes another portion of his so-called profits. Then as he bestows labour, sometimes of the most arduous and exhausting character, in the management of his business, he obtains, just as any other labourer does, wages for his care and superintendence. And lastly, in case his occupation involves any risk of loss, he requires, again in the aggregate of his so-called profits, to insure himself against such contingencies. He would do so indeed under the natural competition of trade, though his prudence and foresight may enable him to reduce these contingencies to a minimum.

Accumulation of Wealth for the purpose of Capital. The wealth of a country may be stationary, progressive, or retrograde. The first state is of course, like a mathematical point, wholly hypothetical. The last is, unfortunately for mankind, too frequently witnessed when the government of any country is negligent or rapacious, or the moral character of the community is discredited. The same result may ensue from any great change in the conditions of commerce. Thus the decline of the trading republics of Italy, and of the Hanse Towns, is to be chiefly ascribed to the discovery of other commercial routes than those of which the ancient centres of commercial enterprise almost possessed the monopoly. But when the energies of any country are untrammelled, and the disposition to save is general (even though the rate of interest may be low), and investments may be made which satisfy the community, wealth will be enormously accumulated.

The accumulation of wealth in this and other countries can of course only be guessed at. The elements of the calculation, however, are to be found (1) in the investments of a permanent character which have been made, as in new shares, stocks, and similar employments of industrial capital; (2) in loans to foreign governments and foreign enterprises; (3) in buildings and in permanent improvements of the soil; (4) in the mechanism of foreign and home trade. It must be remembered, however, that as the primary form of capital is the first necessaries of life, wealth may be accumulated more rapidly than the processes for which it may be employed are discovered; that those industries only absorb capital which directly or indirectly produce food or procure it in exchange; and that all other employments or industries, although they may benefit those who follow them, merely absorb wealth, diminish the general stock of food, and represent waste.

In the United States and the British Colonies the accumulation of wealth is still more rapid. In these communities almost all persons are engaged in business. There is no merely spending class, for very few persons live on the bare income of property. The habits of society do not encourage or indeed permit great personal expenditure; the rate of profit is high, and accumulations are therefore encouraged; and the country affords boundless fields for industrial enterprise, while the raw produce of these countries finds a ready market over the whole civilised world.

Capital, as has been stated, is antecedent to the employment of labour, and is devoted to its maintenance. Wealth will not be employed as capital except with a view to profit; and it must be employed in the sustentation of labour. Hence it is the interest of the capitalist to discover the most productive labour, because this gives him the largest advantage in the use of his capital; and it is the interest of those who live by wages to protect and foster capital, because the greater the capital, the larger is the rate of wages, the fuller and more continuous is the employment. Unfortunately, however, labourers have not always seen the function which capital fulfils, nor have capitalists always interpreted the productiveness of labour sagaciously. Like some married people, they have been at cross purposes when they should have been at one; for labour and capital, as long as they are not reciprocally benefiting each other, are paralysed and powerless. The two blades of a good pair of scissors are not more useless when separate, and more effectual when united, than labour and capital are when disjoined and combined. It is idle then for labourers to talk of the tyranny of capitalists in the mass. Capitalists have a common purpose—the attainment of profit. But unless they were united in a vast partnership, a thing manifestly impossible, they have diverse and competing interests; in fact, no competition is more active than the competition which regulates profits. There is none, I may add, which is more beneficent to the general community. Employers may be individually harsh, but it is to their own detriment; for the labourer will always, if he be free to choose, seek the best market, and the best market is that in which he can earn the most, and in the least onerous fashion. So again capitalists will employ their capital most readily where the risks are the least and the mutual confidence of employer and employed are most fully sustained. It is wholly unreasonable to suppose that men prefer an atmosphere of vexation and risk and suspicion to one of ease, security, and good faith. Everything, in short, which facilitates the relations of labour and capital, tends to raise the wages of the former, and to moderate the profits of the latter, because it eliminates risk, encourages accumulation, and suggests the employment of capital at home.

On the other hand it is an error for capitalists to overlook the efficiency or productiveness of the labour which they employ. Of course they require competent skill, and are ready judges of such skill as is required. But this is by no means the only condition of efficiency. A man may be a skilful but a worthless workman. He may be underfed, and incapable of that muscular exertion which is essential to the right discharge of his labour. He may be overworked, and the last hours of his day's labour may be unprofitable. He may be irregular in his energies, negligent when he is unwatched, careless at all times. It is impossible to estimate how much labour is wasted by preventible causes, by general bad faith or indifference on the part of workmen; but it is certain that the waste is enormous. This harmony of the two interests, however, is one of those problems which lie on the border-land of economical and moral science. But the discovery of the means by which such a harmony may be effected is a problem of great and urgent interest, because on its solution depends the continuous development of public wealth in this as in other countries.

Capital then is what men save and use. They save it in order to set labour in motion, whether the labour be their own or that of others, and to make it more effective. The capital of a country consists in its food, and in its power of obtaining food, i.e; its tools or machines; its money, in so far as that money is an instrument of production or exchange; all improvements in the natural powers of the soil which tend directly to increased produce from the soil; and lastly, the acquired skill or power of labour itself. These, as all aids to production, are part of the capital of a community. A nation is all the poorer by the exportation of what might be used as capital, in whatever form that capital is exported. As a rule, however, wealth is not exported unless it be accumulated in excess of the wants of the country in which it is gathered.

As wealth is gained by saving, so it is wasted by such consumption as is not reproductive. It does not indeed follow that such consumption is in itself an evil. But if a community does not save as much as it consumes, its wealth is declining; if it does not save more, its wealth is stationary. In those wide regions of western and central Asia which were once peopled by thriving communities, wealth has been destroyed, and a desert usurps the place of ancient civilisation. In China it is probable that wealth is nearly stationary. In Europe and the New World, especially among the Anglo-Saxon races, it is accumulated rapidly. The best test of rapidly increasing capital is rapidly increasing population; for population must perish unless capital maintains it.

Credit however is not wealth, still less capital, except in a metaphorical sense. The moral qualities of a borrower are, in a way, part of *his* capital, in something like the same way that his intellectual and physical powers are, in so far as they are rendered available for increasing the productive agencies in which he is engaged; and similarly, the moral qualities of a nation are, in a sense, sources of economical prosperity, but only as conditions. Without credit, capital would be accumulated by those only who could use it for their own purposes, i. e. there would be neither lenders nor borrowers. Such a state of things, it is plain, would seriously hamper the progress of any nation, and as between nations would render trade all but impossible. But wealth always represents a value embodied in some physical object.

CHAPTER VII.

Labour and Wages.

THE wages of labour are determined by the same causes which determine the value of all other economical quantities, and which may be put into the form of two questions: first, How much did it cost to produce the labour? next, What is the relation between the supply of labour and the demand for it? The answer to the first question will involve the answer to another question: What is it which causes labour to be variously remunerated? The answer to the second is founded on the proportion which industry bears to population. For a while we will assume that the demand for labour and the corresponding supply are exactly *in equilibrio*, and then having seen that the cost of production (no other cause interfering) governs the rate of wages, we can discuss the cause which, disturbing the equilibrium of demand and supply, disturb also the proportion between the cost of producing labour and the rate at which it is remunerated.

The production of labour involves cost. Capital, in other words, is invested in the maintenance and education of children, just as it is in the improvement of the soil, in the production of machines, in the breeding of animals, in the discovery and adaptation of various economies and forces. It is only because the child is not, for certain moral and political reasons, saleable, that this investment of capital in the maintenance and education of children is not as manifest as it is in those other objects to which allusion has been made. In the slave-holding states of the American Union, where labour was saleable, an infant had its price, which rose as the child reached adolescence, according as he represented a greater expenditure of labour in maintenance and instruction. In certain agricultural districts of England we have seen an analogous phenomenon in the establishment of children's gangs. A contractor hires these children from their parents; and he is able to hire them, because at their tender years the sale of their labour is not at their own discretion, and they are temporarily the property of their parents. Now it is plain that the value of such a child's labour depends on his strength, and, in some degree, on his quickness and intelligence—matters on the whole of maintenance and instruction.

Every adult labourer, then, as Adam Smith recognised, represents in his existence and capacity for labour a certain amount of capital expended. Now capital is accumulated and expended with a view to profit, and must be replaced. Again, just as a steam-engine must be supplied with fuel and other necessary appliances for its activity, so the labourer, who needs continuous subsistence in order to exhibit continuous activity, must be maintained. Here however we must note a difference. The character of a labourer's maintenance is matter of general habit or tradition. It cannot be determined at the discretion of his employer. The owner of a steam-engine may study the cheapest way in which he may supply the fuel needed for the force he calls into operation; but he cannot study these economies in dealing with free labour. He can dictate the quantity and kind of food which a labourer shall consume only when he is called upon to maintain the labourer without bargaining for his services, as for example when he supports him in a workhouse or a prison, or can exercise the authority of a master over a slave.

The food of a labourer has a powerful influence over that part of the rate of wages which is relative to his maintenance. If his customary food is costly, his wages will be proportionate, in so far as they designate the amount necessary to his subsistence. In England the staple food of the labourer has for many ages been wheat; in Scotland it is generally oatmeal; in Ireland it was, in great degree is still, potatoes; in many parts of Europe it is barley or rye. That part of the rate of wages which is devoted to the personal subsistence of the labourer will be determined, on an average, by the cost of that on which he principally subsists.

Weight for weight, the proportional value of wheat, barley, or rye, and oats, in English markets, may be represented, on an average, by the numbers 100, 75, and 42. These numbers are not exact, but are accurate enough for the purpose of comparison. Now we may safely predict that, other things being the same, such part of the rate of wages as is relative to the subsistence of the labourer, and of those whose subsistence he provides, will be proportionate to the value of the kind of food on which he and they subsist. To this condition we may add the cost of the house which he ordinarily inhabits, and of the clothing which he ordinarily wears. These are part of that supply which is necessary to the work of the man, in the same way that food and stable-room are needed for cattle, fuel and other appliances for the continuous working of a machine. We shall see hereafter that other important consequences ensue, whenever we witness the fact that the labourers of any country insist on a high standard of living.

The capital invested in the maintenance and instruction of a labourer must be replaced. Like every other machine, the labourer, sooner or later, wears out. Now just as in the long run, and on an average, capital will not be invested in objects in which, after a lapse of time, it is consumed, unless the profit on the capital is accompanied by a further payment, out of which the capital is virtually replaced, so wages will be increased or diminished in proportion to the period during which the labourer is effective. When any calling, however humble it may be, is surrounded by risks to health or life, or where the labourer is almost inevitably short-lived, there the rate of wages rises above the maintenance of the labourer and the cost of making him effective. The labour of a collier is of the lowest kind. It needs no special training or aptitude. But it is highly paid, even when compared with many kinds of skilled labour, only because it is dangerous. The wages of a needle-grinder were very high, for his occupation was so deadly that few workmen in this craft used to live beyond forty years of age. So with other dry grinders. Since the discovery of means by which the risks of these callings are diminished, the wages of these labourers are said to have fallen. It is a scientific induction that the wages of labour are always proportionate to the period during which the labourer can ply his calling.

But the causes which determine the wages of a collier, a husbandman, a carpenter, a mason, an engineer, determine with equal force the wages of a barrister, a physician, a clergyman, or any other professional agent, who enters into the competition for employment. Let us suppose that supply and demand in all these callings are *in equilibrio*, and that the aggregate earnings of a husbandman are £40, of an artizan £60, of a person following one of the three above-mentioned professions £500 per annum. The payment made to each will represent interest on capital expended in fitting the labourer for his calling, replacement of capital exhausted in the gradual wearing out of the human machine, and insurance against the risk which must attend all human labour, the duration of which is not and cannot be determined with any precision.

We must therefore recognise that the term 'labour,' in order that we may be able to give it an intelligible meaning, and to interpret the economical phænomena which accompany it, as well as the laws which regulate its remuneration, can be used in no restricted sense. When a physician attends a patient, a barrister defends a prisoner or supports a claim at law by his advocacy, the payment which either receives for his services is as much wages for labour as the compensation made to a ploughman is when he has finished his day's work. Furthermore, the causes which regulate the remuneration of both physician and barrister are exactly identical with those which govern the wages of manual labour, though the analysis is a little more obscure, the elements as might be expected, being a little more numerous.

We have hitherto assumed that there is an equilibrium between supply and demand, that there is just as much labour as capital can hire, just as much capital as labour requires, in order to maintain the ordinary standard of comfort needed by the labourer. And in truth, if no artificial hindrance is put in the way, this equilibrium is a state to which society continually and on an average tends, though it must be admitted that there occur some occasions on which the supply of capital is in excess of the average proportion, more occasions on which the supply of labour is in excess of the capital available for its maintenance.

CHAPTER VIII.

The Growth of Population.

IT may be well at this point of our inquiry to connect the theory of population with the analysis of wages and labour. This theory, which was first investigated accurately by Mr. Malthus, may be briefly stated as follows :—Under certain circumstances, there is a tendency for the numbers of any people to increase up to the means of subsistence—of comfortable subsistence, if the habits of the people are such as to make them unwilling to lower their standard of living; of bare subsistence, if they are content with poor and cheap food, scanty clothing, and mean lodging. Should anything occur to permanently depress the condition of the great mass of the people, it does not follow that population will be checked; for the people may accommodate themselves to this new position and accept an humbler and, as we shall see, more precarious state of life. But of

VIII.]   THE GROWTH OF POPULATION.   69

course they cannot subsist without the means of subsistence, and cannot increase beyond the bare necessaries of life.

The theory alleged by Malthus was, it must be admitted, stated repulsively, and was disfigured by an analogy which was at best of a general and metaphorical character. He said, for example, that the checks to this tendency were vice, misery, and moral restraint. Vice, as we know, shortens the lives of many. But it does not necessarily lessen population, at any rate during the age in which the excess or redundancy is most felt. As long as the vicious live they subsist on the produce of labour, and except in so far as they labour themselves, they diminish the resources available for productive labour by their demand and their consumption. And again, it is only when misery kills that it checks population, and then only in the same way that vice does, by shortening life, not of necessity by diminishing numbers. The third check, moral restraint, is far more effectual. Mr. Malthus meant abstinence from marriage, and thereupon such social habits as on a large scale would notably diminish the number of births. This restraint, as has been observed by the critics and commentators on Mr. Malthus and his theory, need not be dignified by the title of moral; it is sufficient that it should be voluntary.

Restraints imposed on marriage by law, with a view to checking births, or more frequently for the purpose of limiting the number of persons engaged in certain occupations, are rarely effectual, and, as a rule, involve worse evils. Thus, for example, the regulations by which marriage is surrounded in Bavaria, and in particular at

Munich, have often been adverted to, and have been incautiously praised by Mr. Mill. These rules are not intended in the public interest, but in that of certain guilds of artisans and traders. These people have two objects: one is to keep up prices; the other is to diminish the liability, to which they are subject, of maintaining such members of their fraternity as are incapacitated for labour. Hence they check marriage. But they do not care to check concubinage; and thus the number of illegitimate births in Munich is nearly as large as that of legitimate. On the other hand, public opinion is much more energetic when it is arrayed against rash and imprudent marriage and analogous misconduct. Thus we are told that the general prosperity of the Norwegian peasants is greatly aided by the custom which prevails there of discouraging marriage till such time as young persons are possessed of a small farm, and such savings as are needed to stock it.

In our own country, self-respect, the dread of falling from a higher to a lower social position, and perhaps the natural anxiety of parents that their children should occupy no worse a place and have no less advantages than they themselves enjoy, are powerful hindrances to rash and premature marriages among the middle classes of society. Such prudential motives, however, seldom operate on the very poor. Agricultural labourers marry early and improvidently; so do most artizans: they have indeed few checks, except those which are imposed by others; as for example, the difficulty of getting a house on the estate where they work, or the bastardy laws, which put the maintenance of an illegitimate child on its putative parent, or the paternal authority and control of their employers. When we consider how low their condition ordinarily has been, and how little risk there is of their sinking further, we may fairly conclude that the ordinary morality of the poorer classes in England has been due to external preventives, and not to any self-restraint or self-respect.

The customary food of a people, as it has its effect on the rate of wages, so it powerfully affects the growth of population. As was said before, wheat has been the staple food of the English nation for ages; barley and oats are, or were, the common subsistence of the Scotch; oats and potatoes of the Irish; rye of the eastern nations of Europe; rice of the many Asiatic communities. Now as wages cannot descend below the amount necessary to procure this food, so again population will not increase beyond the power of attaining it. If the customary food becomes scarce and dear, a community, if it can do so, will temporarily, may permanently in rare cases, descend to a lower and cheaper kind. In the interval marriage will be checked. It has been noticed over and over again that marriages, and subsequently births, are affected adversely by dear, favourably by cheap years, i.e. by scanty or abundant harvests.

It will be seen, then, that a community which subsists habitually on dear food, is in a position of peculiar advantage when compared with another which lives on cheap food; one for instance which lives on wheat, as contrasted with another which lives on rice or potatoes, and this quite apart from the prudence or incautiousness of the people. Two instances will illustrate this rule. The Irish famine of 1846 was due to the sudden disease which affected the potato. It was equally severe in the northern part of Scotland, and particularly in the western Highlands; its effects, as we all know, were terrible: but the same disease affected the same plant in England. That, however, which was distress to the English, was death to the Irish and the Highlanders; they had nothing else to resort to; they subsisted on the cheapest food. Now were such a calamity as the potato disease to attack wheat in England, formidable as the consequences would be, they would not be destructive. The weakest and the poorest would no doubt be sacrificed, but the nation might and would resort to cheaper kinds of food.

No doubt the Irish, whose personal morality is high, were exceedingly imprudent. They married on a potato-field, and at a cottier's rent. But, on the other hand, the Belgian peasantry are among the most thrifty in the world. It is a general practice, as I have been informed on the best authority (that of M. Van de Weyer, the late minister for Belgium), for the people of that prosperous country to save half their income. Their diligence is untiring: they have turned sandy wastes into fertile fields. But again, their chief maintenance in the period referred to was roots, and especially potatoes. The distress which they endured was hardly less than that which fell to the lot of the Irish. Famine-struck by the unexpected calamity, these thrifty but starving peasants clamoured at the gates of the Belgian towns for food, and were driven away only by the bayonet. They perished by thousands. Their imprudence consisted in their choice of food. A nation, in short, which is contented to live on cheap food, is always within the risk of famine. The English, who live on wheat, have never endured a real famine since 1315–1316. With the Irish it has been a periodical visitation. So it has with the Hindoos, who live on the cheapest kinds of grain. Here the risk is even more imminent, the event more frequent; for drought is a more common phenomenon than (as was the case with the potato) organic disease in the plant.

During the middle ages the custom of monasticism, and the celibacy of the clergy, formed, we cannot doubt, very effective checks to population. It is not easy to estimate the population of England and Wales up to the middle of the sixteenth century; it was, however, probably not more than 2,000,000. But the monks, nuns, and priests could not have been much less than a twentieth of the population. They abstained from marriage, but were to a great extent engaged in agriculture and other industrial occupations. When these establishments were broken up, and this remedy for an overplus of population was no longer available, considerable distress ensued. I do not say that this distress was caused by the confiscation of the religious houses, but I do not see any reason to doubt that the existing distress was exaggerated by this great social change and its inevitable consequences.

Among the illustrations given of his theory by Mr. Malthus, was one which has been already alluded to. It was, that food increases in an arithmetical, population in a geometrical ratio. This generality has been adversely commented on, and with justice. The supposed relation is a mere hypothesis. Population cannot, for obvious reasons, increase faster than the means of life. In a rough way, we may say that there are as many people in England as there are quarters of wheat with which to feed them. Population, then, increases with the increase of quarters of wheat, whether these quarters are grown at home or imported from abroad. Now it is possible to state with tolerable precision what was the general rate of increase five hundred years ago. It was about on the whole one-seventh of that which can be obtained at the present time from equal areas of arable land. The population of England and Wales was not, I have said, more than 2,000,000 from the fourteenth to the sixteenth centuries. At the present time it is ten times that amount. Of these, about 15,000,000 are fed from native produce; the rest subsist on imported food.

Many economists of great reputation have been concerned at the risk which society runs from the contingency of over-population. The alarm I am persuaded is futile. First, the supply of food is a 'condition precedent,' as lawyers say, to the growth of population itself. Next, the area from which this country can procure food is, day by day, increasing in width. The risk of famine is far more remote than it was fifty or sixty years ago. We draw our supplies of food from all regions. A perpetual harvest contributes to our wants. All over the world corn is being reaped for the sustenance of such industries as can exchange the products of their labour for that of the agriculturist. Food is the raw material of labour, and just as cotton and wool and other textile materials are gathered from all quarters of the earth, so is food forthcoming. England, and other great industrial countries, resemble in the density of their population and the necessity of their consumption, when contrasted with those thinly-peopled nations of the world from which they draw their supplies of food, great cities surrounded by a fertile plain. Nor is it probable that the supply will be cut off.

A city, to be sure, may be beleaguered by a hostile army, and suffer a famine. So if we had the misfortune or the folly (both we may hope inconceivable) to quarrel with the whole civilised world, we might not perhaps be visited by famine, but should certainly be afflicted by dearth. So, again, if the whole available area of the globe were so occupied that the produce of the soil in each country were wholly consumed by its people, densely-peopled countries, like populous cities, might starve. But we need contemplate no such contingency. In the first place, it must be ages off; and in the next, fair warning of the event, when ages have past, will be given. To dread such a result is to dread a cataclysm or a glacial epoch, to distress oneself, not only with the sorrows of Hecuba, but with the grief of a future creation.

At the time at which Malthus wrote, there was reason in the alarm. The nation was sunk in penury. A succession of deficient harvests, never, I believe, paralleled since the beginning of the fourteenth century, the period alluded to before, was aggravated by an exhausting foreign war. The only people who prospered were the merchants and manufacturers, for the northern counties were commencing that career of industrial success which has raised this country to the position of the first producer of the world. But the mass of the people had no share in these partial and imperfect benefits. Pauperism was devouring the farmers, the landowners, the retail traders. The fiscal system of the country was absolutely destructive. Taxes were imposed on raw materials, and worst of all, prohibitions were put on the importation of that which, as I have said, is the raw material of labour, food. Everybody, with some few exceptions, believed in the necessity of protection. The genius of financiers was directed towards fostering exportation, checking importation. The trade with the East was in the hands of a company which was much more busied with aggressive politics than with successful commerce. The United States were in their infancy, and the wounds of the War of Independence were not closed. The greatest part of the New World was under the wasteful tyranny and exclusive control of Spain. Europe, then our best and nearly our only market, was entering into the gigantic war with Napoleon. Even if food had been forthcoming, our corn laws, the silly dream of which was a fixed and invariable price, would have checked the market by rendering it wholly uncertain. No wonder, then, that Malthus, grasping the fundamental truth, that population and the supply of food must be exactly relevant, laid down crudely the harsh laws which appeared to him to check or control the growth of that which was already over-abundant. At the present time, indeed, the significance of the inquiry into the causes of population has become less important, less likely to arrest attention. The fear of deficient supply (on the hypothesis that the course of the seasons throughout the world is nearly uniform, and that the process of collection and distribution is continually economised and improved), and the alarms which some persons feel as to the future of this country when its population seems to increase rapidly and to depend more and more on foreign markets for the supply of food, are as rational as the dread entertained in the time of the Stuarts that the excessive growth of London must sooner or later end in dearth or even famine.

But though there seems no risk of over-population

in any country whose fiscal system is sound, and whose foreign trade is encouraged by being freed from restrictions, temporary instances of an excessive supply of labour do occur, and furnish apparent exceptions to the general principle laid down in the foregoing pages, as to the remuneration of labour being on an average due to the cost of producing it. In the same way there cannot be general, but there may be particular over-production.

For example, the remuneration of those who are engaged in what are called the liberal professions, represents a less percentage on the outlay incurred in fitting persons for these professions than *cæteris paribus* is awarded to humbler offices. Here however social position forms part of the incentive to entering into these callings, and therefore diminishes the remuneration. People press into a calling which is held in honour, which gives independence or dignity. The payment made on an average to a barrister, a physician, a clergyman, an officer in the regular army, is less, when the labour given is considered and the preparation requisite for fulfilling the function is estimated, than that awarded to a retail trader. It is not that men are paid by reputation and social standing, but that men compete for these objects, and thereupon compete against each other with greater energy for such remunerations as these callings afford. And conversely, when any discredit attaches to the calling, the competition is scanty and the remuneration is high. As Adam Smith says, the labour performed by a common hangman is easy, but the remuneration is very high. The office is in the fullest sense discreditable; there is no competition for filling it; the service, it seems, must needs be performed, and the functionary can exact what terms he pleases, short, of course, of such a sum as would attract others (who might conquer their squeamishness by their desire of gain) into the field of operations.

Again, the risk of an over-supply of labour attends such offices as are liable to the unforeseen caprices of fashion. Female costume is, it seems, affected, in wealthy countries at least, by extraordinary and unintelligible fickleness. Sudden changes occur, the origin of which cannot be traced, the duration of which cannot be anticipated. Those who minister to these precarious demands are consequently liable, more than any other artisans, to the contingency of over-production, to the revulsion of demand, and to the suspension of occupation. A few years ago, every woman who made any pretension to dress according to the custom of the day, surrounded herself with a congeries of parallel steel hoops. It is said that fifty tons of crinoline wire were turned out weekly from factories, chiefly in Yorkshire. The fashion has passed away, and the demand for the material and the labour has ceased. Thousands of persons once engaged in this production are now reduced to enforced idleness, or constrained to betake themselves to some other occupation. Again, a few years ago women decked themselves plentifully with ribbons. This fashion changed: where a hundred yards had been sold, one was hardly purchased, and the looms of a multitude of silk operatives were idle. To quote another instance. At the present time women are pleased to walk about bareheaded. The straw-platters of Bedfordshire, Bucks, Hertfordshire, and Essex were reduced from a condition of tolerable prosperity to one of great penury and distress.

The most serious inconvenience however ensues, when

the supply of any important raw material is materially diminished or arrested. As a rule, the phenomenon of a glut in the labour market attends any great exaltation in the price of food; for food, as has been stated more than once, is the raw material of labour, must be procured at any sacrifice, and therefore when it happens to be very dear, the consumption of such articles as are of voluntary use must needs be diminished. In dear years the home trade is stunted, that industry which is ordinarily engaged in matters of domestic convenience, comfort, taste, or luxury, is less in demand, and the only labour which is likely to be engaged is that which is occupied in production for such foreign markets as, directly or indirectly, can contribute to the demand for food. When however the deficiency of the raw material is on a grand scale, as happened a dozen years ago with the supply of cotton, the gravest consequences follow—consequences a little palliated by the growth of analogous industries, but not materially remedied.

Excess of labour is not peculiar to the mechanical or manual occupations in which men engage. The proximity of persons in the higher classes of society to the margin of bare subsistence is not indeed witnessed frequently, but it is constantly seen to be close upon the margin of comfortable or decent or customary subsistence. It is seldom, for example, that a poor clergyman, or medical practitioner, or barrister, is literally starving; but he may be, and constantly is, close upon penury, and forced to unbecoming or squalid shifts. On the whole, to be sure, these cases are exceptional, and when persons become more alive to the conditions under which different kinds of labour can subsist, will become scarcer; but every one is aware of how urgently these prudential motives to which Malthus referred are present with the professional classes.

CHAPTER IX.

Restrictions on Occupations.

OF course all persons who are engaged in any calling are aware that the demand for the labour or products of labour in that calling remaining stationary, greater competition will mean diminished remuneration. As a rule, too, those who practise any craft or profession are slow to believe that an increased supply will be met by a corresponding demand, and therefore feel naturally concerned to occupy and retain the market for their own labour or products. They attempt to bring about or maintain this result, either by keeping up prices artificially, or by putting artificial checks on the supply of labour. Hence ensue some of the most significant phenomena in the working of society—phenomena the interpretation of which is rendered obscure by the fact that a number of irrelevant issues and indirect arguments are alleged in support of the customs adopted by such parties, while the true motives are generally denied.

In the early ages of European social history the control over the market of the trader or producer was secured, or supposed to be secured, by the establishment of guilds or trading companies. These guilds were universal, and the character of such associations is suggested by the great companies which still survive, though in an altered form, in the city of London. The general purpose of these associations was that of prohibition. No trader was allowed to exercise his calling within the privileged district unless he were enrolled in these protected bodies, which ordinarily (in consideration of certain sums given to the Crown, at that time supposed to be the fountain of such privileges) had the right of framing bye-laws for the management of their several trades. It is of course obvious that the companies conceded the right of trade sparingly, and under well-defined and strict regulations. Such guilds exist at the present time in Munich, and exhibit faithfully the character of similar incorporations in England, as they were one or two centuries ago.

In course of time, the Crown assumed to itself the right of permitting associations of merchants a monopoly of particular trades or commerce. The privileges accorded by our monarchs to the merchants of the Hanse Towns, trading as the Alderman and Merchants of the Steelyard, are among the earliest of these mercantile monopolies. The discovery of the New World gave birth to another set of privileged merchants. That of the Cape passage, and of the sea route to the East, were the occasions out of which a third set of adventurers were chartered. At last, when the Crown began to grant monopolies of home trade and production to particular individuals the country became indignant, and the prerogative was surrendered.

But it was found that the grant of trading privileges and monopolies might form an important branch of public revenue; and as soon as Parliament took the complete control of the supplies into its own hands, the grant of these powers, always in consideration of sums applied to the public service, became frequent. This was the day of the Bank of England, the South Sea Company, and a host of similar associations. Of these companies none however has exercised so vast an influence as the East India Company, which, before it was transformed into a body of fund-holders, conquered and governed a vast empire as well as carried on trade.

The example of England was followed by other nations. Holland and France adopted the same expedients; the latter with but scanty success, the former with a well-defined and vigorous policy. The Dutch East India Company was a very powerful body, and at the present day, Holland is the only European state which draws a large revenue for public purposes from its possessions in the Indian Archipelago. But the theory of all these companies was one; they sought to keep up prices by restraining supply. Of course these monopolists could not prevent smuggling, or, as the East India Company called it, 'interloping;' while the incessant wars and the necessary police of the seas, to say nothing of the deadening influence of trade privileges, soon lowered the profits and curtailed the trade of these associations.

There is nothing which gives a better illustration of the mischief attending these trade monopolies than the history of the East India Company's traffic. The people of England, dazzled with the astonishing growth of the empire of Hindostan, and the political influence which is supposed to be involved in the maintenance of our supremacy in India, is apt to forget the losses and the sacrifices which the establishment of the empire has cost us. It was the proximate cause of the American War of

Independence. The severance of those colonies from the British crown is not, as we now are aware, matter for regret; but the lurking hostility of the two families of the British race is matter of profound regret and continual danger. But not to enter on this part of the historical question, it is sufficient to say, that for more than a century and a half the produce of the Indian peninsula and of the Chinese empire was lessened in English markets by the monopoly of these imperial traders. The art of navigation in tropical waters, the foundation of independent colonies in the islands of the Pacific, were arrested by the trade jealousies of the East India Company. Every stranger in their eyes was a rival, every colonist an interloper. They prevented the acclimatisation of Europeans in India, they checked the development of native produce. And conversely, since their monopoly has been rescinded, hardly a generation ago, the passage from the East to Europe has been so shortened, that a freight from thence to England is reduced to one-fourth, the time required to one-third, and the produce of India and China have been powerfully stimulated by the freedom of trade.

It is by machinery like this that in times past trading companies, having induced the executive or the legislative power of the country to grant them special privileges, have sought, but almost invariably in vain, to derive certain benefits from a monopoly, and in order to stereotype these benefits, have attempted to keep up prices artificially. The defence alleged for the practice has professedly been derived from the principles of natural justice. It has been said that it would have been impossible for private individuals to have ventured on trade with those distant countries; that it was necessary to incur vast outlay, not only in vessels, and merchandise exported for purposes of exchange, but in factories and the like; and that it would have been unfair, had others, who had taken no part in the venture, and had not incurred the risks of the experiment, been enabled to enter on the fruits of those labours which had been undertaken. It is not difficult to see that these charges were either visionary or unnecessary. It has been found possible to carry on trade with foreign countries, though they have been only newly discovered, or only newly opened to such trade, without it being necessary to adopt the expedients which the founders of the East India Company thought proper in their early relations with Hindostan.

Similar or analogous restrictions have been adopted by various classes of persons who carry on trade or practise professions at home, or have been imposed by law. Thus no person has been allowed to engage in a branch of business unless he has passed through a period of apprenticeship, or has completed a formal course of study, or has consented to a series of bye-laws framed for the purpose of narrowing the number of persons who may be employed. In the same way, entrance into the medical and legal professions is restricted to those who have attended a certain curriculum of study, and the practice of these professions is guarded by a number of regulations. The functions too are divided: the etiquette of the law requires the presence of two functionaries, an attorney and a barrister, whenever the agency of a court of law is required. Similarly, though here the distinction is less rigorous, the ordinary medical practitioner is distinguished from the more dignified physician. In all cases, the restrictions put on these callings are justified on the plea of the public good. It is averred, that were these rules swept away, great injury would ensue by the introduction of unqualified or dishonest practitioners. But the police of these bye-laws is, unfortunately, no guarantee against dishonesty, and the regulations by which both these professions guard against the intrusion of incompetent persons are far later than the concession of professional privilege in the case of medicine, and are hardly operative at all in the case of law. It does not, in short, seem possible to doubt, that the purpose of all these restrictions has originally been to raise prices, by imposing obstacles on practice; and it may well be questioned, whether the testimonium of a board of examiners has not been gifted with greater importance than it deserves when, instead of being treated as a certificate of proficiency, it is turned into a licence to practise.

We do not indeed imagine that any great inconvenience follows on these regulations. The use of legal and medical services is, to a great extent voluntary; and the advantages of competition are, on the whole, secured by the fact that though these persons are united together against those who lie outside the privileged body, they compete eagerly against each other. I have referred to these facts because they illustrate the causes which tend to derange the operation of that fundamental law of wages and labour, that the remuneration of a service is due on an average to the cost of producing the labourer.

The effect, however, of various attempts to artificially inflate the rate of wages on the one hand, or to artificially depress it on the other, in certain commoner and more necessary callings, is far more important, and far more deserving of consideration. The machinery which has been employed to depress the rate is older, and the policy adopted in both cases has produced such important consequences on the social history of this country, and is now dominant in so many important industries, that it will be well to give a short sketch of the course which this policy has taken, before we proceed to analyse the social effects of these endeavours to interfere with the natural relations of supply and demand in the labour market.

Five hundred years ago and upwards the whole of Europe was afflicted with a plague of uncommon severity. According to contemporary accounts, more than half the population perished; and though probably the loss was exaggerated, there can be no doubt that labour became so scarce and dear that a complete revolution ensued in the tenure and cultivation of land. In order to obviate these inconveniences, the landowners of the day attempted to regulate the rate of wages by acts of parliament: at first, by enacting that no more wages should be paid than had been customary before the visitation of the great plague, and by restricting husbandmen and their children to the calling which they had hitherto followed, and to the place in which they were born; next, by fixing rates of wages from time to time in parliament; and finally, by leaving the right of fixing the rate with the justices of the peace, who, as employers of labour, or at least as letting their lands to employers of labour, would be interested in prescribing and enforcing low rates of wages. These provisions of course were only temporarily operative; they could not affect in any notable degree the wages of artisans, and in practice it was found that they had only a partial operation on those kinds of labour the dearth of which was the original cause of these legislative enactments. Of course, as far as possible, the labourers retaliated. They rose in insurrection, and once, under Wat Tyler, nearly overthrew the constitution. Fresh laws were enacted, severe punishments were inflicted, but it was not possible for a long time to break down the opposition to the law. The Lollards, Oldcastle, Cade, and others, were all combatants on behalf of labourers as opposed to landowners. It appears that, on the whole, the labourers succeeded in bettering their condition; serfage was extinguished, and an influential class of yeomanry, partly possessed of free and copyhold estates, partly the beneficial lessees of the various monastic corporations, arose.

A great alteration took place in the middle of the sixteenth century. It was due partly to the confiscation of the church lands; partly to a change in the method of tillage, and the adoption of sheep-farming in lieu of corn-growing; partly to the debasement of the currency; partly to the depreciation of money—always a serious evil to those who live by wages; partly to the growth of population. These and other concurrent causes led to the enactment of a poor-law, followed subsequently by the law of settlement which put the burden of maintaining the destitute poor on the parish of their birth or legal adoption, and by implication forbad or restricted the migration of labourers in search of employment. This law of parochial settlement, which had a great influence in lowering the rate of wages, was modified at last indirectly by the rise of the great industries in the north of England, by cotton manufactories, and by the increase of iron and other hardware products. The demand for labour became urgent, and the migration from agricultural regions to those in which these industries were carried on became great and uninterrupted. The employers of labour in the north of England were too eager for labour to care for the risk that it might become a burden on the parochial rates. But meanwhile the laws against the combinations of labourers remained on the statute-book, though they were gradually becoming obsolete, and were seen to be unjust and invidious. In 1825, i. e. 476 years after the enactment of the first statute of labourers, they were repealed.

With the repeal of these laws commences that organised system of combination known familiarly under the name of a trades-union. The purpose of a trades-union is to keep up the price of labour, and if possible to enhance it. In order to effect this, restrictions are put on the number of persons entering into the employment, by insisting on apprenticeship, and regulating the number of apprentices kept by any employer. Restrictions are put upon the mode in which work is done, upon the hours during which labour is employed, on the rate of wages paid to those who work over-time, on job or piece-work, and in particular on the rate of wages themselves. Obedience to these regulations is enforced among the members of the union by fines, and in cases where the offence according to the bye-laws is great or reiterated, by expulsion from the benefits of the union. Those who do not belong to the union, and take work when the interests of the union are supposed to be in danger, have been slighted, threatened, or even maltreated, some acts of extreme ferocity having been sometimes committed. The machinery adopted against the employer is a strike, i. e. a refusal to work, the time in which this strike is decided on being generally one which is critical to the employer. Naturally, workmen on strike look with great dislike on such other workmen as take employment under the master whom they have made war against, and strive to deter them by persuasives more or less cogent, or even by acts more or less violent; since the success of the manœuvre consists in starving the master's capital. In the abstract, it must be admitted that these arrangements represent no more than the joint-stock principle applied to labour. On the other hand, employers also naturally combine, and obviate these threats or these acts by a retaliatory process called a 'lock-out,' the lock-out being, as a rule, more general than a strike, and being of course felt more severely by the men. In order to carry out the organisation of a trades-union, large funds are subscribed, out of which labourers on strike or locked-out are supported. It may be added, that trades-unions answering to the above general description are almost peculiar to this country, great hindrances being put in other countries on the use of the machinery by which the ultimate ends of the union are achieved.

Now my reader will remember that the rate of profit, by which, as we have seen, must be understood the interest on advances, is in a manner fixed. It may rise by competition for capital; it may sink by a superfluity of wealth seeking employment as capital. It fluctuates most largely when advances are made for short terms; it varies very little on permanent investments. The occupation of a man's own capital in his own business is of a permanent character; the assistance which he obtains from bankers and other dealers in money is of a short or precarious character; and as a rule, therefore, the rate of profit is the quantity which is large enough to induce persons to save or employ wealth as capital. If it falls too low, the owner will not save, or, which is the same in an economical sense, will hoard or reserve his wealth. Interest or profit is, as Mr. Senior used to say, the wages of abstinence; but no man gets wages unless he works, nor does any man get profit or interest unless he lends, either indirectly to an employer of labour, or directly in the employment of labour.

It will be clear then that the machinery of a trades-union cannot increase wages by depressing the profits of capital. On the contrary, if these profits are rendered insecure, the rate payable to the employer will increase with the risk. This increase is not, to speak exactly, a rise in the rate of interest; but a compensation or insurance for and against the contingency of loss. And in just the same way that superior intelligence, activity, and skill (qualities, it will be remembered, which make labour more effective, and which are therefore in an economical analysis to be classed with labour itself), invariably obtain an increase of remuneration as compared with the labour of those who are deficient in these qualities, or devoid of them; so when they are applied to the management of capital, they raise the amount which the capitalist is enabled to appropriate under the general name of profits. The ingenuity which substitutes machinery for muscular force, which discovers a short way of transacting business, which eliminates a superfluous intermediary in trade, which satisfies a new want or supplies an old want at an easier rate, aids its possessor towards what is familiarly called 'making a fortune.' This fortune is obtained really by an increase of effective labour. But in just the same way, the intelligence which can anticipate disaffection among artisans, which can prophesy a strike, or see that labour is under particular circumstances unable to dictate terms to employers, and which is therefore cautious or bold as the case may be, takes advantage, to its own profit or gain, of the very organisation which at first sight is directed against it. The labourer seeks to get more out of the capitalist, and the effect is that the capitalist gets all that the labourer gets, and something over, out of the public. In popular language, the struggle of a trades-union is supposed to lie between labour and capital; in effect it lies between the labourer and the purchaser, the man who sells the service and the man who buys it, and to whom the employer is only an intermediary. To this rule there is one exception, which I will state.

The effect of a combination to raise the rate of wages will be found to vary with the relation of the labour to the product: in no case will it fall on the capitalist; i.e. the person who advances the wages.

If, by any arrangement, the combination of agricultural labourers should raise the rate of wages without making their labour more productive or valuable to the employer, the loss would not fall on the farmer but on the landlord; i.e. the increased cost must be compensated out of rent. Rent is all that remains out of the price of the articles produced from the soil, after the cost of production is satisfied. When the farmer has received interest on his capital, is insured against the risks of weather, and is paid for his own labour in superintendence, and the like, the residual value of that which he obtains from the soil is paid by him to his landlord as rent. Just the same facts apply to the rent of a house in a crowded thoroughfare as are manifest in the process of ordinary agricultural business, though in the former case the facts are more complex. A man pays £500 a year for a shop in Cheapside, and only one-fifth of such a rent for equal accommodation in a country town, because the returns of a Cheapside business, as a rule, leave such a margin over the ordinary compensation obtained by a trader, from which the owner of the house can levy this rent.

If rents fall by reason of such a combination, no one but the landlord will be injured: for the origin of his rent, in so far as it is merely compensation for the use of the natural powers of the soil, is entirely due to the competition of purchasers for the products of land. There is no rent in countries where land is cheap, abundant, and naturally fertile: there could be no rent, if the cost of production swallowed up the whole return from the soil. Such a result, in an indirect way, was actually almost reached under the old poor-law, when in some country districts the rate amounted to twenty shillings in the pound, and therefore if the assessment to the poor-rate and the net rent of the land approximated, rents were wellnigh or entirely extinguished. As I have said above, it was because the cost of production during the middle ages was relatively so high, that the rent of land was so low; and it is because the cost of production has so marvellously diminished that in our own day the rent of land is so high.

When this book was first written, the probability of a

combination of agricultural labourers with a view to raising the rate of wages seemed to be very remote. The labourer did not appear to possess the resolution necessary for the experiment, and the machinery by which such a resolution could get effect, seemed all but unattainable. To the surprise of every one, however, farm labourers combined on a large scale, managed their union with singular perseverance and energy, and have unquestionably secured a considerable advance in wages, especially as they have devoted no small part of their funds in transferring labourers from over-crowded districts to places where labour is in demand, and in encouraging emigration.

Now that such a combination has been effected, the incidence of the event will be very probably obviated by the large use of machinery in agricultural operations. This use is increasing, and is rapidly increasing. Labour was in excess, and had to be maintained; the incentive therefore to substitute mechanical for muscular forces was formerly weak. But if at some future time the use of such machinery becomes universal, the result will be that wages will be lowered till such time as labourers again emigrate from the district; and rents will rise until the emigration takes place and another rise in agricultural wages is effected, accompanied by no corresponding increase in the efficiency of labour; for whatever be the way in which the cost of production from the soil is economised, the benefit, as long as competition for the product exists, will enure to the landlord only; and conversely, when the cost is enhanced, the loss will fall on the landowner only in the end.

When the product on which labour is exercised is capable of importation from abroad, the effect of a combination to raise wages, supposing it to be effectual, will not raise prices beyond the amount at which the article can be produced and imported from abroad. Thus, for example, if a piece of English silk cost eight shillings a yard, and could be produced, but for the restrictions and charges of the unions, at seven shillings, and if foreign silks, produced under these cheaper conditions, are allowed free importation, the price of the home product must fall, and the manufacture will either be abandoned or the labourer must accept lower prices. Such indeed was only lately the case in this country. Up to the time in which the commercial treaty with France was negotiated, foreign silks were burdened with a fifteen per cent. *ad valorem* duty. During the continuance of this duty the silk-throwsters and weavers took incredible pains to raise wages by the adoption of trades-union regulations. The natural remedy for dear labour (by which I do not mean high wages, but high wages for inferior labour), i. e. the adoption of improved machinery, was not available, for most of the best silk fabrics were manufactured at their own looms, and in their own lodgings, by the silk-weavers. Hence when the duty was remitted, the price fell, the home-silk manufacture shrunk in the competition, and the weavers were wellnigh ruined. Such at least was said to be the case at Coventry. Exactly the same circumstances have attended other processes, which at one time or another have been sustained by protection. There is therefore a natural limit to the operation of a trades-union, or of any combination for the purpose of raising wages, when the article produced can be freely imported from abroad; and hence the union of such labourers as are engaged in these occupations would be practically harmless to the purchaser, though it might, perhaps does, operate injuriously on the aggregate interest of the country.

Much more important however is the operation of a trades-union on those products which cannot be imported from abroad. Here, supposing the combination to be effectual, the rise in price may be continued as long as the purchaser will submit to the enhancement; or until he economises its use. According to the terms of my hypothesis, he can substitute nothing for the article produced, and must use it in a greater or less degree. Such, for example, are the materials for house-building, and the labour engaged on constructing houses; and it is upon these, technically known as the building trades, that the union is reputed to be most active and effectual. Here there is hardly any operation on which artificial restraints are not imposed: the making of bricks and tiles, the cutting of stones, the process of building, the work of carpenters and joiners, of smiths, and whoever else contribute to the result, is limited by specific regulations, and controlled by jealous supervision. The number of apprentices, the hours of labour, the method of labour, the quantity of labour, the quickness and slowness of labour, and a variety of other particulars, are determined by the rules of the union or the custom of the trade. And the effect, it may be predicted, is that houses are bad and dear—dearest and worst for the working classes themselves; for of course the necessaries of life consume a far greater portion of the incomes of the poor than they do of the incomes of the rich. It may indeed be doubted whether the real benefit of a rise in the price of labour has ensued; and whether such an increase as has been effected in the money wages of labour, may be more than compensative for the general rise in most prices, which has characterised late years; or at least has not been due to the operation of natural causes, which are quite independent of a trades-union: but it cannot be doubted, I think, that the manipulation of labour by trades-unions has heightened prices, and heightened them to the consumer, without in the least degree diminishing the gains of the employer.

It has been said, epigrammatically, that trades-unions are a machinery by which ten per cent. of the working classes combine in order to rob the remaining ninety per cent. Let us state the grounds upon which this epigram is founded. The amount available for the payment of wages is all the food and other necessaries which a country can produce or procure. We may not, to be sure, know what the amount exactly is, but it is certain, notwithstanding, for it is all the capital which a community uses productively; everything which is paid for services, of whatever kind these services may be. We have seen that certain classes of labourers have exceedingly limited powers in this direction: they are those who are engaged on such products as can be freely imported from abroad. Hence some artisans have striven to develope, as yet without success, an international trades-union. The only labourers whose discretion is apparently uncontrolled in this direction, are those who produce such necessaries as can only be supplied at home. Now it is clear that no act on the part of labourers can increase the amount of wealth available as capital in the country, but that it can only decrease it; either by causing it to be withdrawn from productive operations, or by inducing the possessor to export it in foreign loans, or for the subvention of foreign industry. If therefore a trades-union succeeds in extorting a larger share of this fund on behalf of the operatives who enter into the combination, it can do so only by leaving less to those who are unable or unwilling to enter into a union. It does not deserve therefore the sympathy either of other labourers or of consumers; not of the former, because it diminishes the resources available for them; not of the latter, because it heightens the price of the articles which they buy, and curtails the comforts which they might enjoy. And it need hardly be said, that most men are in one way or the other labourers, and that all men are consumers. Moreover if the union, while it raises prices, does not raise wages, it is of no real or even apparent benefit to those on whose behalf the union is constituted; it is even more mischievous, for in this case it inflicts a wrong on all, a wrong which only ceases to be wanton, when it is shewn to be done ignorantly.

The case however will be made still more clear if we take a hypothetical instance. I have the greatest aversion to the introduction of hypothetical cases into a subject like Political Economy, in which a flaw in the reasoning, an error in induction, has often had serious consequences. But the hypothesis is so remote, and yet the inference from it is so manifest, and its partial application to existing facts is so plain, that I hope my reader will see at once the apology for its introduction, and the lesson which it conveys. Suppose that all men could combine for the purpose of raising wages, and that a Japanese system of complete exclusion from the other markets of the world were adopted; suppose that the people of these islands determined to supply all their wants from their own resources, and repudiate all commercial intercourse with the rest of mankind; because, unless this were done, some of those articles which can be imported from abroad would come into competition with the products of some labour at home, and so interfere with the efforts of this universal determination to put an artificial protection on labour. Now on my hypothesis, as all money wages would rise, all prices would rise. The labourer would get more money, but he could buy less with it. He would be nominally richer, but virtually in the same position as he was before he set to work with such great pains to achieve a larger remuneration for his services; and ultimately, unless some labourers were more powerful than others, and therefore got better terms in the distribution of that which was produced by the joint labour of the community, all would be on the same level; with this sole difference, that the trade of the country would be annihilated, its industry reduced to the lowest level, and its people demoralised by the search after a good which is about as real and tangible as the philosopher's stone or perpetual motion. Some labourers in any country may be guilty of a partial folly and a partial wrong, but a universal folly means the annihilation of the place which the misguided country occupies among nations; and a universal wrong is universal barbarism.

The sentiment which is manifested so strongly in a trades-union, and which might develope such serious results, is identical with the fallacy of Protection. Nobody has ever doubted—if no necessity arose for levying an income for public purposes, and therefore if it were impossible to say that any person's enjoyments or resources or powers were curtailed or limited—that trade should be as free as the winds. The principle of Protection was excused because it was thought that some interests were crippled by taxation, or because it was insisted that they were, and therefore that compensation should be secured them by giving them a sole market; that as they were taxed, they should have and enjoy a right to tax others. The cry of 'peculiar burdens' always intends a claim for peculiar privileges. As we have seen, there was a time in which labour was peculiarly burdened, and particularly manual labour. It was tied to the spot, it was hampered by restrictions; its own raw material, i.e. its food, was taxed, wastefully and wantonly; its operations were checked by a host of foolish and vexatious imposts and excises. It would have shown wonderful sagacity and intelligence, if the mechanics and artisans of this country, after the labour laws were abolished, had not retaliated, because they knew that protective regulations are delusive; it would have shown wonderful patience and virtue, if they had decided that wrongs are never cured by wrongs, and that the past, in which employers had armed themselves against labour, was no wise precedent in pursuance of which labourers should arm themselves against employers. For it is one of the consequences—and one of the worst consequences—of bad laws, that when they cease to operate, and are even repealed, they leave a feeling of revenge and hatred behind them, and that the most inveterate antipathies are nourished and strengthened by the fact that certain classes of society have used the law to do injustice.

It must be observed, however, that there are other

aspects, from which these combinations of labourers may be estimated. They may have served to develope an intelligent acuteness in artisans, have suggested lessons of public and private duty, have discouraged (in the vast majority of cases) the harsh expedients of violence, have materially extended the growth of benefit societies, those reciprocal charities which the proudest man may take, without losing his self-respect; have assisted the political education of artisans. But I am speaking of course of their economical characteristics only.

In quitting this subject we should repeat that the principle of trades-unions is not confined to certain operatives. Its consequences on the general industry of the country are however more significant when it is dominant upon manual labour, because it affects or might affect the general prosperity of the British nation. There are a thousand restrictions on the freedom of labour in other and only less important branches of human industry, a thousand artificial hindrances put on the right of individuals to make the best use of their faculties and opportunities. But as time goes on, and the conditions of civil society are more carefully studied and recognised; the more fully men see that the prosperity of mankind is due to the acceptance of a few principles; the more we get rid of those prejudices, fears, and hatreds which hinder the true progress of mankind, and which spring originally, and have such vitality as they possess, from the evil passions and selfish appetites of men; the more surely shall we gain our true ends in aiming at social perfection and just civil government.

If therefore the adoption of these restrictive combinations is no security for economical progress, but a hindrance to it, and may be a danger ; what remedies can we propose for the elevation of labour above the actual degradation in which it is placed in some callings, from the uneasy and hostile attitude which it takes in others? Many schemes have been suggested, several principles have been announced, some of which I will attempt to discuss in order.

I. The first and most obvious remedy is the diminution of the number of persons competing for wages. Many economists have been profoundly impressed by the reasonings of Malthus, and have inferred instantly that the cure for the depression of the rate of wages is to be discovered in wholesale emigration in the first instance, and in prudential restrictions, either personal or legal, on marriage in the next. I have already observed that legal restrictions on marriage lead, as evidence affirms, to evils which are morally far worse, and more subversive of social order, than any encouragement to marriage, however indiscreet. But voluntary migration generally takes away the best, the most thrifty, the most active, the most hopeful of the population. Such has been the case in the Scotch Highlands, and in Ireland. The same cause is at work, with increasing rapidity, in the English agricultural districts. Emigration on a large scale has never been made the business of government in this country, which has only colonised with convicts. Colonisation will be a very poor remedy for over-population, a very scanty corrective to low wages, unless it is undertaken on a large scale, is general in its character, and is carried on under the superintendence of a wise and judicious executive. The British colonies, even in a fuller sense than the United States, are colonies developed under the principle of selection, and are of a voluntary character; the colonisation which relieves society, is that of both sexes and of nearly all ages, and perhaps, except criminals, of all classes of society. Neither the labour nor the capital of this country is benefited by expatriating the cream of the working and small-farmer classes—a contingency which we shall see fulfilled in a formidable shape when the working people in England are thrifty and a general exodus begins. The facts indeed that great colonies have been founded by men of Anglo-Saxon origin, that they are growing rapidly, that they form a commercial, and should form a great political connexion with this country, are matter of congratulation to statesmen; but these phenomena do not, as economical facts, bear, except very slightly, on the correctives of a redundant population or of low wages. Enterprise and energy are valuable qualities in a people, and therefore are too good to lose, when they are most fully manifested. The indirect benefits of colonisation have been and will be large, but the causes which have led to the foundation of the British colonies are historically not over creditable to the government whose policy made them originally expedient, or to the social state which still makes them almost necessary.

II. Thrifty habits on the part of the population, i.e. such a custom of forethought as enables the labourer, by virtue of being possessed of some savings, to transfer his labour to a better market. It is said that the labourers of Cumberland and Westmoreland, where the highest rate of wages is secured, never allow themselves to be destitute of such a sum of money as will enable them to emigrate, in case the ordinary rate of wages shows signs of yielding to the pressure for employment. With these men such a sum is a sacred fund, which is laid up against this last emergency, as the Athenians laid up of old a hoard of 1000 talents in the Acropolis, against the risk of siege or the appearance of a hostile fleet in their port. For although a labourer, able to work, and ordinarily in such a position as will secure him employment, does really, as I have said above, represent a sum of capital fixed in himself, as certainly as capital is invested in improving land and buying goods; so, equally with the agriculturist and the tradesman, he should have some stock of money or other hoard which he can draw on when the seasons are unfriendly or business is slack, in order that he may save himself from the chance of being obliged to sell his crop or his goods, or his labour indeed, at a loss. It is a maxim in business that no man should have all his funds in such a shape as is not immediately convertible into cash, except at a serious loss, but should have a hoard or reserve from which he can draw, when the times are untoward. In practice the labourer makes no reserve except against sickness, or, in case he belongs to a trades-union, against the enforced idleness of a strike or lock-out. But he makes no provision against a falling market for labour and the consequent risk of diminished wages.

A labour fund of such a kind would be of great service against the contingencies alluded to. It would be above all others a substitute for the organisation of a trades-union, it would supply all the possible benefits, and obviate all the disadvantages, of such a combination. An illustration of the working of such a system, though in an imperfect form, has come before my notice, as recounted to me by one of the largest employers of labour in the Manchester district. This employer, during the course of the year 1866, was visited by a deputation of some of his factory hands, with a request for a rise in wages. He recognised the justice of the claim, and forthwith conceded it. A short time after this arrangement had been made, one of his best hands came to him and said that he was about to quit his work. On being asked why he did so, since the claims made were at once agreed to, he answered, that the men with whom he was associated had come to the conclusion that the union was a great waste of power, that they had abandoned it, and in place of it created a fund, out of which one or more of their number should be selected by ballot to visit other labour markets, especially those of the United States; that he had been thus selected, and was on the point of going on this tour of discovery; and that if he reported favourably of the places to which he went, the hands would as prudently as possible withdraw themselves to the more favourable market.

The chief reason why artisans and mechanics are so much at the mercy of employers in the first instance, and of trades-unions in the next, is because they live from hand to mouth. A man who is absolutely without any reserve of his own to fall back upon, must take such terms as are offered him; whereas if he thought proper to save a portion of his income, he could make far better terms with his employer, or at least, if these terms are not before him, betake himself to a market where he would be better paid.

III. Co-operation. This is the favourite expedient of those who, looking to the condition of the working classes, attempt to provide a remedy for the evils attached to that condition. It is supposed that if working men could unite in themselves the functions of capital and labour, they would, in the first place, make much more of their time and labour; in the next, be better able to distribute the proceeds of their labour, according to the intelligence, capacity, diligence, and perseverance of the several workers; in the third, discover the real conditions which underlie the production of wealth; and in the fourth, discover a real remedy for those inconveniences for which the trades-union is admitted to be an imperfect counterpoise. There are, however, many kinds of co-operation, in all of which, it should be observed, there is an attempt to eliminate some intermediary in the process of production and sale, whose services under this system might, it is hoped, be dispensed with.

The most obvious and familiar is co-operation of supply. Such a scheme, now becoming very general, is exhibited on a large scale by the 'Rochdale Pioneers.' The artisans who framed this association at first purposed, as many reformers do, to reconstruct society at large. Such a plan, vast, impracticable, and I need hardly say absurd, broke down; but the preliminaries of the plan succeeded, in the form of a grocer's shop or store. It is not extraordinary that such a plan should succeed. Common honesty and intelligence in keeping accounts are indispensable; but every purchaser is, more or less, and as a rule, sufficiently competent to judge of the goodness or badness of grocery. But the co-operation of production, though growing, has not been so general, or successful. Skill in buying and selling, in management and control, are not so readily available for the projectors of such a scheme. The intelligence which can organise and carry out a great manufactory is of such value and rarity, that the possessor of these faculties would hardly be content to remain an artisan, or on the wages of an artisan, when he can easily better himself in the calling which he follows by managing for a capitalist, or becoming a capitalist and employer himself.

The inclination which such a person would feel towards quitting the superintendence of a co-operative store would be strengthened, if, as is commonly reported, the committees of these stores or manufacturing associations are unwilling to recognise the authority, or remunerate at a proper rate, the services of their managers. But such managers, though they are from one point of view the servants of the association, are from another the masters of it, and must be masters, if the undertaking is to succeed in detail, just as the ministers of a popular government are also its rulers.

The systems of co-operation on the continent have either sought the necessary capital from the state, or have obtained it by a combination of workers from their joint resources, or by their joint credit. The national workshops founded in Paris during the epoch of the revolutionary government of 1848 were of the former character; those of Germany, instituted under the scheme of M. Schultze Delitzsch, are of the other kind. We need not dwell at length on the former. A scheme which needs the support of the state for its organisation must obtain the necessary funds from taxation or from loan. In the latter case, the action of the government is nothing but the diversion of capital from one branch of industry to another; in the former, though a tax may be nothing but a curtailment of an individual's enjoyments, the strongest plea of necessity must be alleged to justify such an appropriation, while in the great majority of cases such a tax would be a mere diversion of capital from a man's own ends to that of another, without even so much as giving him interest on his advances.

The plan of M. Schultze Delitzsch, as gathered from the excellent report of Mr. Morier (Correspondence of Her Majesty's Missions Abroad on Trades Unions, 1867), is as follows:—'If it be found possible to lend a producer, i.e. an artisan, capital at the ordinary rate of interest, he will be able not only to obtain the wages of his labour, but the profits of trade, i.e. in our nomenclature, the wages of superintendence ordinarily secured by the employer. It is true that the risk of lending an individual capital is so great, that it cannot be done at the ordinary rate of interest, for the labourer has nothing but his labour to pledge, i.e. inconvertible capital, and the trader has his stock in trade, i.e. convertible capital. Besides, with all the will to pay, the artisan may be disabled by sickness or accident; and thus the disposition to lend is restrained by two risks, that of dishonesty and incapacity. If, however, the loan is made to more than one artisan, the risks both of dishonesty and incapacity diminish with the increase of the number of co-operators. The insurance against incapacity is calculated on the ordinary risks of life and health; that against personal dishonesty may be obtained by information as to the borrower's character, and by accumulating motives to honesty. This scheme is formulated in two sentences—the minimum of risk, the maximum of responsibility.'

In order to accomplish these results, M. Delitzsch established credit banks on a peculiar principle. The capital of the bank is provided either by the contributions or deposits of the artisans, or from the advances of capitalists, the latter being the most considerable. The members of the association of credit banks can alone borrow. They need not, it appears, be possessed of capital themselves, but they must be able to work, and in regular employment. The best guarantee, however, of their fitness for association, and one which can be easily and most satisfactorily fulfilled, is the possession of a share in the bank. The principle of unlimited liability is the keystone of the system. If the assets of the business fail, the creditor may recover on the private property of the associates, each and all being jointly and severally liable to the debts of the association. In this way the maximum of responsibility is attained. It should be added, that the object of the credit bank is the interest of the borrower, not of the lender; and yet, according to Mr. Morier, the credit banks have become exceedingly lucrative to the lenders. The safety of the bank consists in its rigid limitation to the loans required by members of the association, and, as has been said, to the maximum of responsibility annexed to the personal property of the borrower—a responsibility which is made to continue for twelve months after any member ceases to belong to the association. The principle of the accumulation of the stock capital is, that ultimately it should amount to fifty per cent. of the borrowed capital. Each member is to have one share, and the shares must be all alike. The cardinal rule in loans is, not to lend for a longer time than the bank can borrow, and the general practice is to limit the time to three months.

Here then is a scheme, in active and successful working, by which the labourer can unite the functions and earn the wages of labourer and employer, by superseding the necessity of using the services of the latter functionary. The reason why this personage exists in modern trade and manufacture arises from the fact that he has security on which to borrow, and that general interest in the welldoing of the work which gives unity to the plan of operations stimulates economy in the details, and provides supervision over the whole mass of transactions. He subsists, in short, by the weakness of unassociated and irresponsible labour. Supply these two defects in the action of artisans, and the advantages obtained by the intermediary employer become an additional remuneration to the operative. Of course the high rate of interest obtained by these credit banks (Mr. Morier informs us that it is as much as eight to ten per cent., especially on short loans), is a merely temporary phenomenon, which only results from the fact that at present the borrowers obtain in their competition with employers all, or nearly all, the advantages which the ordinary trader or manufacturer accumulates. When the time comes—and come it will, should the system succeed largely and be largely adopted—that the associations practically compete against each other, the margin will inevitably be narrower, and the terms of interest lower.

IV. Association of Employers with Operatives. The jealousies, quarrels, and frequent strikes of labourers, and when these do not occur, the negligence, inefficiency, and slovenliness of the persons employed, have suggested to some employers, that it would be well to take such men into a sort of modified partnership, so that two things might be effected: first, that the workmen should be informed of the course of business and rate of profit; next, that he should be stimulated to activity and intelligent industry by motives of self-interest. Several years ago, M. Leclaire attempted some such scheme in Paris with the happiest and the most abiding results. The idea and the practice is of course not novel; for the custom of allowing certain subordinates in many kinds of trade a commission on goods sold is familiar. But the modern practice, now it appears increasing, is to lower the rate of wages by a certain percentage, and to offer the employé a share, calculated on an average at the residue, in the profits of the business. The objection alleged against the plan—an objection which may probably be fatal to its adoption in several kinds of business—is that it necessitates the abandonment of that secrecy which it is believed is essential at all times, and particularly in some emergencies, to success. The value of secrecy may be overrated, probably is; but its significance is felt, and will in all likelihood be felt more and more as the principle of limited liability is adopted. In some kinds of business, however, secrecy is of no importance. Thus, to take an example in which the association of employers and operatives has been tried, and, as I am informed, with great and uninterrupted success; I have learnt from Mr. H. Briggs, one of the partners in a colliery near Barnsley, that his firm had been harassed by incessant discontent, claims, and strikes on the part of the colliers. It appeared to the partners that these inconveniences might be obviated if some plan could be devised by which the colliers could be made to feel an interest in the success of the undertaking. It was thereupon resolved to turn the colliery into a joint-stock company, to pay the workmen, in part at least, according to the market price, and to encourage them in the purchase of share capital. The plan succeeded admirably for a time, and the inconveniences felt under the old arrangement were obviated. Latterly, however, the arrangement has been annulled, owing to disputes arising from the fluctuations in the coal market.

My reader will see, however, that all these remedies for low wages, or rather all these expedients by which it is attempted to instruct operatives in the economical conditions under which wages are paid for work, and by which the labourer is enabled to better his own position in life, respect certain classes of labour only, and leave out of calculation the function of the peasant. Here in point of fact we have other difficulties to contend with. The system of farming in England is increasingly that of large as opposed to small culture. This is not the place in which to discuss the relative advantages of either method. The system of tenure in England is favourable to the accumulation of land in few hands; and the passion for becoming the possessor of a vast estate, and founding a family, is aided by the direct enactments of law and its indirect sanctions. This again is not the place in which to discuss the social and economical consequences of such a system. But of one thing we may be clear: if the advantages be great, the sacrifices are great also; if the large farm system be favourable to production—a position by no means proved ; if the accumulation of real estate gives a solidity to public interests, and provides a variety of social safeguards—an hypothesis by no means certain;—these customs also condemn the largest part of the agricultural population to a condition from which there is not, except by a general emigration, any escape. Society does not exist merely for the accumulation of the largest amount of material products, still less in order to give facilities for their being accumulated in favour of a few persons. It must take into account (if it be true to its mission, if it would escape pressing, imminent dangers, and would obviate certain decline) the machinery by which wealth is distributed. This fact is the more manifest when the legal system which may be endured, though as I have said with great hardship, in a country which is largely devoted to commerce and manufacture, is made to apply to another in which agriculture alone is practised. If we needed an example of such a state of things, we should find it easily in the chronic disaffection of Ireland, a disaffection which late legislation has only partially remedied.

CHAPTER X.

On the Causes which depress the Rate of Wages.

My readers will remember, that according to the theory of wages given above, the remuneration of a labourer is generally relative to the cost of producing his services: and that wages are partly interest on capital; partly a sinking fund, the operation of which is the replacement of wealth as it is gradually extinguished by the growing age or declining strength, or certain wearing out of the labourer; partly an insurance against the risk of the premature extinction, or of any extraordinary liability to a suspension of work, in the case of the labourer. Hence such callings as involve risks are invariably paid more highly than others are in which no such risk is present; and such callings also as concentrate risks always secure greater wages than others, the following of which does not tend towards an easy destruction of the vital powers.

It will be clear therefore, if these charges and risks are compensated by certain legal provisions, which transfer the risk from the labourer to some other parties, an economy will be induced on wages. If, for example, a large percentage of labourers is reared and instructed at the public cost, up to the age in which their labour becomes available, the tendency of such an arrangement will be to lower the wages of those who are not so maintained and instructed. This rule holds good, whatever be the labour which is seeking employment and wages. For example, a common practice with wealthy and benevolent persons in bygone ages was the foundation of colleges, in which persons destined for the Christian ministry should be gratuitously boarded, lodged, and taught. The recipients of this benefaction were undoubtedly advantaged, for they went into the market to compete against the labour of others who were not so circumstanced. But they diminished the earnings of the latter; for the aggregate earnings of any one class of labourers is proportioned, as I have said several times, to the aggregate cost of producing all those who are, at any given time, competing to supply a service which is in general demand.

The fact to which I allude was recognised and commented on by Adam Smith, who rightly explained the low earnings of clergymen on the ground that the education of many among them, both at school and in the University, was practically gratuitous. And just the same facts apply to the fulfilment of other analogous functions. To communicate a high education requires a person of high learning and considerable skill. Now setting aside those who would do their best to supply this service to mankind for other than the wages which an economist recognises (such persons being few at all times, and not causing any marked effect upon the general rate of remuneration), the fact that there exist large endowments in aid of the highest education, in the shape of salaries to teachers, has a depressing effect on the rate of remuneration obtained by those who are unendowed; and this in two ways, first by increasing the number of those who enter on these callings, secondly by lowering the earnings of all. For just as the aggregate earnings of any class of labourers is proportioned to the aggregate cost of producing these labourers, so the amount distributed among the several labourers, *cæteris paribus*, is not increased by that which is added to the general fund from permanent sources, but diminished to a tantamount degree by it; for all other things being considered, the profits of all occupations tend to an equality, and all conditions being fulfilled, are never far distant from this equality.

What then, may be asked by the way, is the use of educational endowments? Are they not an inconvenience and an evil, if they reduce the rate of remuneration in the case of one class of workers, by the permanent quantity which they add to the gross remuneration divisible, but not divisible equally, among all those who are employed in the same function? Whatever benefit may be conferred by them on individuals, are they not a wrong to others, either by the fact that they depress their earnings, or by checking free competition in the field of employment, because they limit temptation, in some degree at least, to those who are endowed? It does not seem to be a fact that they restrain competition for the endowment; for as a rule, those occupations in which there are occasional prizes are more eagerly entered on than those are in which the rate of remuneration is generally uniform.

The excuses for the existence and continuance of educational endowments are two, one of these relating to the teacher, the other to the pupil. Neither however is, strictly speaking, of an economical character. The need or the advantage of these aids is to be found in the facts that the economical value of high education, or even in some cases of education at all, is only slowly and imperfectly appreciated by the public, and that the free competition of labourers, with what is implied in this competition—ample opportunity for the development of the individual's natural abilities and capacities—is in reality a merely hypothetical state, which has never yet occurred in the actual working of society.

Let us see what Education is. Properly speaking, it is the cultivation of the reflective faculties, with the view of making the acquisition of knowledge easier and the process of thought and reason more rapid. The benefit of a high education, that is, one in which these faculties are most thoroughly sharpened and trained, is of manifest significance to the possessor of such powers. But as the number of such persons as possess this education determines in general the intellectual position of a nation among other nations, it is of great importance to a nation that high education should be cultivated and used. Public opinion, however, appreciates this fact very slowly and very indistinctly. It confounds education with the knowledge of facts, whereas it really is the possession of method. It affects to prefer 'common sense,' which is in effect a rough and imperfect education. It is prone to limit education, even when it does acknowledge its value, to the simpler and more familiar branches of it, those the use of which is common and convenient; and to disparage its higher growths, the use of which is obvious and less material. Lastly, even when it is available for service, society is very slow to employ it, partly from prejudice, partly from fear, partly because it is often sharply corrected by it, partly because it prefers other agencies which are more familiar and in appearance more submissive. Hence, as the demand for the higher education is slow, and the use of it is great (owing perhaps to the fact that society is artificially constituted and a variety of interests are protected in it), it is argued, and with much reason, that this education should be also protected, and protected in the least invidious form, that is, by permanent endowments or grants in aid of it. The same reason applies to a minor, but by no means unimportant subject, assisted education in art. The value of the service is undoubted, but at present it could not be secured by the ordinary agencies of public competition. The government therefore interposes, and rightly estimating the value of the process, fills up the deficiency of public or general opinion. It provides, in short, that a teaching which would not otherwise be given, but is of great public importance, should be supplied or supported. On the other hand, when the service is capable of easy valuation, and is in fair demand, there is no necessity that government should aid the acquisition of such knowledge as is necessary towards rendering the service. Many of the arguments used in favour of claiming public assistance for special education have no economical justification. When any particular branch of industry is in demand, the assistance which government may give to the education of such an industry becomes a mere means for lowering wages in that industry. It is therefore of no ultimate good to the labourer and is a wrong to the public, because the assistance can be given only by the machinery of taxation, i.e. by levies extracted from the savings of other industries.

Secondly, it is of great importance to the pupil. Individuals have different capacities, different impulses, different degrees of activity or diligence. The possessor of these faculties, under certain moral conditions, is of greater service to society than another would be in whom these characteristics are defective or wanting. Now if the progress of such persons could be secured by any process of natural selection, if the higher intellectual powers and qualities were as certain of making their way as bodily powers and lower intellectual gifts can, there would be no need for any artificial selection by examination or certificate and for the artificial stimulants of rewards and aids. But it will probably be a long time before society can dispense with these assistances, and meanwhile its business is to make such use of the forces as are at its disposal, as will enable it to select and promote the greatest diligence and capacity, wherever it may be placed by birth or fortune.

These statements however as to the depressing effect

of endowments on the wages of unendowed teachers, and of similar endowments on the remuneration of unassisted pupils, do not refer to general education. If the whole community were taught at the public charge, no one could suffer exceptionally, or gain exceptionally; but all could gain, in so far as the instruction given increased the powers of labour by diminishing the amount of muscular or nervous exertion, and so enhanced the enjoyments of society. An educated people works less and earns more than one which is untaught can. The reason is obvious, if the reader will recall the definition of education given above—that, namely, which makes it to consist in the cultivation of the reflective faculties. Men in whom these faculties are developed see the end before them and the means to its achievement with greater clearness, and combine both ends and means with greater dexterity and swiftness, than uninstructed people can. To take one of the simplest and most familiar instances: a recruit who knows how to read and write can learn his drill in half the time in which a totally ignorant person can. Now it is said that it costs, on an average, £100 to teach each man to be a soldier. The sum may be exaggerated, but this does not affect the illustration. The British army is about 250,000 men, and according to this estimate it has cost £25,000,000 to instruct it in its calling. If we suppose that the average duration of service is ten years, and that primary education could reduce the cost by one-half, there is an annual outlay of £2,500,000 which could be made £1,250,000 by the use of the economy of primary education. There are other and similar economies in manufacture and trade: for example, it is computed that the adoption of a decimal system in currency, weights, and measures, would save the services of half the clerks employed on the railways of Great Britain.

A high standard of general education, as it promotes efficiency in the labourer, tends also to raise the rate of wages. Men who reflect on the conditions which surround labour, do not rashly incur risks; they make labour scarce in the best way in which it can be made scarce, by forethought; they make labour cheap in the best way in which it can be made cheap, by increasing its efficiency, and thereupon the demand for it. For cheapness and dearness in matters of political economy do not mean low and high prices, low and high wages, but efficiency and inefficiency, capacity and incapacity. The dearest labourer is not the man who gets most for his labour, but the man who does least for his money. This is, I admit, a truism; but it is a truism which, like many other axioms, is apt to be forgotten, equally by employers of labour and labourers themselves.

The maintenance of labourers during nonage, during temporary incapacity for work, after the time in which they become incapable of work, and during the intervals in which they are capable but unwilling or unable to work, is provided for in this country by laws which have been in existence for nearly three hundred years. They are peculiar to England, having been lately introduced into Scotland and Ireland, and existing, even in these countries, only in a qualified form. They have produced, as I shall attempt to show, special and important economical consequences—consequences which remain, although the machinery of relief accorded under what are technically called the poor-laws, has been materially modified Practically the English poor-law is a legal, and therefore compulsory, system of insurance against the risks incurred by certain kinds of inferior labour.

The feeling which has led men to consider it their duty to provide for the pressing wants of their poorer fellow-creatures is not the impulse of a social law, but of a corporate sympathy. It had no place in the ethics, public or private, of ancient civilisation in the West; it sprang in the first place from the national wants and the national weakness of the Jewish race, was imported into early Christianity, and has been a special characteristic of the latter religion. It was copied by Mohammed, and it has since been endorsed by many publicists and economists, who have ignored or repudiated that theory of human obligations by which this social rule has been sanctioned. If we look on men as merely possessed of animal life, it is clearly the interest of those who are strong in any sense and can work, to eliminate those who are weak and cannot contribute to the general aggregate of products and services. All the lower animals do so; they starve or kill their weaker fellows; they are unable to exchange services, but they know how to economise resources, and are wholly merciless or indifferent to the weak and ailing. The right to live on the part of all human beings now existent, till such time as they perish by natural causes, is a maxim which has no counterpart in the physical world, has no necessary connexion with social laws. It is a modern equivalent of Jewish sympathy, confined by the Jews to their own race, but extended by Christian teaching into a duty incumbent on all such men as are brought up under a Christian code. There is no part of political economy which diverges so widely from the rules of social morality and habit, and seems to contradict them so pointedly, as that interpretation which this science is constrained to pronounce as the aids given by charity or sympathy to weakness, suffering and incapacity. Undoubtedly, if we considered society as a mere machine for collecting and distributing material enjoyments, and for stimulating the means by which these enjoyments could be enlarged and economised, we should leave the weak and unprotected poor to perish, if indeed we did not peremptorily arrest such a tax on the resources of those who work and possess, and which is levied on behalf of those who are destitute and incapable, by violently extinguishing such useless lives. And, as my readers are aware, there do arise, happily under rare circumstances, occasions on which the economical view of human life necessarily overrides the moral and religious.

Here it will be desirable to give a short sketch of the history of those enactments which are known collectively and familiarly as the poor-laws. They are in effect a means for bestowing assistance on the destitute poor (in the failure of voluntary effort to meet the want) by a public charity, to which all contribute according to their income, or in some cases according to their expenditure. It is needless to say that any discrimination in interpreting the claims of such recipients must be of a very general character, and that (if a few broad lines of distinction be laid down between the measure and manner of relief in cases of infancy, sickness, and old age, as contrasted with able-bodied destitution) all are equally entitled to assistance when in want.

Before the Reformation, and during the time in which the numerous monasteries were in being, the wants of such poor as were reduced to penury by great necessity were relieved through these sources of charity. Land was generally distributed, the leases of corporations were easy or beneficial, guilds supported their own poor, excessive population was probably checked by the celibacy of the monastic and clerical orders, and, according to all testimony, absolute want was on the whole unknown. The scene changed after the epoch referred to. The monastic lands were divided among the rapacious and prodigal courtiers of Henry, the guild estates, which were the medieval benefit societies, among those of Edward; sheep-farming, the obvious resource of landowners without capital or enterprise, became general; and the mass of the population fell into great distress. Added to these several changes was the great wrong inflicted on the community by the issue of base money under Henry VIII and his son. Any disturbance of the currency affects the working classes, that is, those who live by weekly and on the whole fixed wages, far more severely than it does other ranks. These evils are greatly aggravated when the government commits, as Henry VIII committed, a vast fraud. Every circumstance then of society, all the policy of the court, tended to the aggrandisement of the few and the misery of the many. In Henry's time population and misery were kept down by excessive executions, the laws regularly sacrificing thousands yearly on the gallows. The reign of Elizabeth was milder, but the destruction of capital had been effected, and its accumulation was slow. England fell into the rear of other nations, and the government attempted to meet the suffering of the time by levying a local tax for the relief of the impotent, and by providing the machinery of employment of the able-bodied poor. It has been said that the latter provision was neglected; it is hardly necessary to say that it is economically impossible, as a permanent arrangement.

The necessity which arose in the days of Elizabeth was as urgent in those of Charles II, while the machinery of relief was found totally inadequate. Pauperism began to be burdensome, and the owners of the soil strove to confine it within such limits as could laid down. Hence the law of parochial settlement, under which the liabilities of the parish on which the pauper was chargeable were defined. The strictest precautions were taken as time passed on to prevent these liabilities from being transferred from one parish to another. As far as possible the peasant was literally tied to the soil; if he attempted to quit the place of his settlement, and reside in a new parish, his intrusion was watched with the greatest jealousy, and he was liable to eviction in case the parochial authorities of his adoptive parish suspected that he could by any possibility come on the rates. When an employer wished to engage a servant from a foreign parish, he was not permitted to do so unless he entered into a recognizance, often to a considerable amount, to the effect that the incomer should not obtain the settlement, else the bond to be good against the employer. Parochial registers are full of such acknowledgments. The stringency of the law of settlement was far more severe than the old manorial view of frankpledge; but the law was so obscure, perhaps necessarily so obscure, that the litigation between parishes, each trying to throw the burden of maintaining paupers on the other, was enormous, incessant, and ruinously expensive. The law served only one notable end: the legal learning connected with the law itself, and the adjudged cases under it, was so vast that many a distinguished practitioner owed his elevation on the bench to well-pleaded settlement cases. Meanwhile the cost of maintaining the poor increased greatly. Under the allowance system, by which payments in money were made to parents in proportion to the largeness of their families, the burden became intolerable. Some labourers actually saved small fortunes during the great continental war, out of these parochial doles. At last the rates threatened to swallow up rent, and in some parishes actually did so. In 1835 the law was altered, out-door relief was as a rule prohibited, and most of the incapable and able-bodied paupers were collected into workhouses.

During the prevalence of this system, however, all parishes were not equally affected. The limits of a parish, though ancient, are artificial and arbitrary, being, it appears, generally the boundaries of some manor, whose extent was accidental. In fact they were not settled till the system of parochial relief began. In some of these parishes parcels of land had been freely alienated, and there were many proprietors. These were called 'open.' In others, the estate of the proprietor was unbroken, and only one person owned the soil. In some, again, a few proprietors, who could easily act in concert, were in possession. These were called 'close.' When there were one or a few of these large owners, it was the object of the proprietors to extinguish all outlying freeholds, and to constitute the boundaries of the parish into a ring fence. Landowners paid many times their worth for these fragments; for the possession of a 'close parish' rendered it possible to improve the property in a peculiar way.

The process was to evict the tenants and to pull down the cottages, so as to force the labourers to migrate to some adjoining 'open parish,' in which they might dwell, and from which they might go to and fro on their work in the 'close parish.' The employer, to be sure, if there were degrees of labour, got only inferior labour; but this, in the general beggary, was a comparatively trifling evil by the side of heavy rates and decreasing rents. The policy was general, and on the whole successful. Farm-labourers even now are deficient in those parishes in which the whole of the soil is owned by one or a few proprietors.

The act of 1834-5 remedied this evil to some extent, for it distributed certain of the charges over the whole union. But up to the year 1864 each parish bore the greater part of the charge of such paupers as lived within its boundaries, whether they worked within the parish or without it; and the change of that year, notwithstanding its obvious equity, was resisted fiercely by the owners of close parishes, was achieved with difficulty, and is by no means perfect yet (1875). The pleas put forward against the change were amusing and contradictory. At one time it was said that the poor would be neglected if the charges were levied on the whole union instead of being confined to the locality in which the necessity arose; at another time it was averred that the interest of the rate-payers would be neglected if the guardians could spend out of a common fund.

After this sketch we shall perhaps be able to see

the economical bearing of a rate in aid of wages. It is a means for paying a portion of wages indirectly. Were poor-rates abolished—and perhaps it is under the circumstances impossible to do so now—the labourer must receive, in lieu of this aid, such an increase as would enable him to do that for himself which the poor-law does for him, to insure him against sickness and old age, and to provide for the nonage of his orphan children. In those parts of England in which the contingency of coming upon the rates is dreaded as a disgrace, the labourer strives by benefit and other societies to secure himself against such a risk. To do this, he sets aside a part of his wages. But where no such feeling exists, wages are lowered to the bare margin of such subsistence as is customary with the labourer, prudential motives are ignored, the labourer is indifferent to seeking a better market for his labour, and he becomes immoveable and unthinking. In a parish or district where the labourers are thoroughly pauperised the lowest morality prevails, family feeling, filial and parental duty, almost wholly die out, and the people become nearly brutal. 'The parish,' they say, 'is bound to find them;' they have no care, life is bounded by animal pleasures and enjoyments, and they cherish neither hope nor thought. These traits still exist in the rural population, though there is hope that they are being slowly modified, to be subsequently effaced.

If the burden of supplementing low wages by the machinery of a poor-rate were cast on the employers of labour only, the process, though it would still bear with it the moral evils adverted to, would yet be equitable. But this is not the practice. The employer, though paying most of the rate in agricultural parishes, does not pay the whole rate. The rate is collected from all occupiers, whether employers of labour or not. The farmer of course reckons the ordinary rate as part of his outgoings, and regulates his power of agreeing to rent accordingly. But the ordinary occupier has, by the machinery of the poor-law, to supplement the wages of the labourer, who is underpaid by the amount of the rate, from his own resources and for the benefit of the employer. It is from the fact that people confound the moral obligation of maintaining their distressed and starving fellow-creatures with the systematic supply of a fund, the object of which is to aid and increase wages indirectly, that the economical significance of a poor-law is not more generally discerned, and the incidence of the rate is not more clearly recognised.

The legal aid of labour, then, lowers wages, annuls prudential motives, checks industry and improvement, and disposes labour to be passive and immoveable. The poor-law was, as I have said, peculiar to England: it prevails in no other country. Up to the Irish famine of 1846, it had not been adopted in that island; up to the disruption of the Scotch kirk, and the scarcity of the same epoch, it was existent only in a very modified form in Scotland. Even now in both these countries it is administered severely, and with a wise severity. As a consequence, the ill-fed Irish labourer and the thrifty Scotch peasant are incomparably more enterprising and alert than the English farm-labourer; though the Irish have never colonised independently, and the Lowland Scotch are of the same race with ourselves.

We shall moreover find, as we study history by the

light of jurisprudence and political economy, that laws and customs have effects which last beyond their actual existence. The repeal or modification of a law is not always and instantly followed, as legislators are apt to dream, by the social reform which the change is intended to effect. The consequence of past legislation endures beyond its legal life. We have not yet escaped, and we shall not escape for a long time yet, the results of those laws which were devised in 1349, by which attempts were made to coerce and control the wages of labour. Similarly we still suffer from the law of settlement, enacted now nearly two hundred years ago, though modified thirty years since, and all but repealed lately. To study a nation's history we must study its laws: not alone such laws as are the spontaneous development of the principles and the policy in which a nation is self-contained, and which form its lineaments; but those which have been established in the interest of a section of the community, and maintained for the benefit of the few. The history of this country, its policy, its trade, its habits, its character, have all been affected by the legislation of bygone centuries. Thus the studies of the antiquary become constantly the key to those problems which baffle the publicist and amaze the economist: for the present life of the nation is founded on the past, in the accumulation of its labours, and in the waste of its errors and shortcomings; just as its pedigree is a commingling of races, its arts and its literature an inheritance from forgotten or undiscovered ancestors; its constitution, the spoils of many a victory, the losses of many a defeat; its character, the product of many habits, some perhaps natural, most acquired, all of which converge in the present, though their source is distant and often hopelessly undiscoverable.

The effect of machinery on the rate of wages at first sight appears to be necessarily depressing. Men substitute mechanical for muscular forces because they are cheaper, that is, enable them to dispense with some part of the manual labour hitherto occupied in the work for whose production machinery is employed as a substitute. Some workmen must, it appears, be thrown out of employment, and the effect of a glut of labour in the particular calling which has been modified, is, it seems, inevitable. So obvious, on a superficial estimate of the consequences, is the impression that labour prices will fall as machinery is adopted, that we cannot wonder at the hostility which workmen have constantly displayed when their labour is threatened by the competition of machinery. In practice, however, these results do not ensue, and for several reasons.

In the first place, and in the great majority of cases, the development of machinery is the escape from the dearness of labour, i. e. its dearness in an economical sense, its largeness as an item in the cost of production. But when the cost of production is diminished and the market for the product is wide and increasing, the labourer is in greater demand, and the products of labour are supplied at cheaper rates. If he is superseded in one direction, he is required in another; for all capital must be employed in the maintenance of labour; and as an enlarged business and a consequent aggregation of profit are developed, larger demands are made on the labour in the market. If the economy of labour did not increase production and stimulate demand, the substitution of machinery for manual exertion would be a loss to the labourer; but as we see in such a contingency, labour would not be superseded by machinery. Machinery then benefits the labourer in two ways: first by accumulating capital for his subsistence; next by diminishing the cost of the articles he consumes. Under each case it increases his actual wages: in the first by enlarging their amount, in the second by increasing their power of purchase. For example, the cost of manufacturing a yard of cotton cloth has been lowered by the use of machinery to one-twentieth at least of the outlay originally incurred in the process; but the labour required to meet the demand of an enlarged market has brought masses of people to the great centres of this industry, while the product of this labour has been brought within the familiar use and convenience of thousands or even millions who, before such reductions in the cost of production, were either debarred from its use or stinted in supply.

Next, it rarely happens that labour of any kind is so special in its character as to render the labourer unfit for analogous labour. Thus, for example, a smith may be engaged generally in forging or worming screws. These screws are now made by machinery to a very great extent; but the smith, though this part of his work may be cut off, is still a smith, and capable of a variety of other occupations known as smith's work. The simpler the labour is, the more ready is the change. The training of an artisan is in the method of doing a variety of things, although in practice he generally betakes himself to one only. It is especially in agriculture that specialities of labour are extinguished, and without immediate compensation. Thirty years ago all corn, or nearly all corn, was threshed by the flail: at the present time, the sound of the flail has all but passed away, and before long the art of the thresher will be quite extinct. But the circumstances which require that the agricultural labourer must be instructed in a variety of operations also prevent any material lowering of his condition. He must, to supply the demand of the farmer, be able to live; and should any of the customary occupations of indoor work be taken away from him, his general wages must be compensated in order that he may exist.

Even though labour be extinguished totally, and without compensation in its own way, yet if it be able to transport itself to new industries, the evil lasts but a short time, and is immediately counterbalanced by a demand for other kinds of labour. It is possible—to judge from the local diminution of population, it is probable—that the introduction of machinery has diminished the general demand for agricultural labour, or in other words, that equal quantities of produce are grown and secured at less cost in wages. But concurrently with this state of things, there has continued a great and increasing demand for skilled and unskilled labour in manufacturing districts. In effect, labour which was wasted in agriculture, as long as the process might be cheapened and was not cheapened, is economised and transferred to manufactures. It is true that all the beneficial effects of a diminished supply of labour have not been appropriated by the farm hand, for in the absence of any effective control over the labour of children and women, the wages of adults are lowered by the competition of those who should be precluded in whole or in part from such occupations. But the extension of the factory acts to agricultural operations is merely matter of delay.

It is seldom the case, then, that the displacement of labour, when the result is due to machinery, implies more than a temporary inconvenience to the labourer whose work has been superseded. To the mass of labourers it is a positive gain. The adoption of mechanical forces is at once the effect of a desire to economise the cost of production, and a stimulus to the demand for labour in other directions. It means a greater outlay of energy, with the object of compensating a lower rate of profit on each transaction by a higher aggregate of profit on a larger number of transactions. Thus in so far as he is a consumer of produce, the labourer is directly benefited; for the adoption of machinery in manufacture is always most obvious in articles of general or universal consumption, because it is in these that the market is most rapidly widened, and that additional outlay obtains its earliest and most permanent profit.

CHAPTER XI.

Profit and Interest.

I HAVE already observed that the rate of profit is to be identified with the rate of interest. Whatever else is secured to the capitalist, beyond the average rate of interest, is either wages of labour, i.e. the labour of superintendence, superior intelligence, and tact, and the task of supplying the purchaser with what he wants, all which are kinds of labour, wherein great skill is ordinarily necessary; or the replacement of outlay; or insurance against risk. It will be found that every instance of common or average trade-profits is susceptible of this division, and that exceptional rates of trade-profit are due to exceptional ability, invention, or as people sometimes say, good fortune.

Suppose, for example, that a man invests £1000 in the business of a grocer, and borrows another £1000 from his banker in the shape either of an advance to his credit or in the discount of bills which he draws. Let us also suppose that he pays, on the average, five per cent. for the convenience granted him by his banker; this being the average rate of interest on mercantile advances, abundantly secured by goods or credit. Let us add that he derives an income of £400 a year from this sum invested in business. Of this sum he has £350 to spend or save from, since £50 must be transferred to the banker in payment of interest for the sum advanced. Of the remaining £350, a seventh part is the interest on his own capital, such an amount as he would-have gained had he lent his money to another person. The remaining three-fourths of his income, is wages for his labour, and insurance against the risk of bad debts and other similar contingencies. It is as much wages as the salary of a clerk is, or the commission of an agent who buys and sells with other people's money, or the fee of a lawyer or physician, or the payments made for manual labour to artisans and farm hands.

The only circumstance which obscures this analysis of what are called 'trade-profits,' is the fact that in certain occupations a source of income, originally nothing but wages, accumulates so as to form a fund, closely analogous in its characteristics to capital, and, like capital, capable of direct sale at a valuation. This is commonly known as 'good-will' or 'connexion.' As a man is able to increase his business, he is also able, in accordance with the principle of the division of labour, to substitute for that direct labour which he formerly gave, other labour subordinated to himself and superintended by him. The extent to which this labour can be introduced and superintended is a variable quantity. There is no doubt a limit of greatness as well as smallness, in which the profitable employment of capital is checked, the superintendence becoming too vast for any individual mind, and too complicated for the effectual working of any subordinate machinery. It is said that this limit of largeness has been reached in some railways and in certain joint-stock enterprises, and that the control of the whole organisation is incomplete and *pro tanto* unprofitable, from the very greatness and complexity of the undertaking. So on the other hand we are very familiar with cases in which the shrewdness and intelligence of traders are checked and wasted by lack of capital.

The good-will or connexion of a business, considered apart from the capital and labour of the trader, is partly due to the reputation of the trader, partly to the indolence of those who deal with him. In a great many articles, the buyer is a good deal at the mercy of the seller. Only a practised eye can detect the amount of alloy in an ornament professedly manufactured of gold. The quality of cloth is not easily decided on by an inexperienced purchaser. Even articles of common use may be so skilfully adulterated, that ordinary customers cannot detect the fraud. But as long as fraudulent sellers abound, trustworthiness and integrity are marketable qualities, whether they exist in the trader or the labourer, or, as we should say, in whatever kind of labour they are present. Of course if guarantees can be given that goods will be honestly supplied, by any other process than the personal integrity of the trader, or from any other motive than the sense of prudent self-interest, which is at the bottom of all honest dealing in trade, that part of 'good-will' or 'connexion' which depends on the real or supposed exercise of these qualities will be proportionately extinguished. Now such a displacement of the voluntary exercise of moral qualities in trade, by means of what may be called a self-acting honesty, is not undiscovered. I am not of course referring to the honesty of a servant or manager, who does not embezzle or peculate, but to that for which the public is constrained to pay, the integrity which warrants a real sale of that which is professed to be sold.

Now this was done by the promoters of the 'Rochdale Equitable Pioneers.' I cannot do better than quote the case in the words of Messrs. Ludlow and Lloyd Jones. Speaking of the establishment of co-operative stores, these gentlemen say, that 'the great difficulty with the first stores was to bring custom; and failing in this, they broke down.' 'In Rochdale, however,' they say to the public, 'invest in the trading capital here, and you shall have five per cent. on your money, inasmuch as we bind ourselves not to put it to risk by speculative trading, no credit being given; in the next place, whatever remains as profit, after paying interest on capital, will be divided as bonus on the amount of money spent in the store by each member.' 'The advantages of this proposal soon began to make themselves apparent. Presuming a hundred men invested twenty shillings each, one shilling each would be due to them at the expiration of the year, as five per cent. interest on their separate investments. They had each done precisely the same as investers, and each was justly entitled to the same reward. But custom is as necessary as capital for the production of profit, and in contributing this all-important element, they almost necessarily differed from each other. The family income made a difference; the number in the family made an important difference. In fact, a poor workman with a large family was a far more profitable customer than a well-paid artisan with a small one. These former men, therefore, the most difficult to move, because usually the most encumbered by debt, were the most directly appealed to by this new plan. *There was no interest in buying inferior articles and selling them at high prices, no temptation to adulterate anything sold, no inducement to give short weight and measure, inasmuch as everything taken from the consumer by fraud would go back to him again as increased bonus.'* (Progress of the Working Classes, p. 133.) This society, which commenced with a capital of £28 in 1844, and with twenty-eight members, had 7021 members in 1874, a capital of £162,768, did business to the amount of £287,212, and divided a 'profit' of £31,957, having steadily increased in all these elements, except during the disastrous year of the cotton famine, 1862.

My reader will observe in this passage that the word 'profit' is used in the ambiguous sense which common language ordinarily assigns to it. The Rochdale co-operators, or, as they quaintly called themselves, pioneers, took the common prices of retail trade (in which as I have said are included risk and labour, highly paid when the business is small, still highly paid when the business is large; for no man will reduce his rate of remuneration below that which is necessary to secure custom), and sold at these rates. The difference between the price at which they could have sold, when all expenses were paid, and the price at which they did sell, was conventional, and in a manner arbitrary. Some difference was necessary, in order to secure custom, or, more correctly, to induce it. In fact, of course, the so-called profit had been paid already when the customer bought his goods, and need not, in order to carry out the principle on which these stores are founded, have been added to the cost and divided at the end of the year. But it is very hard for people to forget traditions and experiences, and the Rochdale co-operators did wisely in deferring to habits of trade, to customary expressions.

The system, however, which they adopted, when the ambiguity referred to is cleared away, will illustrate to us what is one of the sources of 'connexion' or 'good-will.' It is very hard work for a man to build up a character for commercial integrity. Perhaps no labour of his life is so severe as this, none which needs more constant watchfulness. There is a story told of a certain Colonel Charteris, who was a notorious cheat and swindler. He once said that he would give £5000 if he could get a good character; and when he was asked why he valued it so highly, answered, that he could immediately borrow £10,000 upon it. But we see from the case given above that, if it be possible to bring about what I may call a sort of mechanical morality, a saving may be effected, and society be all the better off, in just the same way as it is when physical forces are employed in place of manual labour. There is no reason why we should not economise moral forces, when they are susceptible of a market-price, as well as those which are muscular or intellectual.

Another cause of connexion or good-will is the indolence of customers. They wish to have the fact of a man's business brought to them, and not this only, but the favour of their purchases canvassed. Hence the prodigious outlay on advertisements, and the gross trade-falsehoods which are prevalent, as to the merits of particular goods, the skill of particular traders, the impossibility of securing such advantages elsewhere as those which the advertiser offers. These devices are developed most fully in this country, and have probably had something to do with those frauds which have discredited several branches of our trade, in the imitation of trade-marks, and of other special signs by which producers in credit seek to prevent others from appropriating dishonestly a part of their reputation. The same desire to attract customers, and the weakness which leads customers to rely on such attractions as merely guide the eye, give a fictitious value to certain streets, and cause extravagant expenditure on shop-fronts and other decorations. These causes of expense—for of course they must needs be paid by the customer, who simply bears the charge for gilding the trap in which he is to be caught—are obviated under the co-operative system described above; for those dealers have no need to advertise their wares, or spend their capital on an attractive outside, or incur heavy rents in a fashionable or crowded locality, in order to get custom. The machinery of their combination secures them those advantages, which the ordinary trader, whose sole object is the benefit of the seller, can hardly obtain, except with heavy outlay and trouble; though when he does obtain them, he finds that they ordinarily possess accumulated value.

Having then explained the anomalous position occupied by 'connexion' and 'good-will,' and having therefore shown that all business-returns, after capital is replaced and loss insured against, are divisible into wages and profit, i.e. profit proper or interest; it will be convenient to say a little about the position which interest on money assumes in all acts and processes which bear an economical value.

My reader will remember that money is a measure of value, and is accepted in lieu of goods and services, because it is easily disposed of, and is, under ordinary circumstances, more susceptible of exchange than any other commodity. But he will also remember that people take money in order to get rid of it; for as long as they keep it, it brings them no further advantage than a dormant power of exchange. And as men take money only for what it will fetch and buy, so when they lend money, they do not really lend pieces of gold and silver, but that which pieces of gold and silver will purchase, i.e. labour or goods. The lender surrenders his right to buy goods or hire labour, or use goods which he has bought or might buy, in order that another person may effect the purchase. But as persons exchange with a view to some ulterior advantage, the surrender of this right of purchase or exchange must be compensated by an offer of some of the advantages attending that transaction, which is completed by the interposition of money. You cannot induce a man to surrender these rights without offering him some equivalent. This equivalent is profit proper, or interest; and hence Mr. Senior defined interest to be 'the wages of abstinence.' The owner of the money abandons his beneficial use of the money to another. He may give it if he will, or lend it without interest. These, however, are exceptional acts, the great majority of lenders performing this function of relinquishing their own use to others on condition of gaining some benefit by doing so.

For a long time, however, partly in consequence of some inveterate misconceptions as to the nature of money, partly from traditions derived from certain religious feelings, the levy of interest on advances was discouraged, reprobated, and even forbidden. Thus, for example, so sagacious an analyst as Aristotle objected to the payment of interest, on the ground that it was the productive addition to an unproductive object. This view seems to have been traditional, for it is found, under another figure, i.e. of the rivers and the sea, in the 'Clouds' of Aristophanes. It is quoted in Bastiat's works as a popular delusion among certain socialists of modern times. We find, however, how gross the fallacy is, when we recognise what is really the economical position of money, and see that to repudiate interest on advances is in effect to prohibit a rate of profit, a regulation manifestly absurd if carried out, because it would effectually stop all exchange by stopping the motive to exchange, and so be destructive of society.

The levy of interest was forbidden to the Jews. Various reasons have been assigned for this prohibition. The two most obvious are, first the desire on the part of the Jewish lawgiver to prevent the accumulation of great fortunes by individuals; secondly, the motive of inculcating mutual good-will and benevolence among a race peculiarly keen in striving to obtain pecuniary advantages. From the Jewish code, in which the avoidance of usury forms a peculiar and repeated command, the prohibition of usury was imported into the morals of Christian societies. The office of a lender on interest was viewed with suspicion, and even treated with infamy. It was forbidden to Christians, and was practised at first almost entirely by Jews, though it was in course of time taken up by the Lombard merchants, who were either indifferent to ecclesiastical censures, or were too important in the economy of society at that time to be repressed.

After the English Reformation, the claiming and giving of interest was legalised, though under the supervision of government, and at fixed rates; a distinction being taken between interest, which was admitted to be fair, and usury, which was treated as rapacious, excessive, unlawful. It is only in the present age that all restrictions have been abandoned, and the rate of interest left to the discretion of lenders and borrowers, as they may agree; the courts of equity interfering, as in other cases, to prevent fraud and over-reaching. It should be added, that the usury laws were attacked in the most conclusive manner by Bentham, who greatly contributed in this, as in other subjects, to important social and legal reforms.

The first condition under which loans are made on interest, is that the interest be not only paid, but the principal sum be restored at the termination of the period during which the loan is to continue. Unless security of such a kind be given, loans will not be made at all: unless the security be satisfactory or complete, loans will not be offered except at exorbitant rates of interest, the rate varying with the greatness or smallness of the risk incurred. These rates however are only interest in appearance, the difference between them, and such rates as are accepted on perfectly valid security, being only variations in the rate of insurance, though here again popular language is misleading. The reason, nine cases out of ten, why persons pay highly for accommodation, is because they have no security, or no good security, to offer. This may affect individuals, or classes in the community, or the community itself. Merchants whose personal honour is suspected, or whose prudence is questionable, find it difficult to get assistance in what is called the money market. Mercantile credit may be generally low, and governments may be justly distrusted, because they have been guilty of breaches of faith towards the public creditor.

As a rule, mercantile credit is higher than government credit. The maintenance of perfect good faith, especially in countries where trade is open to severe competition, where penalties are inflicted on fraudulent bankruptcy, and the profitable employment of capital is limited, is of absolute necessity to the trader. He dares not break his engagements, except to the ruin of his reputation. But the case is somewhat different with a government. The security which it offers, the pledge namely of the industry exercised by its subjects, is more permanent than that which a merchant offers. It contains the present property and the future earnings of the nation whose government borrows. But the security is apt to be repudiated, especially when the obligation is entered into by an irresponsible or profligate government. There is not, I believe, a single European government, with the exception of our own, which has not repudiated its obligations in whole or in part, either by refusing altogether to pay interest on its debts, or by forcibly converting high into low rates of interest, and thus depreciating violently the saleable value of the security or principal. Even this country ran considerable risk of partial repudiation after the close of the great continental war, during the debates which preceded the resumption of cash payments by the Bank of England. Now though the lender in such a case is powerless against the present action of a repudiating and dishonest government, and cannot prosecute it, coerce it, or chastise it, yet he can put it under a future disability, and he does so very effectually. Governments are apt to be borrowers, but a defaulting government borrows in a very narrow and reluctant market. It may be, and frequently is, absolutely excluded from the market. The police of the stock-exchange is exceedingly weak in attack, but it is exceedingly powerful in its defensive or retaliatory action. It may be pillaged, but its memory is very long, and its revenge is ample. Charles I and his son Charles II never committed more fatal errors than they did when they robbed the exchequer and appropriated the goldsmiths' money.

Another circumstance which determines the rate of interest is the abundance or scarcity of capital. There is a point in the rate of interest, no doubt hypothetical, below which capital will not be accumulated for lending, and on the margin of which it is less abundantly accumulated. The ordinary or average rate of interest is itself determined, supposing the community accumulates in any notable degree, by the amount of demand which there exists for capital, in other words, by the number of channels into which it may be profitably diverted and employed, and by the amount of compensation which will satisfy the lender. In penurious and thrifty countries, especially those in which there are few objects on which capital may be safely and advantageously lent, the rate is low. Such for example was the case with Holland, and in some degree is so still. During a great part of the last century, money in that country would fetch only from two to two-and-a-half per cent. on loans. On the other hand, the rate of interest in Australia is very high, not because the security which can be offered is inadequate, but because the available quantity of loanable capital is small, and the competition of borrowers, who can employ the labour of superintendence in its beneficial employment, is great. The reason why this competition is keen is manifest. Most persons are actively engaged in production, and thus though many may save, few are willing to transfer their savings from their own occupations to those of others; whereas in old countries, the savings of many are accumulated for the loans of comparatively few. Again, the beneficial employments of capital are far more numerous. Land is abundant and cheap, labour, though expensive, is productive. The commoner manufactures are protected by the distance of fully-settled countries and the cost of transit; and even the more costly products of labour enjoy certain advantages by the same causes. Hence all persons can be, as a rule, beneficially engaged. When wages are very high, rates of interest are very high also; for a rise in the rate of wages implies an increasing demand for labour; an increasing demand can be sustained only by an increase in the capital which maintains labour; and such capital can be borrowed only by continually offering better terms to the lender, as long as the demand is in existence. The reverse of these phenomena is discerned in old and fully-settled countries, especially when the people are parsimonious, indisposed to venture or speculate, and tenacious of old habits and customs.

Here however it would be well to refer to some cases, not on the whole common in this country, but frequent in continental ones; the apparent occurrence, so to speak, of different rates of interest on the same kind of security. Thus, for example, in France and Belgium, particularly in the latter country, the price of land is so high that agricultural plots are often purchased at such rates, that the capital sum invested, as measured in rent, will not give more than from one-and-a-half to two per cent. interest. But the same purchaser, should he pledge his land on mortgage, will give from four to five per cent. on advances. That is to say, the buyer who gives fifty pounds an acre for land, and can only get one pound per acre rent, will, if he becomes a borrower, be obliged to pay two pounds or two pounds ten shillings for every fifty pounds which he borrows, though he offers a security purchased at so high a price, and generally saleable at as high a price, for the loan which he wishes to contract.

Part of this discrepancy may be accounted for by the passion of proprietorship. There is no inclination so strong among men as that of possessing land. Land is visible, enduring, personal. It is well known that, within certain intelligible limits, a divided estate will fetch a higher price than an aggregate does; because it answers the demand of a larger, and, on the whole, of a keener body of competing purchasers. An estate too may be heavily mortgaged, and yet the interest of the mortgagor in his estate may be unimpaired, or even made more intense, for a proprietor reserves rights against a mortgagee, and though he may lose some part of the control over his property, these rights are only suspended or in abeyance.

Next, the rent of land, or the interest issuing from the purchase of land, is a very different thing from the cultivation of it. Writers, especially those writers who take a political view of economic science and an aristocratic view of politics, are perpetually confounding, either wilfully or ignorantly, land as an investment and land as a machine. Land as an investment is possessed of a few intelligible properties. Its value can be determined at any given time, and is, on the whole, relative to the rate of interest; though as this value is continually increasing, partly from the cause mentioned above, partly from causes which will be discussed in a subsequent chapter, the rate of interest on investment in land is low; in other words, land is dear. But land as an instrument or machine has vast powers, powers as yet only partially discovered, but continually comprehended and appropriated by intelligence and industry. It is in the discovery of these powers that absolute proprietorship busies itself, with alacrity and success; for a precarious occupation, while it may make and appropriate discoveries of which the occupier cannot be deprived, is necessarily indifferent to those which the occupier cannot secure. The pains which an owner will take, for the purpose of improving his land, are incredibly greater than those which the farmer can or will take, and though it may be sometimes the case that part of his labour is wasted, or as far as he is concerned, is comparatively unremunerative, it is far better for the country at large that such work should be given, than that it should not be exercised at all. Labour no doubt should be as productive as possible, but labour which is scantily productive has a value, which is not possessed by indolence or indifference. If land in a rich country, like our own, were generally distributed, the United Kingdom would be as carefully cultivated as a garden is.

We have hitherto considered interest, that is, the sum of money or value promised at a future date, and promised in consideration of capital advanced to the borrower. Such interest, if the security be valid and ample, is generally liable to very slight variations. An excellent example of such interest is the rate at which advances on mortgage of freehold land are compensated. The great majority of advances however are made in another form, and are known as discounts.

When a trader borrows, he generally borrows on the debts owing to him; his debtor acknowledges the debt in a technical form, known as a bill of exchange. In this bill, which is an open letter, the creditor calls on the debtor to pay at a given date, generally three months from that at which the obligation is drawn, a specified sum of money, for which value has been received. The process by which the debtor acknowledges the bill, and accepts the responsibility, is by formally declaring his responsibility, and by specifying the place at which the bill is payable. Formerly this used to be the debtor's counting-house, and the practice of making the bill payable at this locality may linger still. But in almost all cases, at present, the debtor, or as he is called the acceptor, agrees to pay it at his bankers', who treat the bill when it is presented for payment as they would a check, and debit their customer, the acceptor, with the amount. Many millions in value of such bills are weekly cleared through the London bankers, and these clearances represent a large but by no means an exhaustive amount of these commercial instruments. It should be added, that a share in the responsibility involved in a bill of exchange attaches to all those through whose hands it passes, and who are said to endorse it. This responsibility in the persons of such endorsers as have a very high credit, is, relatively to those whose credit is inferior, as in similar cases, a marketable commodity. Thus, for example, if the current rate of discount on bills of exchange known as first class is five per cent., but a trader whose reputation is not so accredited is constrained to pay six per cent., the bill may be subsequently endorsed by a firm of high character, and be re-discounted at a lower rate, the endorsing house reaping the benefit of the transaction. This kind of business was, it is said, attempted on a large scale by the once notorious house of Overend and Gurney, but was summarily put an end to by the Bank of England. The process has nothing in it which is inconsistent with the ordinary principles of trade; for, as we have seen several times, a high commercial reputation is acquired with great difficulty, and, like other objects of laborious acquisition and economical value, bears a price in the market.

The fact that discount is a deduction from the present value of a security the payment of which is postponed, while interest is the compensation made for the past use of an advance, constitutes no real difference between discount and interest. How then comes it to pass that great variations occur in the rate of discount, while the rate of interest varies very little? Thus, in the year 1866, discounts were as high as ten per cent., and had remained at that amount for some months. At the close of 1867 they were as low as two per cent. But for the last ten years the interest obtainable from a first class security has stood with little change at four per cent. The cause of this difference, of the uncertainty of the one, and the comparative unchangeableness of the other, is partly to be found in the difference between the objects on which the loan is made, partly in the peculiar character of the obligation incurred.

Mercantile bills are generally drawn for short periods. Now, assuming that the transactions are perfectly safe, in other words, that there is no doubt at all that the bill will be met at the time when it becomes due, the fact that the loan is for short periods tends to reduce the rate, because, as the ordinary lender on these transactions wishes, it makes his money as manageable as possible. Of all securities, bills of exchange are the most easily saleable, because the interval at which the advance is to be recovered is short. A banker cannot afford, even at the prospect of securing a larger rate of interest, to have his capital locked up in long advances; he has liabilities to which he is perpetually exposed, and the best way in which he can gain a profit on his capital, and yet make it as accessible as possible, is to advance it on short loans. But the competition of lenders on short periods, when money is at an average amount, is sharper than the competition of lenders for long periods. Still more sharp is the competition of the former class of lenders when money is abundant. The advantage of lending money at short dates makes a good mercantile bill a more convenient form of investment than any other security is, and so, whatever be the average rate of discount, it follows that at certain periods low rates prevail. The same causes operate with increasing force when, for certain reasons, the supply of money is very abundant. But, on the other hand, when the supply of money is short, the competition of borrowers raises the rate to a height which is far in excess of the ordinary rate of interest. No great increase can be suddenly made in the amount of capital available for discounting bills, and the consequence is, that as the market tightens, in the language of the Exchange, the rate of discount rises.

Another cause which leads to great fluctuations in the rate of discount, is the peculiar character of the obligation incurred. The Bill of Exchange, as I have said, is an order written by the drawer, and addressed to the acceptor. Now this acceptor stipulates that at a future date he will pay a certain sum of money. His power of fulfilling this obligation depends on the prospect which he has of obtaining at the end of the period a certain portion of the precious metals, or of their equivalents. The amount of this fund for payment is, ordinarily, enough and to spare for the purpose of liquidation. The trader has his capital, as a rule, invested in commodities, by the sale of which he purposes to create and meet obligations as they are needed or become due. But if business becomes dull, or the market falls, or supply is checked, or the amount of money available for all discounts is seriously diminished by the efflux of specie from the Bank and the diminution of its capacity for making bonus, the power which the borrower has of supplying himself from this fund is curtailed, and the competition of borrowers for a limited supply of assistance becoming keen, the rate of discount naturally rises. The difficulty however of meeting the obligation already created is not so great as that of creating other obligations. For, as the trader knows very well that unemployed capital is loss, and strives to reduce the amount of such unemployed capital to the lowest possible quantity, he regularly anticipates the liquidation of those obligations under which buyers lie to him, and, as they are paid, issues new bills drawn for new debts. These new bills then supply the means by which his purchases can be made and his trade be carried on. It is true that he might contract his trade by purchasing less and selling less under such emergencies, but to shorten his accommodation is not only to shorten his power of purchase, but to interrupt his transactions, to diminish his connexion. He will, therefore, frequently consent to pay as large a discount for his bills as will absorb all his business profits, because the temporary evil of a high rate of discount is not so serious as the permanent evil of a contracted or interrupted business. I am speaking, of course, of bona fide trade, conducted with a reasonable hope of profit, which is affected, in so far as it enters into the market to borrow, by such high rates of discount as have been induced by speculative purchases and the losses of a declining market, although it may never have contributed in the least degree to the speculation and the reaction, and therefore is compelled to reduce its operations or lose its profits by events with which it has not had any relations, and over which it has never had any control. This explanation will I hope be enough to render, in some degree, intelligible the causes which lead to fluctuations in the rate of discount, as compared with those which affect the rate of interest. I shall have to enter into a fuller statement when I deal with the question of foreign trade.

CHAPTER XII.

The Rent of Land.

THE payment made for the use of the soil, known under the name of the rent of land, has attracted the attention of English economists, to a far greater extent than it has that of those who have derived most of their information from foreign countries. The reason is, that the occupation of land in this country is peculiar, and the phenomena of rent are more manifest. In this country the cultivator of the soil and the owner of the soil are, as a rule, different persons; in other countries they are, as a rule, the same; or, when they are not the same, the owner of the soil rather occupies the position of a perpetual lessor, or mortgagee, than that of a landlord whose contracts with his tenants are constantly liable to revision, and who is able to exercise a considerable control over the acts of the person who occupies and works the soil.

XII.]   THE RENT OF LAND.   153

Rent has been defined to be the payment made for the natural powers of the soil. This definition is somewhat vague, because it must be limited by several conditions before it becomes true, and when it is true, it becomes necessary again to define the meaning of the expression 'natural powers.' For it will be seen that as long as any part of the territory of a country is unoccupied and unappropriated, rent will not be paid for such natural powers as such a residue possesses in common with other occupied and appropriated soils; and rent will be paid for the use of the appropriated soil only because it is nearer to the market, and its produce may therefore be more easily disposed of. But it would be a mere figure of speech to say that the demand of purchasers for agricultural produce, and the nearness of a field to such a market, had anything to do with the natural powers of the soil.

For example, fertile land in the western parts of the United States is almost worthless, or at any rate is worth no more than a dollar an acre, the price at which the government, which has assumed an ownership in all the land lying within the political limits of the United States, is accustomed to sell it. Land however which lies within ten miles of the city of New York, may bring a rent perhaps as high as any within ten miles of London. The reason why, within the same political community, in two tracts, possessing equal natural powers, the rent of the one is nil, and that of the other is high, is to be found, not in the natural powers, but in the artificial demand of a dense and near population. Before this demand arises therefore, rent will not be paid, for a primary condition of rent is demand for the produce, a demand which becomes more urgent as population increases. Hence the growth of population is intimately connected with the rent of land.

But again, there is no doubt that certain natural powers must exist in land before produce can be obtained from it. Neither corn, nor grass, nor roots, which directly or indirectly form the food of man, will grow on the surface of a rock, or on soils whose chemical properties render them incapable of sustaining vegetation, nor, except, partially, on such soils as those whose vegetative constituents are defective. Beyond the conditions that cultivable land must be pulverised and watered, in order that plants may get root and grow, it is necessary that they should also contain certain other constituents which are not found naturally in air and water. Thus, for example, all wheat-growing soils must contain potash, phosphorus, iron, manganese, and sulphur, to judge from the analysis of the grain. These constituents exist in various degrees in various soils, and are supplied in various proportions of sufficiency and solubility by those soils which possess them.

So again, though heat and light and water are generally distributed over the surface of the earth, the extent of their distribution may variably affect the productive powers of the soil. Excessive heat, joined to excessive moisture, is peculiarly favourable to vegetable growth. But it is unfriendly to human life, and these natural forces are therefore, in so far as man cannot live under their influence, of no economical value. But they are also unfavourable to the growth of the most valuable kinds of human food. The best wheat, as a rule, is grown close to the margin of those climates in which it will not grow at all, and becomes inferior the more southerly the soil on which it is cultivated. Fertility, to constitute an economical quantity, must be capable of appropriation and be appropriated.

Again, the demands of population may be very urgent, but rent may be scanty or almost unattainable. I have alluded in a previous chapter to the very different value of land in England, as measured by rent, five hundred years ago and at the present time. While corn has risen about nine times in nominal or money value since that period, the rent of the same plots of arable land has risen from forty to sixty times, while much land which could bear no rent at all has become available for this purpose. But the pressure of population was just as keen during the period referred to as it now is, in point of fact far more keen, for dearths, now happily infrequent, were common in those times, and there was just as much eagerness to cultivate poor soils as there now is.

The common theory entertained about the occupation of land is, that the best soils were first cultivated, that is, those soils the cultivation of which cost least labour in proportion to the produce attained; that as population increased, poorer soils were taken into cultivation; and that, under these circumstances, the better land yielded a rent, the inferior land just paying for the cost of cultivation, and leaving no margin over from which rent could be derived. The theory is quite hypothetical, and has absolutely no historical foundation. It may account for the difference between the rent of two plots of land, both equally open to the same stimulants of demand and the same facilities or difficulties of supplying the demand, but it does not give any real account of the mode by which rents have arisen and have increased. Now there is no great discovery in telling any one, that difference between rents arises from difference in the relative fertility of soils. Every man who rents or lets land is perfectly familiar with this fact.

There is not a shadow of evidence in support of the statement, that inferior lands have been occupied and cultivated as population increases. The increase of population has not preceded but followed this occupation and cultivation. It is not the pressure of population on the means of subsistence which has led men to cultivate inferior soils, but the fact that these soils being cultivated in another way, or taken into cultivation, an increased population became possible. How could an increased population have stimulated greater labour in agriculture, when agriculture must have supplied the means on which that increased population could have existed? To make increased population the cause of improved agriculture, is to commit the absurd blunder of confounding cause and effect. Had this theory of rent been merely speculative, no harm would have happened. But it has been carried out into that of population, and a number of imaginary dangers and safeguards have been suggested, from this presumed origin of rent. Similarly in handling the question of population, a great many fallacies have been defended, and a great many wrong practices encouraged. Nor is it true as a fact, that the increase of agricultural produce has been achieved by increased labour, or greater relative cost. The development of agriculture, the advantageous cultivation of inferior soils, goes on simultaneously with the numerical decline of that part of the population which labours on and is directly subsisted by the soil, and is obtained, as the evidence of farming rent proves, by diminished cost.

The question may be asked however, What was the origin of that theory which is alluded to above, and which conceives that rents have arisen from the necessity that has existed of taking inferior lands into cultivation as population pressed on the means of subsistence? The answer is to be found in the same exceptional set of circumstances which originated and confirmed the Malthusian theory of population. The ordinary resources of the community, owing to a succession of deficient harvests, and to the cessation of foreign supplies, consequent upon an exhausting and general foreign war, were curtailed. The laws of the time starved the people. It was therefore advantageous, under an abnormal set of circumstances, to take lands into cultivation which, under the ordinary conditions of supply, would never have repaid the charges of agriculture. Hence arose the notion that rent was invariably due to those causes, to which an inquiry into economical history shows it can be only exceptionally due. If by any mischance, or mismanagement, that fraction of the British population (now amounting as a rule to one-fourth of the whole) which subsists on imported corn were suddenly deprived of this supply, and the produce of the world were shut out from the British market (a contingency which we may fairly conceive impossible, since we have got rid of the mischievous follies which characterised the political system under which our fathers lived), the same circumstances would occur which induced, sixty years ago, the cultivation of grain on poor land, and which gave colour to the opinion that rent was due to the pressure of population on the means of subsistence.

The occupation of inferior soils and the increased fertility of land long cultivated is due to the growth of agricultural art, and is stimulated at once by demand and by high prices of labour. In just the same way as a manufacturer strives to attain greater results at less cost of labour, and thereupon invents, economises, and adds new and cheaper forces, so the agriculturist busies himself in such inventions and economies as increase his gains, by diminishing the charge of labour, and by effecting a greater return for his outlay. The progress of agriculture, just as with other arts, is due to a judicious interpretation of forces, an intelligent self-interest. There must be a demand, in order that improvement may be stimulated, but we know also, that the demand may be urgent, but the improvement may be slow or nonexistent. To improve agriculture needs capital, industry, intelligence, a sense of security, and a conviction that cost incurred will be remunerated. And this is just what has happened in the history of the art of agriculture. We cannot see this better than by comparing the process of agriculture five hundred years ago with that of the present time.

In those days, then, half the arable land lay in fallow. The amount produced was, to take wheat as an example, about eight bushels the acre in ordinary years, i.e. less than a third of an average crop at the present time. There were no artificial grasses. Clover was not known, nor any of the familiar roots. As a consequence, there was little or no winter feed, except such coarse hay as could be made and spared. Cattle were small, and stunted by the privations and hard fare of winter. The average weight of a good ox was under four cwts. Sheep too were small, poor, and came very slowly to maturity. The average weight of a fleece was not more than two pounds. With ill-fed cattle, there was little or no strong manure. Iron was very dear, costing, to take wheat as a standard of relative value, nine times as much as it does now. But the number of persons engaged in agriculture was nearly as numerous as it now is. It embraced, to be sure, nearly the whole population, though all their labour did not produce an eighth part of that which is gathered at present. Permanent improvements of the soil too were very imperfectly carried out, not for want of will, but for want of knowledge. The farmers of the time were shrewd enough, but they knew very little. Rough draining, ditching, and ridging were used in wet soils, and this drainage was sometimes done on a large scale where land admitted its use. But their ploughing was superficial, and as for selecting breeds of cattle, though they had many varieties of oxen and sheep, it was premature to think of it. No selection could be effectual when the stock was half starved in the winter; for improvement in the breed of cattle is only possible when food is plentiful and regularly supplied.

The development of agricultural science, and its application to practical farming, is not the result of a pressure of population upon the means of subsistence (such an event would rather check than aid it), but the effect of intelligent self-interest. The customary demand existed, and if the farmer could satisfy it at one-third the cost, he could at least be able to appropriate a portion of that percentage. Hence the introduction of roots, originally, it seems, from Holland, the discovery of artificial grasses, the supply of artificial manures, the analysis of the chemical properties possessed by the soil, the adaptation of mechanical forces to agricultural processes, and the selection of seeds and cattle. All these discoveries and adaptations have increased produce, or diminished cost, or both.

Now if these discoveries and substitutions had not been conditioned by the occupation of a large area of the earth's surface, most of the benefit would have been the property of the producer, the labourer, and the consumer. Everybody is now sharing in the benefit of Watt's and Arkwright's discoveries, for the commodity is cheapened, and the process is free. The general benefit of these agricultural discoveries lies in the fact that a large portion of the population was liberated for other productive energies, and that the resources of society were *pro tanto* increased. But the particular or special benefit lies with the owner of the soil, the person who licenses another to use it, and who is able, by reason of the fact that the instrument of agriculture is limited in extent, to exact, in accordance with a social law, a certain compensation from the occupier. The landowners of a country, in short, are, as agriculture advances, in the position which a nation would find itself in relation to the interest of money in case the capital which could be borrowed were a rigid and invariable quantity, and its productive use were regularly increased. The landowners possess just such a capital, and they are continually enabled to raise the interest on advances of land, as the science of cultivation increases.

. Assuming then that the demand for the produce of

land is constant, we shall find that the proper definition of rent is:—all that remains in the price at which the produce of land is sold, when the cost of production and the farmer's profit are deducted. If the average produce of a farm is worth £1000, and the average cost of production and profit are £800, the average rent of the farm will infallibly be, should the land be let by open competition, £200. Of course, as in other business, exceptional skill, early adaptation of new discoveries, judgment in interpreting the rise and fall of markets, will give one farmer an advantage over another; but if agricultural skill be generally diffused, nothing will prevent the excess of price over cost from finding its way to the landowner in the shape of rent.

The landowners in this country, whose influence was overwhelming in the legislature, were well enough aware that high prices of agricultural produce involved high rents for land. They had unhappily adopted, at least those who were most intelligent among them, the position that rent is due to the pressure of population, and the consequent occupation of inferior soils; and they therefore strove to starve population, and force this unproductive cultivation, by excluding the general mass of the population from the foreign market of supply. To some slight extent, and in appearance to a large extent, they succeeded; for the machinery of the poor-law enabled them to put part of the charge of labour on the general public, i.e. on those who did not employ labour with a view to profit. But in the greater part of this scheme they failed, and inflicted on themselves evils similar to those which they strove to put on others, and to a great extent did put. They wished to keep the people poor, in order that they might maintain a high price of wheat. They kept the people poor, and they lowered rents, because they could not appropriate more in the shape of rent than the quantity by which the demand of purchasers could exalt the price of produce over the cost of production, and as they narrowed the circle of purchasers, they lowered the motives of improvement, and stinted the powers of the cultivator.

For throughout the whole of the controversy on the nature of rent, people argued persistently, as though everything was to be measured by wheat. Wheat was the staple food of the people, and therefore, every process of production was to be referred to this standard. But the staple food of the people is one thing, the staple industry of the home-producer is another. To limit the latter by the former, unless under compulsion, is prodigious folly. But this was done by the corn-laws, which prevented the farmer from seeking to supply a market for other agricultural produce, by forcing him to devote all his energies to the production of wheat. The act was only less absurd than it would be to abandon all the cultivation of grain in the south of England, in order to take up with that of vineyards.

At the present time we know better. The farmer, it is true, grows wheat, it may be advantageously, but also it may be necessarily, as one in the rotation of crops. But he also grows other kinds of grain, and especially provides meat and dairy produce; articles in which he is naturally protected, because they cannot be imported, or cannot be easily imported from foreign countries. Now no one pretends to say that the soil of Great Britain has gone out of cultivation since the repeal of the corn-laws, or is occupied less beneficially for the landowner. On the contrary, there has been, as we know-from the income-tax returns, a regular annual rise in rent, since the repeal of the corn-laws. The fact is, if the farmer has lost on the cultivation of wheat, he has gained on that of barley, probably on that of oats, while the price of meat is doubled, and butter and milk, especially in country places, are nearly thrice the price they were twenty years ago. The farmer, in short, has turned that to account which free-trade in corn has silently taught him; he has allowed the American farmer and the Russian peasant to supply the people of this country with a certain quantity of the grain which they need, and has occupied himself in producing that which pays him better, and ultimately increases the margin from which rent is payable. The cheaper the artisan or other labourer can get bread, the better able is he to buy meat, for the larger overplus there is in wages above the price of the first necessaries of life, the larger means are there for buying the secondary necessaries, its comforts, and its luxuries. A densely-peopled country like England is, as I have said before, like a vast city, to which the less-peopled parts of the civilised world are an agricultural country, which is glad to send its overplus of provisions in exchange for the luxuries and conveniences of a manufacturing region.

Since therefore the rent of land is all that is over and above the price at which the produce of land is sold, after the cost of production is deducted, we shall find that what measures the rent of agricultural land, equally measures the rent of business premises. A large trading house in one of the great London thoroughfares may be let at, say £2000 per annum of rent. Now some part of this sum is interest on capital expended in the building itself. Let this amount to £10,000, and, at six per cent., be £600 a year: the remaining £1400 is ground-rent, i. e. is a payment made for a particular site because it has certain conveniences, productive powers, or, to use an analogous term, fertilities, which another site, on which a building equally costly might be erected, would not possess. The person who rents such premises believes, and no doubt with good reason, that it is worth his while to pay this large rent, because he recovers it in the business qualities of the site. And we may be quite sure that, roughly and on an average, the superior business properties of such a site as I have described are worth just the difference between the rent of an equally costly building in a locality which has no such advantages, and the rent of a place which has them. Exactly the same rule will apply to the rent of a coal or other mine, a shooting moor, a salmon stream, or any other right of using the surface of the earth by purchase from its owner.

These facts, which explain the origin of rent and the measure of its extension, will also account for great fertility or capacity on the part of some soils not being followed by the rent which apparently should be derivable from them. For example, it is constantly the case that land which has only lately been taken into cultivation (such for example as the gentler declivities of chalk downs) will bear a rent of, say eighteen shillings an acre, while old arable land will bear no more than thirty shillings, and this while the produce of wheat on the former is not more than twelve bushels, that of the latter is twenty-eight bushels the acre. On investigation, and on all other crops being taken into account, this seeming discrepancy will always be explained by the comparative cost of production. It will be found for instance that the cost of ploughing, dressing, and manuring the richer land is greater, that the capital employed is more to the acre, that it costs more to get the crop in, and so forth; and that we may be quite sure of the formula (supposing the rent in each case were to be equally determined by competition) being as follows:—As eighteen shillings are to thirty shillings, and as twelve bushels of wheat, &c. are to twenty-eight bushels, so is the cost of producing the smaller quantity to the cost of producing the larger.

Thus it comes to pass that the rent of grass or meadow·land is so much higher than that of arable. It costs less to cultivate it, and the margin of rent is greater. The farmer can always pay more, the less capital he needs for cultivation. This fact is equally clear in the history of rent derived from the same parcels of land Arable rents, as I have said, have risen from forty to sixty times, natural meadow-land rents have risen from ten to twelve times only; for that which was possessed of these qualities five hundred years ago was, with some slight differences, cultivated with as little cost as it now is.

As the rent of land is that which remains over and above the cost of production, it is paid last, i.e. when all the other contributories are satisfied. Such a state of things is perhaps never historically exhibited, for as a rural population, however poor, can always be made to pay some tax, so they may be always made to pay some rent. Such a rent however is artificial, just as the rent of land would be in those parts of the United States where a dollar an acre is paid for fresh prairie, or in the Australian colonies where a pound an acre is charged for grants of public land, these regulations being accompanied by prohibitions of squatting. The rents of the middle ages were rather taxes than rents, sums extracted from the subject peasantry rather than compensations for the use of a natural agent, the amount of which was limited and the whole appropriated. But though the satisfaction of rent comes last, the amount of rent, as my reader will anticipate, is an increasing quantity. If by some device or invention the produce of the soil could be procured at half the cost at which it is procured at present, nothing could prevent the whole difference from being (other things being equal) paid as rent, just as the product of past inventions has been and is appropriated by the landowner as soon as these inventions are generally used. Such an appropriation is inevitable if we recognise a permanent property in land, and if a right be conferred on the owner of securing all the future as well as the present value of his estate. Such a right has almost invariably been accorded, because it is justly believed that industry in developing the resources of the soil would not be exercised were the ownership imperfect or contingent, or liable to sudden determination on paying the present capital value of the usufruct. If this be the case, it will be seen that the argument is very strong for securing fixity of tenure for the occupier of the soil as well as for the owner.

My reader will now be able to anticipate the causes which will increase rent and those which will diminish it, viz. everything which diminishes or enhances the cost of production. Thus the introduction of machinery, if, as is invariably the case, it is cheaper in the gross than human or animal labour, will tend to increase rents. Of course machinery is costly; but no one would use it except it were cheaper than other labour and unless it lowered the cost of production. And on the other hand, any increase in the cost of labour, any scarcity of labour which cannot be compensated by an increased use of animal or mechanical labour, will tend to, and in the end will ultimately effect, a diminution of rents. Every permanent improvement of the soil, every railway and road, every bettering of the general condition of society, every facility given for production, every stimulus supplied to consumption, raises rent. The landowner sleeps, but thrives. He alone among all the recipients in the distribution of products owes everything to the labour of others, contributes nothing of his own. He inherits part of the fruits of present industry, and has appropriated the lion's share of accumulated intelligence. But if he gets it from no merit or labour of his own, he gets it by the operation of natural causes. The only hindrance to this prosperity is his too frequent wish to be wiser than nature, more eager to grasp than society is to give. Thus he has more than once succeeded in hindering the beneficence of other men, in his desire to intercept their earnings before they begin to pour them into his lap. I have already alluded to the policy which developed and the effects which flowed from the corn-laws.

What has been said applies only to those powers of the soil to whose development the landowner has contributed nothing. Those which are the result of positive outlay on his part, are constituted exactly like every other kind of fixed capital, in the immediate anticipation of profit, and like every similar investment, are followed by profit if the outlay be wise. In some cases, as for example in the draining of Whittlesea Mere and the great enclosure near Beddgelert, the rent of such land may be entirely interest on capital. In the great majority of cases however, as for instance in subsoil and surface draining, the outlay which renders the land more fertile is very small beside the capital value of its unimproved powers. Nor, again, do these statements apply to payments made for the use of houses, and which are familiarly but improperly called rents. These are merely payments, the ground-rent being deducted, for the use of capital invested in buildings, and are exactly analogous to interest on advances; for the tenant borrows a house on which he makes a periodical payment, in just the same way that a borrower gets a loan for which he pays a periodical interest.

CHAPTER XIII.

Various Tenancies of Agricultural Land.

IT was stated at the commencement of the previous chapter that farmers' rents are almost peculiar to England. The nature of rent is not altered in those countries in which a different system prevails; it is only obscured when the same person reaps the wages of his labour and the profits of his capital, and also enjoys the progressive rise in the natural value of land. There are no means by which such a person can be deprived of this natural value and the benefits which accrue to him on his possession, unless government were to give him the present value of his estate, and reducing him to the position of the owner of a perpetual rent-charge, were to appropriate these progressive profits to public ends. To some extent, at least, such a relation between governments and owners is found in the Indian land tenures, where the absolute ownership lies with the king or state, just as it was the characteristic of our own feudal tenures, which held that the ultimate ownership of the soil was the property of the crown, that the relations of feudal tenancy were capable of modification or even reconstruction on this basis, and which, for a time at least, took the improved value of land into account in fines on re-grants or successions.

In many parts of Europe the occupation of the tenant is permanent; but he pays a fixed quantity in money or produce for the use of his farm, generally using the landlord's stock and seed. This kind of tenancy is called *mélayer* in France, from the fact that the produce is ordinarily divided into equal moieties between the landowner and the cultivator. The tenure is as old as the days of republican, or at least of imperial Rome, and arose probably from the system under which a part of the lands, previously possessed by independent governments, but gradually absorbed by the conquests of the republic, were confiscated and re-granted. In *mélayer* tenancy, the motive to improvement is stunted by the fact that the inventor of better agricultural processes has to share the profit of his intelligence or invention with the landowner; that, in short, it produces the same discouragement to agriculturists that tithes in kind do. On the other hand, it is said to be unfavourable to the landowner, whose live stock is likely to be overworked by the tenant.

Such a tenancy prevailed in England for about sixty years. The earliest agricultural records which are preserved to our own time exhibit the surface of the soil divided into manors, the boundaries of which ultimately, as it seems, became parochial limits. In these manors the best and most central lands were possessed by the lord, who generally had, besides, all or most of the natural meadow, if any such existed. This land he cultivated himself, or by the hands of his bailiff, using for farm-work a certain number of hired hands, and such other labour as his feudal dependants were bound to give. These dependants generally occupied lands at labour rents, the liability to labour on the manorial estate, and the right to a share in the manor estate, being, if we may judge from an enormously wide induction, mutual and invariable. The rest of the manor was occupied by free tenants, who were however, besides their obligation to do what was called suit and service in the manor-court or court-baron, liable to fixed annual rents, generally in money, but always so considerable as not to fall far short of the average rack-rent of arable land. Sometimes the parish contained more than one manor, but this is rare.

The estates of these free and serf tenants were scattered up and down the manor, generally in the form of strips containing so many furrows. There were usually also some common pasture and some common wood or turbary, in which latter the villagers had the right, under certain restrictions, of cutting or gathering fuel. The quantity occupied by these peasants was from twenty to fifty acres as a rule, and the distribution of land under these conditions was very general.

After the Great Plague of 1348 this system was rudely broken up. Labour became so costly that the landowner could not cultivate his farm by hired hands, except at a loss. The surviving peasantry, however, who lived on their labour, were incomparably better off. Wages were high, but profits were high also ; and in a short time the condition of the agriculturists, who were part peasant proprietors, part labourers, was greatly improved. They could not however take in hand the large farm of the manor, not being possessed of such capital as would be sufficient to work it. Hence the temporary adoption of a system like the *métayer*. One of the small proprietors of the manor engaged to take the lord's farm and stock at an annual rent, generally in money, and stipulated at the end of the term, which was almost always short, to restore stock and seed, either at a fixed rate, or in the same quantity. This method of cultivation lasted, as I have said, for about sixty years, and was superseded by the growth of a hardy and prosperous yeomanry, who either purchased the land in parcels, or bargained to work it with their own capital and at a money rent.

Peasant proprietorship, i.e. the union in the same person of ownership and occupancy, is by far the most common form in which land is distributed among civilised nations. It prevails over nearly the whole continent of Europe, and is all but universal in the United States. It is found in the Eastern world as generally as in the Western, for it is the rule in India and China. Most persons who have studied its peculiarities agree that it has great advantages, when the government is just, in elevating the character and promoting the social morality of the people. It appears to stimulate economy, to induce habits of parsimony and forethought, to render any legal relief to the poor unnecessary, and to obviate certain tendencies to any over-population, with its consequent degradation and danger.

Peasant proprietors are often heavily burdened with mortgaged debts. It is said that in France the amount of capital invested in mortgage of real estate is not less than £500,000,000 sterling, this estimate being taken from the public registers in which every mortgage, to be legal, must be inscribed. No doubt the real amount is large, but it is certainly less than these figures would imply, for in France it is necessary to go through a form and pay a fee in order to cancel a mortgage, this process being in practice avoided. Hence many estates in France, to judge from the registers, are mortgaged to far more than their real value. Still there is, no doubt, considerable indebtedness in the case of peasant proprietors in a country like France or Belgium.

Such a fact, however, though alleged against peasant proprietorship as a system, is in reality no objection. In the first place, it does not follow that the indebtedness of such persons is greater as a rule than that of persons who possess large estates. As a matter of fact, it is certain that the amount of money which is out on mortgage of real estate in this country, where large proprietorships are general, is very great, and would probably not fall short, all things considered, of that in France. But, besides, my reader will remember the distinction which has been made above between land as an investment of capital and land as an instrument of agriculture. The peasant is far more concerned with the latter aspect of his tenure than he is with the former; though as his mortgage merely stipulates that he should pay such a sum of money, of which the value of his farm at the time when the mortgage is effected is constituted a pledge, he has the power of securing such advantages as the growing value of his land gives him.

For it must be remembered, that as long as society progresses, invents, economises, labours, grows, land is the only article the value of which constantly and invariably increases. The value of gold and silver may fall by the discovery of abundant mines and by economy in reducing ores. The value of corn may decline by the cultivation of land at cheap rates, or by inducing cultivation on other lands where corn could not previously be grown, or by abundant and easy importation from foreign regions. The value of manufactured articles may fall by economy in the production of raw materials and by cheapening the process of production. But as these various saving processes are adopted, and the more fully they are adopted, so the rent of land rises, and rises more certainly. The general distribution therefore of land not only gives those moral advantages to the possessor which observers have discovered, but secures to the general benefit of society, or at any rate to the benefit of a larger number of persons, the advantages which ensue from the growth of society itself.

The real disadvantage of these small holdings—if indeed the inconvenience be not exaggerated—lies in the difficulty which there is in supplying the peasant tenants with that animal or mechanical labour which, though so expensive at first, effects so great a saving afterwards. Suppose it costs £50 to purchase a reaping-machine, and 2*s.* 6*d.* to purchase a reaping-hook, but the annual saving on machine reaping is so great as to diminish the cost of reaping by one half, it is plainly expedient to make the outlay. But it will be expedient only if the farm be wide enough to bring about the saving in question. So, again, improved breeds of horses, cattle, sheep, poultry are really economies, in which a first increased cost is rapidly counterpoised by diminished cost or increased gain. But it is not possible, or at least easy, for the small tenant to effect these beneficial changes. His farm is too small for their economical use, even if his capital be not too scanty for their purchase. So he uses the cheaper implement, but costlier process, the reaping-hook. Hence people point to small tenancies as instances of agriculture being stationary, and assert that when land is held in little parcels, there can be no progress in the art of cultivating the soil. These observations of course apply in chief to the commonest and most general agricultural processes. Vineyards must be trimmed and their produce gathered by hand, silkworms must be fed and reared with the greatest care, and so small cultivation only is possible with a variety of similar products.

It does not appear however that the difficulties are insuperable. Such machines, as for example drilling and threshing machines, are readily hired, and it is possible to conceive that small farmers should co-operate, or form a species of company, by which they might be enabled to purchase such machines by a common subscription, and use them according to a rota to be agreed on between each other. The system of co-operation or co-operate industry is in its infancy as yet, but there seems no reason to doubt that so obvious an application of its principle as that which I have indicated might be readily adopted.

There is yet another kind of tenancy, peculiar to the United Kingdom, but now, it may be hoped, becoming rarer, and which recent legislation will in all probability extinguish entirely. But its history is very instructive. This is the Irish cottier tenancy. A similar kind of holding appears to have once existed in the Scottish Highlands. The Irish system was partly due to historical circumstances, partly to peculiarities in the social life of the people.

The ancient Irish tenancy consisted of a village or district, or, in the phraseology of the island, a 'country,' in which there was a paramount chief, selected (according to what was called the custom of tanistry) as the worthiest and best of the blood, and a number of dependent clansmen. These local chiefs were in their way subordinated to the several lords or native princes who held authority over sections of the island. So completely was the tenure of land a village system in which the various members of the sept, though they possessed personal property, were precarious occupiers of particular plots of land, that on the decease of the chief a fresh allotment of the common estate was made among the members of the sept. The right of the chief was that of maintenance, his duty that of defence. These relations were embodied in an adage, 'Spend me and defend me.'

The English conquest of Ireland introduced the Anglo-Norman law, the basis of which was the assignment of all actual and reversionary rights in the soil to some owner. It held that the ultimate owner of all land was a person, not a community; was an individual, not a clan. There can be no doubt that such a theory of property is more favourable to the progress of society and the accumulation of wealth than a system which gives the individual no right to anything but the produce, and acknowledges no permanent proprietary rights except in the community. Such a view of the comparative merits of the English and Irish law was alleged as a reason, among others, for superseding the latter by the former. My reader will remember however, from what has been previously stated, that in early times the cost of production and the value of the produce were very nearly equal, and that therefore, as the margin of rent, was very narrow, the losses consequent upon these frequent partitions and the insecurity induced upon improvement by the liability to fresh distributions were almost trifling. The case of course was different when land became more valuable, owing to increased skill, diminished cost, and an enlarged population. Five hundred years ago the capital invested in live and dead stock on a well-managed farm was probably worth three times the land. Now it is not worth, as a rule, much more than a third.

This village occupation, in which all the land was treated as the common estate of the sept, appears to have been general among Celtic races. It prevailed till late years in Scotland; it is seen to have existed in Ireland; it was extinguished in Wales by the statute of Rutland (1284). Its abandonment in Ireland was due to a remarkable decision given in the Irish King's Bench in the year 1608. Tanistry and Irish gavelkind, as the system of electing the worthiest to the headship of the clan and re-dividing the estate among all the males of the sept on certain occasions were called, were, it appears, formally recognised by the English law as late as the reign of Elizabeth.

In the year 1608, then, a case was brought before the Irish King's Bench, in which the plaintiff was the tanist, the defendant a donee in tail, i. e. a person in whose behalf an estate tail had been created. The plaintiff defended the custom as reasonable, and appears to have propounded a charter of Elizabeth in which it had been recognised. The defendant, on the other hand, urged that the custom was unreasonable, uncertain, contrary to the English common law, contrary to public policy as discouraging the permanent improvement of the soil, and injurious to the people at large. The pleadings are given in abstract by Sir J. Davis, who was the king's attorney-general in Ireland and counsel for the defendant. The case was before the court for three or four years, and then a judgment was given, in point of law for the defendant, though in point of fact a compromise was effected, the donee in tail taking the castle and certain adjacent lands, the tanist the remainder. But from this time forth it became a rule that tanistry was obsolete and contrary to the law of the three kingdoms; and thus English custom was placed in its room, with such powers of settlement and ownership as the law at the time allowed.

I have adverted to this ancient form of tenure partly because it was a very widespread system in primitive times, partly because, tenaciously as customs relating to the tenure of land are retained by communities, the ancient Celtic rule appears to have been broken through by this judicial decision. It probably lingered a long time in remote localities, but it had no legal status, and could not be pleaded. It appears plain too that as the English law became more strictly followed, the permanent rights of the dependent members of the sept were gradually extinguished, and the customary occupation was reduced to a tenancy at will.

Successive rebellions, confiscations, and immigrations of English settlers did their work in lowering the material condition of the native Irish; a faith hostile to that of the dominant class widened the breach between the English conquerors and the Irish peasantry; and a change in the customary food of the people completed their degradation. This change was the substitution of the potato for oatmeal, or whatever other kind of grain had been used before for food.

A nation increases ordinarily up to the supply of that food which is sufficient to sustain life. If the food be cheaply attained, population will grow rapidly. Again, as the wages of labour are relative to the cost of producing labour, if food be cheaply got, wages will be low. The use of the potato increased the numbers of the Irish, and reduced their wages. Five or six centuries ago the wages of labour in Ireland were as high as those in England. Twenty-five years ago they did not, we are told, amount to much more than a fourth of the rate of English wages. But this abundance of cheap food was grievously counterbalanced by the excessive misery of the people, and the risks, ultimately the occurrence, of famine.

The staple industry of Ireland is agriculture. The population of Ireland was excessive. It is possible, had there been abundant capital in the hands of landowners or farmers, that even this population might have been employed. But neither landowner nor farmer had capital, and it was therefore necessary that the peasantry should subsist by their own labour on the plots of land which they rented. These tenants were called cottiers, and there was the keenest competition for these plots, which were put up from time to time to auction. The system has been to some extent remedied by the famine and the subsequent emigration of a large percentage of the population, because the competition for land has become somewhat less active and wages have increased.

There is nothing to limit the rate at which land will be let when the sole or nearly the sole occupation of a people is agriculture, the price paid for the use of the soil is determined by the competition of an auction, and the population is abundant. Property in the soil, under such circumstances, may be used as a means for inducing a scarcity price on its occupation, and for constantly heightening the price as opportunity arises. It will not be difficult to point out the causes and conditions which bring about such a result.

If a town were besieged by an enemy, or its communication with the supply of agricultural produce were effectually arrested in any other way, the price of food would rise. It would become necessary that the inhabitants should practise economy. It would be to the advantage of those who possessed such granaries as existed in the town or district, to exact the fullest price which the demand of the public for such food as they had to sell might put into their power. To the rise which might thus be effected there is no necessary limit. The people who could not buy might perish, and the demand might slacken; but as long as they had such resources as could tempt the owner of food to dispose of part of his store, so long he could exact the largest price within their means, and they would be constrained to sacrifice everything to the necessity of maintaining life. If the whole available food of the town or region were in the hands of one man, like Bishop Hatto in the German story, he would be moved to sell by only one of two risks—the supply from some new quarter, or the extinction of all demand by the starvation of all those who wished to buy. It is hardly necessary to say that a society, however much it might in the abstract respect the rights of property, would never permit its own destruction, by according to any one man such unlimited powers over the necessities of all the rest. It would assuredly (as has occasionally been done when similar or analogous circumstances have occurred) assume that the right of society to exist was more sacred than the ownership of property. For it would hold that sacredness is accorded to private property because it is by maintaining such rights that society exists and prospers; but that when society is threatened with dissolution, the plea on which the maintenance of property depends is about to disappear. Much more then, when the existence of society and the sustentation of certain private rights became incompatible, would the former override the latter; not only because it is stronger, but because it has more urgent and permanent claims.

Now this condition of absolute scarcity in an object which was nearly as important for the continuous existence of the people as the supply of food to a besieged town, was actually effected in Ireland. This country had but few manufactures, and these were little capable of expansion. The owners of the soil had no capital, or if they had, they were not disposed to employ it in hiring Irish labour. The population was abundant, and either could not or would not relieve itself by emigration. The only means of life available for the people was the cultivation of the soil, not as hired labourers, but as small occupiers. At any cost they must have land. In order to gain temporary possession of it, they were willing to offer rents many times in excess of the possible value of all that could be produced from the soil. These promises to pay were of course never fulfilled, but the occupier gave all that he could; that is, he paid everything which he earned over and above his necessary subsistence and the subsistence of his dependants. He had of course no motive of any kind for prudence or thrift, since the possession of any property, except by stealth, would have been merely a plea for the exaction of arrears of rent. The Irish peasantry were incomparably worse off than the French peasantry were before the Revolution and during the period in which an arbitrary *taille* was exacted from them; for the latter could not be easily dispossessed, and might be able to hoodwink the government agent; while the former was absolutely at the mercy of his landlord, except of course in so far as the full exaction of all the legal rights of the landlord might be attended with personal danger to the agent or his principal. The Irish land system familiarised the peasantry with agrarian outrages, because these outrages were the solitary remedy against oppression—an oppression, it should be added, which was not the less real because it was exercised under those forms of law which to all appearance are universally necessary in every society, in order to protect and enforce voluntary contracts. It is a standing rule in all legal procedure that such contracts must hold good unless they are obtained by force or fraud, and that no plea of temporary necessity can be raised against the fulfilment of obligations which have been consciously entered on.

That there are contracts, which are voluntary indeed, but should not be protected by law, would be admitted on all hands. Immoral bargains are of this kind. But it is a nicer question to determine when the law should interfere either to fix a price, or to strike a balance between the parties among whom the value of a produce is distributed. For example, it would be all but impossible that law or equity should determine the share of the workmen and the capitalist in any product to the development of which both agencies are requisite. Nor is the difficulty less in the case of land. The tenant pays a rent for certain properties inherent in the soil. This rent, as we have seen, constantly tends to being everything which is over and above the cost of producing various articles from the earth, when the demand for such articles enables the producer to sell them at a price in excess of the cost at which they have been produced, this cost including the remuneration of the producer's own labour and the profit on his capital. It is clear then that should this rent, or a portion of this rent, be taken away from the owner of the soil, it will not be to the advantage of any one besides the person who occupies the soil. The portion of rent which the landlord loses the farmer gains; and as, by the very terms of our hypothesis, this rent must be over and above the cost of production, the position of a farmer under such circumstances will be *pro tanto* that of a landowner. He would, for example, be able to borrow on the security of his portion of the natural powers of the soil. Now we know that these natural powers have been enormously developed by the progress of the art of agriculture. The soil of England produces eight times as much food as it produced 500 years ago, three times as much as it did 250 years ago. But to maintain that the present generation of landowners has a natural right to the benefit of every improvement which may be induced hereafter on the use of the soil, is not only an extravagant assumption, but cannot be sustained as long as the legislature insists that owners may be dispossessed of their lands at their present value when public exigencies require the sacrifice. It is plain injustice to take such possessions without making full compensation; but it may be matter of the highest policy, when such compensation is made, to establish a body of farmers whose rent shall be permanently fixed, whose holdings shall be incapable of subdivision below a fixed amount, but whose interest in improving the soil should be stimulated by the security which is given them in the fruit of their own intelligence and labour. And surely, as a matter of equity, the outlay of labour and capital is more naturally entitled to the fruits of an improved market and the economy of continued skill than the passive owner is, the value of whose estate grows as he sleeps. The remedy at least for Irish agricultural distress and agrarian disaffection is fixity of tenure, and this fixity can apparently be attained only by granting a permanent ground-rent, representing the average value of the rack-rent, to the landowner, and by securing him in his income by sufficient powers of distress. To some extent this security has lately been given.

My reader will see also that there is another reason which may justify exceptional action on behalf of the Irish cottier, even though it be conceded that no such stringent remedy is needed in the case of the English and Scotch farmer. The latter can protect himself. He will not consent to rent land at such a rate as will not secure him the ordinary profits on capital, the ordinary compensation for a laborious and anxious superintendence over his farm. Any attempt to extort exorbitant rents would be defeated, for capitalists would decline to take land on disadvantageous terms. They would transfer their capital to other occupations, or seek an outlet for it in the British colonies or foreign countries. In point of fact, agricultural land in England is rather under than over let, rents rarely reaching the maximum which capitalists, especially those who are inclined to farm a few acres highly, are or would be willing to give, and frequently falling below the price at which ordinary tenant farmers eagerly compete for the privilege of occupying farms.

But the case of the Irish peasant is, as we have seen, totally different. With him there is no alternative to agriculture. He must labour on the land, or starve. He has little option now; he had no option when the fullest possible rent was extorted from his exigencies, when he was constrained to pay a scarcity price for the use of land. In one particular only he was better off than the English farm-labourer. He often contrived, as no poor-law induced him to rely on the enforced contributions of others, to secrete a little store which availed him for emigration; for the Irish emigration, great as it was, was spontaneous, and unassisted by government. But pending this movement, he was wholly at the mercy of the landowners, as he now is in a modified degree.

The claim of tenant right—that is, the demand to be compensated for the actual outlay of capital in the improvement of the soil—is in effect an assertion that the farmer is unprotected against the landowner. In England and Scotland the wrong of which the Irish complain is not likely to be committed on a large scale; for public opinion is a powerful corrective to such a practice. The English tenant farmers, as Adam Smith observed, constantly lay out great amounts of capital on the land which they occupy, and are yet unsecured against the cupidity of the landowner. But the insecurity was and is only apparent. The tenant is virtually protected by the disreputable publicity which would be given to a sudden eviction, or a dishonest appropriation of the tenants' improvements. Whether indeed improvement be checked by the fact that the tenancy is legally precarious, is a question which Arthur Young answered negatively, and reasonably so, and which, with equal reason, can be answered now with the same negative.

CHAPTER XIV.

Demand and Supply.

As we have several times seen, the keystone of society, from the point of view which the economist takes, is that capacity for and disposition towards the mutual exchange of services and utilities which is manifested in its members. On this aspect every one wishes to buy and every one wishes to sell.

The words Demand and Supply have been adopted by economists to express those states of mind. But every one who buys, sells; and, *pari ratione*, every one who sells, buys; the completion of demand and supply being an act of exchange in which both are interlaced. My reader will remember that the interposition of money merely postpones the actual termination of the true exchange, by enabling the recipient of money to use his pleasure in selecting the time which shall be most convenient for the completion of the transaction; the function of money being like that implement in mechanics which is called an endless screw.

The origin of demand is the sense of necessity, utility, or convenience. The condition of human life is that it must be maintained by the products of labour. The condition of social life is that different persons should be engaged in different pursuits. A continuous supply of food must be afforded in order that man may exist; and food is got by labour. Hence the earliest and most essential function of labour is the supply of food; the possibility of any other than agricultural labour being practised by any community, depending on the precedent condition that such labourers as are engaged in procuring food can produce more than they must needs consume themselves. The machinery available for these ends must show a surplus produce over that which it expends in maintaining its own activity. As then the demand for food is incessant, so, when the supply is straitened, it is urgent. Under such circumstances every other demand is suspended or circumscribed; for utility and convenience give way to necessity. If however this universal want be readily and fully satisfied, the demand for articles of utility or convenience will vary with the habits and tastes of the individual, and with the power which he has of enjoying or using them.

Only a little less urgent than the demand for food is that for clothing and house-room. In some parts of the world these demands are reduced to a minimum, the natural warmth of the climate enabling persons to dispense with them altogether, or at most to be satisfied with scanty clothing and slight protection from weather.

Now the possessor of any object in demand may, and indeed does, temporarily raise the value of it (i.e. its value at any particular time and to any particular person) to the maximum amount which his intended customer will endure to give. In the great majority of cases now-a-days this debate about the value of an article, called by Adam Smith the higgling of the market, is confined to wholesale purchases and sales. But a generation or two ago the habit of bargaining in matters of retail trade was general. It still is a custom in many European countries. It is all but universal in the East. The adoption of a different plan in small transactions is partly due to indolence, partly to necessity. In the multiplicity of objects which may tempt a purchaser (supply in fully settled countries, as far as the utilities and conveniences of life go, being regularly in excess of demand), it is all but impossible to form an estimate of the exact value of retail commodities; and purchasers prefer to trust in the judgment and honesty of those with whom they deal. Hence, as I said above, 'good-will' and 'connexion.'

The sense of utility or convenience is not absolute, but relative or personal. Mr. De Quincey, in a passage quoted by Mr. Mill, observes, that no supply of hearses in any town would induce customers to buy more than was absolutely necessary. No better instance of limited demand could perhaps be given; for a hearse is no pleasurable object for contemplation, is cumbrous, and does not improve in value by keeping. But it is possible to conceive an eccentric person with a taste for collecting hearses, as men have gathered walking-sticks and fishing-rods by the hundred.

Now this fact that the possessor of any object in demand may, and does, temporarily raise the value of it, is the solution of many social questions, in so far as they are examined from an economical point of view. For reasons fully stated before, the best index of such a demand is the price of the object in question. It is perhaps hardly necessary to say, that the demand must be 'effectual,' i.e. the requisition of the object must imply that the intending purchaser is not only willing but able to render that which the possessor of the object demanded considers an equivalent for such an object. But the importance of the fact which has been stated above is so great that it is desirable to illustrate it abundantly.

The demand for food is incessant, primary, urgent. By food is meant, not the luxuries or conveniences with which the great mass of the people can dispense, but that without which they cannot exist. This, for example, in our country is bread. At any sacrifice bread must be procured. No article then exhibits more clearly the demand of society than bread does. Hence, the demand remaining constant, and the supply falling short, the competition of purchasers will raise the price in a far greater proportion than will be manifested in the case of any other deficient article. For a reason which we shall give below, such a rise will also adversely affect the price at which all other articles can be concurrently sold.

If the adequate or ordinary supply of bread to any community is contained in 10,000,000 quarters of wheat, which under such circumstances is sold at £2 10s. the quarter (the quantity and price are merely hypothetical), the falling off of such a supply will, according to its degree, affect the price of that which is available for sale in a geometrical proportion. If, for example, it fall to 7,500,000 quarters, it must not be supposed that this quantity will sell for £25,000,000 only, i.e. the price at which 10,000,000 quarters used to sell. It will fetch much more. This fact, which is fundamental in the theory of demand and in the history of prices, was noticed long ago by Gregory King. Nor in case the scarcity is so high that sufficient food cannot be procured by all persons, will anything check the rise in price, except the starvation of some. The price will constantly increase, if no aid can be given to the deficiency, until the number of those competing for food has been fully reduced. Happily we have had no experience of this excessive dearth for centuries; nor, in the extension of a free import trade, are we likely to ever experience more than a slight and temporary deficiency. When the dearth is absolute, it may be added, all articles of food, all materials which may avail for the sustentation of life, rise proportionately; though, as a matter of fact, such kinds of food as are not habitually and universally necessary are consumed at an early period in such a scarcity. Domestic animals, though they assist human labour, are maintained by that labour, and in some degree at least subsist from the means on which labour subsists.

Whenever the dearth of the necessaries of life does not amount to absolute famine, the secondary conveniences are sure to become cheaper. A high price of corn always involves (all other circumstances remaining the same) a low price of meat. When people have to stint themselves of necessaries, they abjure luxuries, they economise the use of conveniences. High prices of corn under the pressure of a particular crisis are the indications of a peremptory demand; high prices of other articles are an index of a voluntary demand. Just then as the positive necessaries of life rise in price as they become scarce, so do the comforts and conveniences of life fall in price under the influence of causes which exalt the price of necessaries. In order to interpret the events which affect the price of articles we must not take Mr. De Quincey's hypothetical cases; that of a musical-box on Lake Superior, offered by a dealer who is on the point of departure, to a supposed purchaser who will not have, for many years, the opportunity of a similar purchase; or that of a town to which is offered a superabundance of hearses; but the constant conditions of society, in which, by some occasional dearth in the necessaries of life, we may and shall find that the rise in one article is the inevitable depression of others.

In the long run the price of commodities depends, as we have several times seen, on the cost of production.

At any particular time the price depends upon the demand of the purchaser, the discretion of the seller. The fact that commodities are produced at all depends on the pre-existence of demand for them—a demand which is personal when the producer intends them for his own use or consumption, indirect when the producer employs them as a means of exchange. It is perfectly true that the most urgent demand may not induce a corresponding satisfaction. The article may be absolutely limited in quantity, it may not be procurable for a time, it may not be procurable for want of that capital or industry which is essential to all production; capital being, on an economical analysis, labour maintained by the accumulations of previous labour.

Thus, for example, the number of known pictures painted by the great masters of the art is limited. No power could add to the number, though time or accident may diminish it. The value then which will be assigned to these masterpieces is absolutely relevant to the demand for them. The price which they will fetch is wholly settled by the competition of purchasers. A fashion may exalt this price to an extravagant amount, a fashion may depress the price. Forty or fifty years ago it was the custom for book-collectors to search out Aldine and Elzevir editions of the classics. As a consequence the price at which perfect copies were purchased was often enormous. The fashion it seems has passed away, and books which once cost many pounds would not now fetch as many shillings. But on the other hand, the market value of early English printed books is greatly increased. These indeed are examples of that exceptional demand to which Mr. De Quincey referred when he gave his case of the traveller on Lake Superior and the possessor of a musical-box. The value of the article at the crisis is determined solely by the desire of the purchaser and the rarity of the object which he wishes to appropriate. But such cases are only exceptional, and do not bear in any notable degree on the economy of society.

Far different however is the case with those objects the demand for which is urgent and continued, but the supply of which cannot, for a time at least, be increased. Such was till lately the case with food in this country. Almost all nations depend to a great extent on their own harvest for subsistence from year to year. If they have, either by lack of foreign trade, or by a corn-law imposing prohibitive duties or precarious duties on foreign produce, insulated themselves from the harvests of other countries, and therefore cannot get foreign supplies, they must economise their resources, and put up with hardship, dearth, or even famine. But in order to buy, they must be able to sell. Thus, had the trade in corn during the Irish famine been ever so free, the peasantry of that island could not, any more than the peasantry of Belgium could, have obtained foreign supplies, for they had nothing to offer in exchange. But to sell or buy, they must create a market for the dealer. Thus, during the existence of the sliding-scale system of duties (i.e. a rule that the duties on imported corn rose as home-grown corn fell in price, and fell as it rose), it was all but impossible for foreign corn-growers to anticipate the market, wholly impossible to anticipate the produce of the United Kingdom. Now uncertainty is the most serious obstacle to commerce; and hence the continuance of the sliding-scale system was fatal to regular importations from abroad. It also made the trade of the corn-dealer or corn-speculator, instead of being useful only, unnaturally important. The usefulness of the corn-dealer consists in his economising the supplies of any country during seasons of scarcity by high prices, in economising the supplies during abundant seasons by reserving the surplus for harder times. But when the market was so precarious and fluctuating, as it was during the continuance of our corn-laws, the greatest risks attended the trade of the corn-dealer, and as a consequence, he required, in popular language, large profits for his services. At no period were there such constant and such serious fluctuations in the price of corn as during the existence of those laws, the very object of which was to maintain, as far as possible, a uniform rate of price.

It was not, as my reader may anticipate, any advantage to the producer. If a farmer grew nothing but corn, it is doubtful whether he could have gained anything by the machinery of the corn-laws. In the first place, the markets, as I have said, were subject to violent fluctuations, the gain of which, in so far as it could be secured, fell to the corn-speculator. If a dealer desires above all things a uniform or, as Adam Smith calls it, a natural price, still more does a producer; for a fall may overset the calculations and destroy the profits of a harvest, seeing that the producer cannot, as a dealer may, easily extricate his capital from his investment. And if the farmer's profits were precarious, his landlord (if we remember that rent is all that remains over and above the cost of producing an object in demand) could not enter upon the advantage of high prices.

But a farmer does not produce corn only. The maintenance of animals is, not only for the purpose of the market, but for the development of rural economy, altogether of primary and paramount importance. But, as we have seen, high prices of corn involve low prices of other agricultural produce. Unless wages increase with scarcity (a very rare and exceptional phenomenon), the purchasing power of incomes falls with the increase in the price of the first necessaries of life. Every shilling added to the quarter of corn, or, to be more exact, every farthing added to the price of the quartern loaf, cuts off a certain number of purchasers in the market of meat and dairy produce. Any scarcity, I repeat, in the supply of primary necessaries, lowers the value of secondary necessaries, whether this scarcity be the effect of the seasons, or of legislation, or of such artificial regulations as have the effect of legislation.

But thanks to those changes in our fiscal system which have allowed the free importation of food, the explanation of these facts has become little more than a matter of abstract speculation. There is already, or there is rapidly being effected, a perpetual harvest before those who adopt the practice of free importation and have the power to make their demand effectual by the supply of home produce to foreign markets. The alarms which honest fear endorsed, or which interested parties spread, as to the risks of dependence on foreign supplies, or as to the extent to which the foreign producer of food could supply the wants of those with whom he could enter into a beneficial exchange, have passed away. The real cost of carriage is diminishing yearly. The nominal cost can hardly increase, since a great amount of this cost is in satisfaction of interest on capital already fixed in permanent roads. I mean by 'real cost,' the charges incurred at any given time in performing a service; by 'nominal cost,' the price paid by way of interest or dividend on an irrecoverable outlay. Thus the charges of transit by sea are determined by the real cost of the service rendered, or again, by the working expenses of a railroad; while the nominal cost, in the latter case, would refer only to the dividend derivable from the capital invested in the line. The latter is, if competition be free,'a decreasing quantity.

It does not follow, however, that demand will be satisfied, even though the natural circumstances are favourable to the supply. A few years ago we had a striking illustration of this fact.

The outbreak of the Civil War in the United States arrested the supply of an important raw material of British industry. In 1860, about 621,000 tons of raw cotton were imported into the United Kingdom. In 1862, the quantity fell to 232,000 tons, i. e. to little more than one third of the supply two years before. The circumstances of this exceptional occurrence exhibit with great precision the economical conditions under which demand and supply are related; for although clothing is not so necessary to human life as food is, it is only less necessary, and the raw material of clothing, giving as it does the opportunity of labour to millions, is indirectly as important to those who are engaged in manufacturing it as food itself.

The price of best cotton was quadrupled. Not at once, indeed; for the stock of manufactured articles was very large, and the capitalist employer was placed for a time in a particularly advantageous position. But United

States cotton rose from £60 the ton, at which it was returned in 1860, to £267 in 1864. The rise in Egyptian and Brazilian cotton was nearly as great, while the inferior produce of British India rose from £37 the ton to £169; for it is a rule in the price of objects in demand, that scarcity operates most energetically on the inferior article in the same class. A sudden dearth of labour always raises inferior more than it does skilled labour. High prices of fine wool are accompanied by higher relative prices of common wool. This rule does not apply to the first necessaries of life; for here the urgency of the demand puts an end to all other considerations by dwarfing the desire to appropriate other objects.

Great however as was the rise in raw cotton, it would have certainly been greater still had it been the only raw material available for textile purposes. To some extent the deficiency was supplied by flax, still more by sheep's-wool. But no article could satisfy so many, so varied, and such common uses as cotton does. The demand was exceedingly urgent, the supply very deficient. The agents of the cotton-spinners, already associated for this purpose, since there is always great risk in depending on a single market, scoured the world in order to stimulate the production of cotton and to buy up stocks of the raw material. To a certain extent they succeeded. Imports came from countries which had never supplied cotton before. Egypt and India put forth all their energies in order to fill up the void in the British market. These energies, however, were only imperfectly successful, for in the year 1865, when the American war was over, and the stocks had been liberated, the imports were only 436,000 tons.

The fact is, as demand, to be effectual, must be accompanied by the power to exchange; so supply, to be effectual, must be accompanied by the power to produce. Now in order to produce, capital must be forthcoming, i.e. the means for maintaining labourers. But in order that capital should be provided, first, there must be antecedent saving; next, there must be confidence in the course of production; and lastly, there must be confidence in the development of a market. There was plenty of capital saved; but there was little or no information as to the best way in which a cotton supply could be secured, and no certain prospect of an advantageous market. In other words, there was no capital with which to start the production of cotton on a great scale, for there was no knowledge (perhaps it may be said, there was a perverse blindness) as to the duration of that political difficulty which induced the cessation of the ordinary market.

And yet there is no produce for which there is a wider area of cultivation than that available for the cotton-plant. It grows freely as a perennial in all tropical climates; it flourishes as an annual over that wide belt of land which occupies the warmer part of the temperate zones. Wheat, the geographical range of which is perhaps next in width, cannot grow in the tropics, is always highest in quality the more nearly it approaches the latitude in which it will just ripen, the more nearly it is brought to those climatic conditions in which the human race is most healthy and vigorous.

Since the demand for the necessaries and chief conveniences of life is regulated by those conditions of comparative urgency and comparative rarity, it is manifest that such artificial circumstances as give the seller an exceptional advantage over the purchaser should be discouraged. We have already recognised the mischief and wrong which are involved in the maintenance of a tax on imported food. We have in a previous chapter commented on the effect of those regulations which workmen in particular callings have been able to induce on that labour which is engaged in supplying some of the necessaries of life, the artificial dearness which such arrangements involve, the charge they put on the resources of the labourer himself, and the risk they impose on the continuity of his occupation. Nor must we omit to notice also, that any restriction put on the free transfer of land, any check on the supply of that which is necessary for all social uses, is similarly an artificial assistance given to the seller, an artificial disadvantage put upon the buyer. Whatever may be said about other objects, it is inexpedient on every economical ground to permit the right of settling land; that is, of allowing the decisions of those who are dead to have force against the will or wish of the living. Land and its incidents, in fully settled countries, are absolutely limited in quantity. To permit its accumulation in few hands, to hinder its distribution by permissive enactments and direct legislation, is to give its owner an exceptional advantage against the rest of the community, to unduly enhance its price, to lay a special burden on those who require its use.

Where land is occupied with a view to profit, and is therefore brought under the ordinary conditions of production and exchange, the accumulation and settlement of land in few hands does not affect adversely the purchaser of such articles as can be freely and abundantly imported from abroad, except in so far as the cost of freight gives an advantage to the home producer. It does not of course affect at all the purchaser of such objects as are exported to foreign countries, because here the conditions of competition are necessarily fulfilled. But it does affect the purchaser adversely in the cost of articles which cannot be freely imported. It may be the case that the price of corn (on the hypothesis that the price of land and its use are heightened by the legal accidents which are permitted to surround its transfer or alienation in England) is not seriously affected, but the price of other provisions is. Still more however is the ground-rent of houses affected, and by implication the supply of house accommodation. This artificial enhancement of cost in the supply of this necessary is of course greatest in the case of those whose incomes are small.

Not long ago the greatest part of a considerable port on the north-east coast of England was the property of a great corporation and a wealthy nobleman, the one moiety lying on one side, the other on the other side of the tidal river which constitutes the port. The property of the corporation was (owing in part to the disability imposed on all corporations up to a comparatively recent date of leasing their land for a longer period than forty years) occupied by all or nearly all the poverty and wretchedness of the town. In the course of time this property was alienated, and distributed among a number of purchasers in fee. Almost immediately the tide of misery set in to that part of the town which was the property of the nobleman. The distribution of the corporate estate induced a healthy competition for the possession of building-sites and the erection of suitable dwellings. The aggregation of the nobleman's estate was unfavourable to these circumstances. So, again, it is probable that had there not been an all but universal custom in Lancashire of letting building-sites on what is called *chief*, that is at a perpetual ground-rent, the industry of the Manchester district would hardly have been developed, or if it had been originated, would have been small by comparison with that which has been exhibited under what is, in everything but name, an easy and total alienation of land.

Demand, then, is measured by the necessity of the consumer or purchaser; supply by the power of the producer or seller. The check on the claims of the latter is competition on the part of sellers. Everything however which checks competition on the part of the seller, increases competition on the part of the buyer, and so enables the former to extort more from the necessities of the latter.

CHAPTER XV.

Trade in Money.

WE have been hitherto considering the phenomena of supply and demand as exhibited in the purchase and sale of those material products of industry, those services which society recompenses on economical grounds, and that *locus standi* for all production which is implied generally in the expression 'the rent of land.' The demand and supply of money and capital are so important, the circumstances connected with their harmony and the disturbance of their ordinary relations so intricate, that they need a separate treatment and explanation. The functions of money are complex, and the use of the word is exceedingly ambiguous.

We have already seen that in the first instance the precious metals are produced under the same conditions which govern the production of other articles, occupying as articles of value just that place which other values occupy, a price proportionate to their average cost of production, and distributed among those who require and use them in the same way, though with far greater ease, that other values are distributed. When a country produces the precious metals in such quantities as to always have a surplus over the wants of an internal currency and such domestic arts as employ these metals, the distribution of gold and silver is effected in exactly the same way that any other merchandise is. Australian gold and Mexican silver are exchanged for some kinds of British, colonial, or foreign produce, by the same agencies as distribute cotton or wool. The country which imports them procures them at a cheaper rate than another community does which merely obtains them by the action of the intermediary, since the value of an article produced abroad will be governed by the value of the article against which it is exchanged. The value of gold in Australia is determined by the cost of producing it there. But the value of Australian gold in Great Britain will depend on the value of that against which it is exchanged. So the value of wine is not determined in England by the cost of producing it in Spain, but by the cost at which the goods were produced in exchange for which it is sold to the British importer. In this case gold and silver are mere matter of merchandise.

Gold and silver are articles of mere merchandise, whether in a raw or manufactured form—that is, as dust, ingots, bullion or coin—when they are re-exported from countries which merely receive them for the purpose of distributing them. They are still articles of mere merchandise when they are imported for use in the arts, as for gold and silver plate, or for decoration, whether of furniture or of the person, or in any other way than that of currency. They are still articles of mere merchandise when they are exported in the shape of coin to satisfy obligations created in foreign countries.

But concurrently with these uses of the precious metals, they are employed as the machinery of trade, and as the form in which obligations are expressed, and therefore are to be compulsorily satisfied. In small transactions these obligations are liquidated by the transfer of money, for reasons given in a previous chapter. In transactions between nation and nation, except in cases where gold and silver are the natural products of a country, they are rarely used, the imports and exports of the nation as a rule balancing each other, and the influx and efflux of specie out of or into any one country being determined by causes similar to those which govern the distribution of other products. Nor are all the transactions between the inhabitants of any one country settled by the machinery of the precious metals. The result may be effected by their substitutes. Thus, for example, transactions representing an average of £10,000,000 sterling are daily adjusted in one room in London, the bankers' clearing-house, without the intervention of a sovereign, a shilling, or even a penny. In the absence of these substitutes for the precious metals, the adjustment of these mutual obligations would be so inconvenient as to be practically impossible. Convenience as well as economy induces a community to dispense as far as possible with the machinery of a metallic currency. Every one of these obligations is expressed in quantities of the precious metals. But the business done in three ordinary days at the clearing-house represents more specie than is to be found in all the reserves of all the banks in London. Even if these were the only transactions in which substitutes are found for money, the specie possessed by the London banks would be made to operate as the machinery of trade more than a hundred times a year. The only reason why a similar machinery does not extend itself over the civilised world is, that nations are still barbarous enough to employ different currencies, and to use different codes of commercial law. If these differences were eliminated, as in course of time they will be, there would be no more reason for paying any more attention to the efflux and influx of gold between this and other countries, than to that of the same commodity distributed in varying quantities over the area of any one community. In Adam Smith's time, there was a rate of exchange between London and Edinburgh. In time to come, when the reforms indicated above are effected, the theory of the foreign exchanges will be far more antiquated and unreal than that of the balance of power.

A country then supplies itself with such gold and silver as it needs for the arts in the same way that it supplies itself with other raw materials—by the exchange of its exports. In the same way it obtains such sums of the precious metals as it needs for the purposes of ordinary retail trade and exchange. The amount which it retains of these metals is increased as its home-trade increases, but is diminished by economies in the substitution of symbols for coin. Thus the general use of cheques has tended to diminish the amount of specie circulating in a country, and, were one-pound notes adopted, a further economy would ensue, in so far as such notes when put into circulation represented a larger sum than might be retained by the bank which issued them and was bound to exchange them on demand for gold. There is reason to believe then that the amount of specie circulating within a country varies little from year to year; for, as we have seen before, there is no motive to increase its amount, but every motive to reduce it to the least possible quantity consistent with the fulfilment of those functions for which money is adopted as a measure of value. It is possible that at the beginning of the present century there was nearly as much metallic money in England as there now is; for although the population has doubled, and the wealth of the country has grown in a far greater proportion, it is very likely that the enlarged demand for money is compensated by the increased use of banking and drawing facilities, and the abandonment of the habit of hoarding, a practice which was very general sixty and seventy years ago.

The ordinary supply then of gold and silver, in so far as it is employed in the arts, and employed for the purposes of an internal currency, is effected in the same way as that by which other wants are satisfied. It does not seem that these quantities of the precious metals can be materially diminished, just as they will not be materially increased. There may be, as there was during the great continental war, a demand for specie in order to pay troops; and if paper can be substituted for gold and silver, a drain upon the metallic circulation may take place. But in the absence of such a substitute, but little of these metals will pass out of the home circulation. Dealers in the precious metals find it possible to trench on other resources, the amount of which is far less than that in circulation, but which is far more open to these influences. Gold and silver will hardly be extracted from circulation, except in some slight degree, and usually by offering a premium on them and thereby giving them a temporary and exceptional value. Persons who want to export money generally procure gold in exchange for notes, and thus by contracting the paper circulation, and thereupon by putting an additional strain on the metallic currency, render any effect on the latter increasingly remote and difficult.

A paper circulation purports to give the holder of the note a right to demand the sum specified in the note at his pleasure. Under no other circumstances will paper circulate at par, i.e. be exchanged at the sum which it represents. If the paper has a forced currency, it will circulate only because the solvency and good faith of the issuing parties is trusted; if it be suspected, or the prospect of redeeming the note be distant, it will circulate at a depreciated rate, this rate appearing in the country which uses the note in a rise in prices, and in transactions with foreign countries in an adverse state of the exchanges. For example, the par of exchange, omitting fractions, between England and France, is twenty-five francs, = £1. If however French notes were inconvertible and had a forced circulation, and the suspicion or risk attending on the use of the paper amounted to twenty per cent., the prices of articles purchased in the French market would rise by this or more than this amount, and it would take thirty-one francs, speaking roundly, in paper, to procure an English sovereign. This rise in the value of gold, or, to be more exact, fall in the value of inconvertible paper, is manifested in the national currency of the United States. The discredit attaching to this paper at one period was so considerable that it took more than 280 paper dollars to procure 100 gold dollars. But with the return of peace, and with an abundant revenue, the government was able to grapple with its public debt and its state paper, and to offer a prospect that ere long it might be able to meet the over-issue and resume payments in gold.

As we have seen above, banks of issue find it possible to circulate a far larger amount of paper than the gold on which the paper is based. A bank, for example, may in ordinary times circulate £30,000,000 of notes, and be quite safe from risk if it retains only £10,000,000 of specie, i. e. has its metallic assets only one-third of its liabilities. It takes care of course, if it is dealing honestly with those who use its notes, that the remainder of its liabilities are covered by property, i. e. by bills of exchange arriving at maturity, or by quantities of government securities. It is only obliged to have all its assets in such a position as that they can be easily convertible into specie.

Now it is plain that if it become necessary to transmit a portion of this gold upon which notes are issued, that it is only necessary to present a certain number of these notes in order to get gold in exchange. But it is also clear that if any notable portion of this gold is abstracted, the bank is by so much nearer the position in which its notes bear a high proportion to the specie on which they rest. If the bank then be not empowered to issue notes on government or other securities, it must not only (to maintain such a proportion as that which has been referred to, and which is assumed to be generally necessary in order to sustain the reputation of the bank) diminish its circulation by all the notes returned on its hands, but by more than this amount, i.e. by just so much more as will restore the equilibrium. Thus, for example, if the ordinary circulation be £30,000,000, the ordinary amount of specie £10,000,000, the rest being held say as £10,000,000 of public and £10,000,000 of private securities; and £4,000,000 of gold be abstracted from the reserve, the bank must, to keep itself safe, reduce its public or private securities, or both, by £8,000,000, as well as curtail its notes by £4,000,000. That is, in the event of such an operation, its circulation would fall from £30,000,000 to £18,000,000. In its own interest, however, it would rather lower the amount of its private securities, than resort to a sudden or large sale of its government stock. In practice, too, the inconvenience which would ensue from curtailing the accommodation of the bank, will induce the public to be content with an over-issue of notes, provided always that this over-issue be based upon a security which is readily convertible into specie. The customers of the bank will agree, either formally as they did in 1797, or informally as on many other occasions, to accept and circulate notes, even though the metallic basis be fallen to a very low amount. Experience teaches them that when trade is profitable and credit good, the most rapid and alarming efflux of bullion from any country will be speedily followed by a reflux. The same reasoning which induces persons to economise their stock of the precious metals, instructs them also in the fact that large accumulations of specie are mere hoards from which no economical profit is derivable.

We shall however see that during the course of this operation, by which the metallic reserves of a country are diminished, great injury to traders is certain to temporarily ensue, and that the phenomena of straitened supply and urgent demand are as fully manifested among such traders as they are when society is straitened by a dearth in the necessaries of life.

An efflux of specie may arise from many causes. The purchases of a country may be speculative; or the public may be constrained to buy large supplies of food, in consequence of deficient harvests; or capitalists may have invested largely in foreign loans; or sometimes the credit of a country has been temporarily suspended, and it is therefore necessary to make larger specie payments than heretofore; or a country may be forced to make large purchases of raw material or finished goods in other countries, which do not deal conversely with it. All these causes may produce such a result.

The illustration of these phenomena would however be too lengthy for an elementary work. They have all been exhibited in a marked form within the present century, and have all, as occasion has arisen, created serious embarrassments. It is with the last named case that we are principally concerned.

The object of a merchant is to use his capital as completely as possible. He imports goods, and gives bills to such countries as receive and negotiate bills; he exports goods and draws bills on his customers. The same facts apply, though in a minor degree, to the home trade. Sellers take bills from buyers, unless from the terms of the market the latter can gain a greater advantage from the discount allowed for ready money. But with foreign trade it is necessary that bills of exchange should be drawn, for otherwise the purchase of merchandise would involve the export of specie, the sale of merchandise its import. It is plain however that such a continual export and import of the precious metals would involve risk, and certainly loss; for there is more or less peril in the transit, and there is certain loss involved in locking up part of the machinery of trade.

When therefore trade exists between two countries, the buyers of each country draw bills, which are negotiated generally by means of certain persons who make it their business to effect the exchange and liquidation of these instruments, in consideration of a small premium on the transaction. These bills are set off against one another, and may exactly balance between country and country. In such a case, the trade between two countries is said to be *in equilibrio*, and the exchange at par—i.e. it is no advantage to export the precious metals.

It does not however follow that when Paris holds more bills on London than London does on Paris, that it will be expedient to transmit specie from London to Paris. There may be a third place, for example Hamburg, which owes more to London than it has to receive, and receives more from Paris than it has to pay. This third city then may intervene, and the difference between Paris and London may be settled by this indirect or, as it is called, arbitrated exchange. A fourth or fifth city may be added; and so on through the whole range of the mercantile world, the exports of every country taken together paying for its imports taken together. In a country like our own,

P

which carries on trade with the whole world, exchanges are arbitrated between such commercial centres as can hold convenient intercourse together. If however the imports regularly exceed the exports in one of these regions, and the exports as regularly exceed the imports in another, it is necessary that specie should be shipped. The latter has been the rule between the United States and Great Britain since the Californian discoveries, as it is steadily between Australia and Great Britain. The former has generally ruled between Great Britain on the one hand and France and Hamburg on the other. In this way Great Britain has distributed the mineral treasures of the New World and the Australian continent, each transaction involving a profit or advantage to the community.

A country, however, may regularly import more in value than it exports. Such, it is said, is the case with Russia. In this case, it must either pay the balance in specie, or create some new kind of export with which to meet the cost involved in the excess of imports. Commonly it exports securities, i.e. it turns its private debts into a public debt, on which it pays or agrees to pay interest. It does not follow that a public debt, created by one country and taken by another, represents a sum of money exported to the former; it may be, and commonly is, goods, munitions of war, machinery, railroad plant, or any other valuable commodity. And the exports of securities may be new debts created, or debts hitherto due to the inhabitants of an importing country transferred to some foreigner. We might, for example, supposing we imported more in value than we exported, pay the balance in consols, should foreigners be willing to accept this kind of security in liquidation of their claims.

If, on the other hand, the excess of imports is temporary, it may be, and generally is, liquidated by an efflux of specie; nor will this efflux be arrested until the excess is made to cease, and the irregularity is rectified. The way in which an attempt is made to check an excess of imports, is by raising the rate of discount. Under these circumstances it is supposed, and generally with reason, either that profits must fall, and so business must be straitened, or that consumption must be lessened, and so importation be diminished. But the power of controlling importation depends upon the object imported. It will have but scanty influence on the demand for the necessaries of life. A drain of specie consequent upon large imports of foreign corn will not be checked by a rise in the rate of discount. Such a drain, so far as it operates upon the reserve of gold held by the Bank of England, will continue either until the exporting country is willing to take goods, or until the demand for this produce be satisfied. The importer will readily bear the loss involved in a high rate of discount, because he feels sure that he will be reimbursed by the rising market for food.

But notwithstanding the fact that a drain of specie, in order to purchase food, is not compensated or arrested by a rise in the rate of discount, this rise is necessary and inevitable. As there is less gold, so there are less notes. The paper currency diminishes as specie diminishes; should in this country, for reasons alleged before, diminish more rapidly. For a share of this remaining gold, or its substitute, all importers are competing, in order to complete their bargains, to carry out their purchases. Now as competition for a limited quantity always raises its price, much more does competition raise the price if the limited quantity cannot be readily increased, and its supply is of primary necessity to the person demanding it. Thus it is that discounts, the shape in which money is borrowed among persons engaged in commerce, rise under the effects of a drain and the exigencies of foreign trade, as rapidly and to as great a height as that of food does on the occurrence of a dearth. The borrower of capital has to make the best terms which he can with the lender.

It is no doubt possible, when the rate of discount is exceedingly high, to cause a rapid fall in the price of capital advanced on temporary loan. An increased issue of paper will bring this result about when the drain has reached the highest flow and is on the point of ebbing. The convenience of this excess is so great, and the circulation of such an excess is certain to be so short, if the rebound can be foreseen, that the power of adopting this expedient will always check the rate of discount and turn the tide. Much more certain however is the issue of notes representing smaller sums than those ordinarily circulated. If this expedient be adopted, a certain amount of gold, equivalent to such notes as can be put into circulation, will be liberated from the home currency, and flowing to the bank will fill up the void which has been created, either wholly or partially. Even permission to use such an issue is, as was the case in 1825, sufficient, for the holders of capital anticipate that they will soon be constrained to accept a lower rate of discount, and be obliged to compete as lenders, instead of being an object for the competition of borrowers.

The effect, then, of a drain of gold which has been originated from the necessity of meeting the requirements of foreign purchases in an excess of imports over exports, is all the more manifest when we compare, under the economy of banking, the amount of a foreign trade by the side of the quantity of specie on which it is based, and the service which that specie is made to render to the paper currency at home. The amount of these imports is more than seven times as much, in money value, as the amount of the gold ordinarily retained by the banks. Upon this sum, then, must fall the function of paying for an occasional excess of purchases. But this sum also sustains the internal circulation of paper, and a vast mass of credit expressed in money.

In the ordinary course of things, and when mercantile credit is good, capital is procured by borrowers at something less than the average rate of interest, for loans made for short terms are always more satisfactory to lenders than loans which cannot be readily recovered. Lenders in this case, acting through their agents, that is, bankers, wish, as a rule, to have their assets as available as they can. When, however, loans have been freely made, and the articles towards the purchase of which these loans have contributed fall in value, and therefore a loss is imminent on the purchaser, attempts will be made by borrowers to procure an extension of such loans as they have already contracted, in order to tide over the depression, and to save themselves against the time when diminished importation will enable them to recover, in some degree at least, the present loss. But the readiness of lenders diminishes with the eagerness of borrowers; the price of the assistance, known as the rate of discount, rises, the number of loans is lessened, and they whose commercial position is most unsound, are obliged to suspend their payments. Such occurrences increase the distrust; every man seeks to entrench himself against risk; lenders are more than ever wary, and increase their reserves of capital. The feeling of insecurity may, and does ordinarily, increase, and what is called a commercial panic ensues; that is, a state of things in which loans of any kind are made with the greatest difficulty, even when the security is unexceptionable. The deficiency of loan capital does not occur at an early stage in these proceedings, but when the reaction on prices sets in and the speculation is disappointed. In such cases the difficulty has been met, and always successfully, by permitting an issue of bank notes over and above the fixed legal amount, or by the issue of government paper in aid of merchants, under the form of exchequer bills. These bills are really certificates of indebtedness on the part of government, payable at a fixed date, and bearing interest in the interval. The former expedient was adopted in 1847, 1857, and 1866; the latter in 1792, 1811, 1822, and 1825. 'Commercial distress,' it should be added, almost always arises from over or speculative trading, but its incidence is as severe on prudent as it is on injudicious trading. High rates of interest arrest the profits of those who borrow capital in order to carry on trades in which there is the least possible amount of risk, as well as the gains of those who have borrowed in hopes of getting the advantages of a rising market.

It is possible for a country to carry on a large and increasing foreign trade, and to labour under a severe depression of its industry at home. Such facts characterised the trade of the year 1867, and were very instructive to a student. The exports and imports were increased, but many branches of domestic industry were adversely affected. The price of all metals was very low; the production of textile fabrics was carried on under the disadvantageous condition of a constantly falling market; ship-building was almost arrested. Added to these, there was a general and well founded distrust in the numerous joint-stock enterprises which had been attempted, and which had failed, partly by an over-sanguine confidence, much more by the gross dishonesty of many among their promoters, and the utter inadequacy of the English bankruptcy law in arresting and punishing offences against mercantile credit. There may be low rates of interest, and great stagnation of business, consequent upon speculations carried on at home, and carried on unwisely or dishonestly.

CHAPTER XVI.
The Distribution of Capital.

THE profits on capital tend to equality. The same conditions fulfilled, the rate of profit obtainable from advances of capital must be the same; and the circumstances will not vary, whether the possessor of capital uses it in his own business, or lends it to others. There is, as we have seen before, no real difference between the rate of profit and the rate of interest.

If, therefore, all kinds of business were equally safe, and all borrowers equally trustworthy, capital would be equally distributed over all kinds of labour for the produce of which a demand exists. Insecurity alone, when capital has been accumulated, is a hindrance to its equal flow over every field of industry. This sense of insecurity is entertained either against the intelligence or the integrity of the borrower. Where the average intelligence of traders is insufficient to interpret and provide against the risks of any business, capital will not be attracted to the calling in which such risks arise; or what is in effect the same thing, the apparent rate of profit in such callings must be greater than it is in others. Thus, for example, capital flows more readily to ordinary kinds of agriculture, especially to those which involve but little danger of failure from the contingencies of weather and markets, than it does to exportation for a new and uncertain foreign demand. Again, where the business is liable to periods of depression, or to the chance of sudden cessation, the attractions of such a calling are less than those which belong to a safer industry, and the apparent rate of profit rises; an index that the competition of lenders for such investments or advances is small. I have already stated that the risks of a strike increase the gains of those who engage in such occupations as are liable to these occurrences, and will increase them until such times as, the power of calculating or predicting such emergencies being taken away, the possessor of capital absolutely declines to employ his resources in such occupations.

Frauds and similar malpractices on the part of borrowers are also hindrances to the easy distribution of capital. It has been more than once found impossible to carry on trade in certain articles, because manufacturers, in their haste to get rich, have sold worthless goods, or fabricated the trade marks of their rivals on inferior goods, or have in other ways deceived their customers. Again, the want of trustworthy agents in particular localities is not only a hindrance, but an actual bar to the distribution of capital. The rate of interest or profit would approach identity over the world, if commercial honour were generally dominant, and the police of commercial exchange were universally effective. For this reason, a lax bankruptcy law in one country, and a rigorous administration of such a law in another, are obstacles to the free diffusion of capital. Whenever civilisation advances so far as that there shall be an international code of commercial law, the distribution or circulation of capital between country and country, for instance, between France, Germany and England, will be as easy and obvious, or nearly as easy and obvious, as the distribution of capital over the United Kingdom. Such a reform in the international relations of countries is a mere matter of time, of short time when its expediency is known, just as the adoption of international currencies will be.

Pending these changes in the comity or commercial diplomacy of nations, the distribution of capital over any given country is effected by the ordinary machinery of demand and supply; the exportation of its overplus being effected by investments in foreign stocks and undertakings, and occasionally, but rarely, in loans to finance or banking companies. It remains to comment upon the effect of these extraordinary diversions of capital, which interrupt its natural distribution, and cause it to be abnormally occupied in particular objects. These are loans for state purposes, and protective regulations.

A government may borrow just as a private trader borrows in order to carry out some public work, in which, capital being invested, a regular profit is obtained. Thus, for example, several foreign governments have constructed railways by entering into the money market and contracting loans, the interest on these loans being paid by the tolls taken for the use of works when they are completed. Again, a government may establish a post-office, and invest a large capital obtained on loan in the various conveniences which contribute to such a service, paying the interest, and making a further gain from the rates of postage. Here it is plain that the government borrows just as any other trader does, and may be able, as is done with the post-office system of the United Kingdom, to do the service more cheaply than any individual or joint-stock company could do, and obtain a considerable surplus to the credit of the public revenue.

Again, a government may contract a loan for a purely unproductive purpose. The term is not used in condemnation, for a branch of public expenditure may be in the highest sense necessary or useful, but could not, except by violently straining the use of the term, be considered productive. Thus, for example, a loan made for carrying on a defensive war may be exceedingly necessary; a subsidy paid to a foreign state may be exceedingly politic. But no one would call war expenditure productive, except by a figure of speech, which should include the defence of what is produced in the act of production itself; and still less would any one hold that a subsidy paid to a foreign state should be treated as productive expenditure. In these cases then, when the sum is spent, no periodical profit recurs to the community which has undertaken the expenditure. It does not follow that the sum is squandered, but it is spent and gone, and is irrecoverable in any shape.

Now in both these cases the government which contracts the loan comes into the market to compete with other borrowers. This competition may be felt in a rise in the rate of interest. But it may not be so felt, because the reserves of capital, i.e. the amount of wealth waiting for borrowers, and not lent, may be very large. The possessor of wealth often does that which the possessor of goods does; keeps back part of his property in hopes that there will be a greater demand hereafter, or at least is unwilling to lend except upon undoubted security. If governments merely reduce the amount of this reserve, they will not raise the rate of interest, and so it constantly happens that when the rate of interest is very low, owing to the fact that wealth is accumulated and unemployed, considerable sums may be borrowed by governments without inducing any effect on the rate.

In general, however, the effect is to raise it. In this case capital is directed from its ordinary channel, into another which a government has dug. The ordinary borrower suffers from the enhanced rate; the lender is benefitted. Labour is benefitted, for unemployed wealth or capital less actively employed, is devoted to labour, and in general, as government expenditure is concerned with the commoner kinds of labour, a larger number of labourers are maintained than would have been, in case the capital had been left to the ordinary demands of borrowers for production. If, for example, a government loan, by raising the rate of interest, checks speculative trade, or dwarfs such manufactures as are concerned with the supply of luxuries, and expends the sum borrowed in keeping soldiers, or employing navigators, or in building ships, or constructing docks; it is plain that a larger number of labourers will reap the advantage of government expenditure than would have earned wages in supplying luxuries. A great government expenditure, as has been seen many times, gives all the appearance of activity, plenty, prosperity. Very intelligent persons are deceived by it, and have even imagined that nations are prospering, when, after all, they are squandering their resources. They are misled by the abundance of employment, and the consequent command possessed by labourers over necessaries and conveniences.

When the work is done for which the loan was contracted, there will be, of course, a cessation of the demand for the labour which has been called into activity. If, however, the advantage obtained by the employment is permanent and productive, the expenditure may, and frequently does, call into activity a series of fresh agencies or conveniences which absorb the labour which has been employed in the construction of the work, or compensate for its cessation. Thus, a railway or canal which makes a particular region accessible, or supplies a road and a market for the products of industry, though its completion involves the discharge of the excavators and builders who made it, may open a way for the products of factories, quarries, or collieries. For example, the coal and petroleum-fields of the United States are at a great distance from the sea ; so great, indeed, that the carriage of the former for foreign trade seems almost out of the question, and the cost of conveying the latter is so great that it is proposed to lay down a vast pipe from the interior to the nearest port. If the plan be practicable, it is clear that its adoption would involve a permanent benefit.

The case, however, is different when the expenditure is unproductive. The employment of a large number of persons in military operations and military works may indeed relieve the labouring class by diminishing the number of persons competing for employment in peaceful avocations, and by affording occupation for a larger number of persons than would have been engaged under ordinary circumstances; but the survivors of these works generally return to a market which is understocked with capital, fully stocked with labour, and which is further burdened with the interest payable on the loan contracted for the purpose of unproductive expenditure. The cessation of war expenditure is almost invariably followed by great commercial distress and great industrial languor. It was followed by such a reaction in Great Britain after the Continental war, it was in the United States after the civil war. The causes are not far to seek. In the exhaustion of capital, and in the absorption of resources by heavy and crippling taxation, occupation in some industries ceases altogether, and that in others is narrowed and overcrowded.

In this way, we may understand the seeming paradox of Dr. Chalmers, who urged that a war expenditure should always be paid out of income, and not be met by loans, because, as he averred, a nation which adopts the former expedient pays the cost once, while the employment of the latter is to pay it twice—once in the necessary absorption of capital and its diversion from one kind of employment to another, a second time in the payment of interest and the ultimate repayment of the principal. In case the loan, however, does not raise the rate of interest, and does employ more labourers than would have been employed had it not been negotiated, it does not seem that the negotiation can be called a payment. The second payment is, of course, inevitable.

There is, however, a difference between a loan and a tax. A loan is raised upon property and capital, a tax is generally levied on income. The former may raise prices, the latter generally diminishes enjoyments. The former affects borrowers and lenders, the latter curtails the power of expenditure. The former affects the present convenience of an existing society but slightly, the latter is oppressive. Now as no nation ever admits that it goes to war solely for the interest of the present generation, but always affirms that its military action is essential to the security of the future powers of the community, the plea that the parties who are to get the advantage of this security should undergo the charge of some part of the cost involved in the process of defence or aggrandisement is naturally put forward, and is as naturally irresistible. We are, it is argued, transmitting to posterity a vast and valuable inheritance, which must, like other splendid legacies, be a little burdened. This reasoning was very general during the American civil war, just as it was during our great Continental war, and was accepted as implicitly.

It should be added here, in extenuation of such a course of proceeding, that it is very difficult to apportion a war-tax fairly. If it be put on general expenditure, it weighs most heavily on those who have the largest families, who are the parents of a future nation, who are putting their capital out in the maintenance and education of their children, and are taxed for doing so. Besides, as we have seen before, a tax on the food of a people is a tax on the raw material of labour, and is at once unwise and oppressive. But a tax on luxuries, though not open to the charge of oppressiveness, is uncertain in its incidence, and still more uncertain in its productiveness. There remains an income or rather a property-tax, i.e. a tax on profits. Such a tax is less unjust, if it be fairly levied, than any other; but it is in the worst sense unjust, and continues all the worst evils of the worst taxes on expenditure, when it is unfairly levied, to say nothing of the moral evils which it induces, and which, it appears, are invariably connected with it. There is, however, a growing conviction among enlightened financiers, that, in any case, a large part of war expenditure should be paid out of the income of the nation which undertakes the war; and most nations which take a true view of their duties to the present and the coming generation, seek to apportion the burdens of war among those who undertake the responsibility, and who will hereafter enter on the inheritance.

CHAPTER XVII.

Protection.

AMONG the causes which check the distribution of capital, none is more powerful, and none has operated, and still operates with greater energy, than that control over the natural right of free exchange which is known by the name of protection. There is no society which has not adopted, and which does not still maintain, the propriety of protecting certain interests, whether they be civil ranks, or employments of capital, or kinds of labour. Sometimes the assistance given to particular interests is derived from direct legislative enactment, often it is the result of private combination, of voluntary association, of professional etiquette, and of *esprit de corps*.

No one questions the natural right of free exchange. I assume, of course, that there are such rights as are called natural, and that these are the inalienable conditions under which individuals take their place in social life. Nor do I think it worth while to occupy my reader's time with the contemptible quibble as to whether these rights flow from municipal law, or control it. It is sufficient that in practice municipal law is ultimately amenable to natural justice, because a law which does wrong is worse than violence. We are slowly affirming that society is constituted and that it exists in order that the largest possible freedom may be given to the individual will, in so far as this individual will does not trespass on the will of others; that the most perfect society which we can conceive treats freedom as the normal state, and force as a reserve against violence or wrong-doing; and that the progress of society has been marked, on the part of kings and governments, by the gradual abandonment of the privilege of controlling innocent opinion and innocent action, and by the recognition, in the interests of truth and honour, first of complete toleration, and next of absolute equity in adjudicating on contending interests.

The use of free exchange is the simplest and most obvious of these rights or concessions. It consists in permitting each individual to make the best use which his own experience or judgment gives him of such powers and faculties as he has in the purchase or sale of whatever he wishes to acquire or to relinquish. Free exchange is the economical aspect of free will or personal liberty. Now it will be plain to every one that this right of free exchange is granted only sparingly in this country, and is granted even more sparingly in other countries. But it will be also plain, that if there be such a thing as natural right; if a discretion over a man's own labour and the fruits of it, and its natural consequence, the power of disposing them to the best advantage, are the final purposes of social life; if that theory of government which presumes that the administration can make a man's bargains, direct the employment of his capital, prescribe the field of his labour, is exploded,—the institution of any restriction on the course of free exchange must be perpetually on its trial, and must be justified either on the ground that absolute liberty gives an advantage to the strong against the weak and so frustrates the real ends of government, or on the ground that incontestable reasons of public policy justify interference with free action.

It will not be difficult to give illustrations of the cases in which individual liberty is properly curtailed under each of these circumstances. Government helps, or should help, the weak against the strong in various ways. All civilised communities, nearly all Christian communities, have prohibited a parent from holding such a property in his children as enables him to sell them into slavery. With equal propriety a government may, and sometimes does, superintend all contracts which parents may make for the labour of their children, either by prohibiting such contracts altogether when the children are of tender years, as under the factory acts, or by limiting the hours during which they may labour, as under the same acts. Similar legislation, it appears, is threatened in respect of agricultural gangs. So, again, equity interferes to annul fraudulent contracts, and to protect persons from extortion. For analogous reasons the law checks 'free banking' and the issue of paper money. In the same way the law controls certain trades, regulating, for example, the hours during which public houses may be opened; determining the rates of interest which pawnbrokers may exact on pledges; fixing the maximum fares which public conveyances can charge for the services which they render. In these and many other cases which might be cited, the government is rightly occupied in protecting the weak against the strong, in preventing the holder of a supply, the demand for which is urgent and temporary, from taking advantage of the position which he occupies.

For similar reasons government has interfered with the free course of trade in order to protect discoverers and inventors. The plea on which the old trading companies were sustained, when the rule that the crown or parliament was justified in granting commercial monopolies had been exploded, was, that it would be unfair to those who had developed commerce in some new direction, if other persons who had not incurred the previous expense and risk of opening up the trade were permitted an unrestricted use of the new market. The reasoning was unsound because the facts were false. So, again, on far more plausible and perhaps on solid grounds, the law protects inventors and authors by patents and copyright, when it provides that they who have discovered some new process, or have written or composed a literary work, should have the sole right of manufacture or publication. But the expediency or justice of patent laws and copyright are far too large a subject for the present work.

Again, and in the second place, government may interfere with the freedom of exchange on grounds of public policy. It is easy to find illustrations of such a justifiable interference. In times of peace there is no reason why the sale of gunpowder, firearms, or any other commodity which may be brought within the definition of munitions of war, should be prohibited or controlled. In times of war it is plainly the duty of a government to prevent its subjects, if possible, from supplying the public enemy with such assistance, on the simple principle of self-defence. If a blockade can be justified, much more can the prohibition of such an exportation be defended.

Again, a government may with propriety check the too rapid exhaustion of a limited quantity of any commodity, when that commodity is not only valuable, but is a condition to the economical prosperity of a country. Thus, for example, government may prohibit the exportation of coal, or limit its use to the higher kind of mechanical operations. In this country, the area of whose coal-fields are limited, and in which the quantity of coals which can be worked can be calculated with more or less precision, the manufacturing eminence which Great Britain possesses depends upon the continuity of the supply. Now, if other means fail, it could not be said that the legislature would not be justified, if it be possible, in inducing a forced economy of these resources. The real defence against government interference in such a case lies in the fact that economy is naturally induced by dearness, and that when the scarcity is felt, its effects are far more complete than those which any regulation of the legislature could bring about. But it is possible to give instances in which economy may be enforced by legislative restrictions on exportations. These restrictions should not appear in the form of export duties, for though these duties involve an economy of the article so burdened, they operate also to put those regions in which the article is produced most disadvantageously in a position of artificial sterility; but in the shape of a limitation of the quantity exported. Thus, for example, a check might have been advisedly put on the destruction of cinchona trees, and on the exhaustion of certain other forests in which timber available for industrial and other purposes used to grow, and which have been recklessly consumed.

Again, for obvious reasons, a government may interfere to confirm or annul contracts for the use of that, the quantity of which is limited and the use of paramount importance, and in such cases can properly control the relations subsisting between seller and buyer. The most important illustration of such a justifiable interference is, that which relates to the letting, devising, and settlement of land.

No civil government has ever accepted the doctrine that the absolute ownership of the soil should, or indeed can, be conferred on any individual. The largest present rights in its usufruct, many of which are, historically, usurpations, fall far short of a complete discretion. The community, or the monarch (as a corporation, not as an individual), is invariably presumed to have an ultimate and recoverable interest in the soil. The extent of this remainder interest varies from such a reality as that which forms the dominion of the government in India, to so slender a claim as that with which our modern notion of

English law makes us familiar. It could not indeed be surrendered without reducing society to a deadlock, for there are and must be occasions on which it is necessary to resume, in the public interest, land the usufruct of which is enjoyed by private individuals, after due compensation is made for the present value of the land in question.

The land of any fully settled country is limited. Its adequate cultivation, even under the freest system of importation, is of paramount importance. The largest development of scientific agriculture is not only the measure of population, but also effects the fullest possible distribution of many secondary necessaries or comforts of life. Part of a nation may subsist on imported corn, but a much smaller part can obtain imported meat. But the maintenance of cattle in any country is for the most part relevant to the cultivation of arable land, to the rotation of crops, to the growth of succulent roots. If therefore the arrangements under which land is possessed, or let as farms, are such as to check the development of agriculture, and thereby to diminish the resources or reduce the comforts of a community; or if the system of land tenure is unfavourable to the distribution of wealth, the laws which bring about such a result are fairly open to revision, and the causes which contribute to these evils should be met by the necessary remedies. The common adage that 'a man may do what he will with his own' is false in reference to such property as can be indefinitely increased; it is not only false, but destructive, if it were allowed to extend to the possession of land.

The expression, 'free trade in land,' is used a little

inaccurately. It is commonly employed to designate the abolition of those powers of settling land which are conferred on its possessor by the law of this country, by which he can, by deed or will, grant an estate in land to unborn persons; and for the reversal of a custom which prevails over the greater part of the United Kingdom, by which those estates in land which are known by the names of fee-simple and fee-tail are conferred (in cases of intestacy in fee-simple, or in failure of extinguishment by deed in fee-tail) on the eldest son. It is manifest that these customs and rights tend to aggregate land in few hands.

All rights by which individuals are enabled to determine the course of an estate after their own death are mere creations of law. Except for reasons of public policy, no person can have the smallest claim to control the fortunes of the living after he is dead, or even to devise that which he has accumulated or inherited. Still less can he claim to extend his control over those who are living in favour of such as are unborn. A settlement of land, therefore, is the exercise of the will of a man who is dead, in constraint of the will of a man who is living, and every settlement, whether it be of land or of personal property, is a hindrance to free exchange on the part of the person whose discretion is thus limited. A removal of these constraints or hindrances, an abolition of these privileges and customs, is not free trade in land, but a removal of certain obstructions which preclude a large portion of the soil from being brought into the market. Those who advocate what is called free trade in land, contemplate the subdivision of large estates, the creation of a class of yeomanry, and perhaps the development of peasant proprietorship; for they anticipate that should these customs be taken away, larger quantities of land would be annually submitted to sale in smaller parcels,

Some of the reasons which are alleged in favour of these changes are political. With these we have nothing to do. Some of them are economical, of which there are principally two. It is supposed that small cultivation is more productive than large. It is supposed that the subdivision of land has a direct effect in elevating the condition of the working classes, in giving them a real stake in the country, in encouraging thrift, in diminishing pauperism. Land as an investment pays, it must be admitted, but a poor percentage. But it is certain that it always pays a higher rate than is given as interest in the post-office savings' banks, the obvious and nearly the only investment of the poorer classes. As I have said before, however, land as an instrument should be distinguished from land as an investment, and a class of peasant owners would use land in the former way. It is possible that the minute division of holdings is an economical evil. It is also possible that the accumulation of real estate is another, and a greater economical evil.

Correctly stated, free trade in land consists rather in the removal of the hindrances which the law puts on the conveyance of land. These are, the long period required to constitute a valid title, and, thereupon, the tedious and expensive recital of the title, the tax imposed on its transfer, and the professional charges of conveyancers. Many of the restrictions are traceable to the power of settling land, some are merely legal rules, the relics of far more stringent regulations, originally intended to save the rights of the Crown, or the reversion to the State;

some are relevant to the class interests of legal practitioners. In short, free trade in anything is not only to be referred to the quantity offered for sale, but to the facility with which an exchange can be effected, when any part of the object, be it great or small, is offered. If the custom of primogeniture and the power of settlement were instantly and entirely done away, and no person were enabled to grant a less estate, either by deed or will, than that which is called a fee-simple, it does not follow that there would be free trade in land. The change must be followed by an alteration of the conditions and processes under which a valid conveyance can be made. The interests of the great landowners are protected by the powers of settlement and the custom of primogeniture; but free trade in land is only indirectly affected by these peculiarities of tenure.

I have adverted in a previous chapter (ix.) to the protection which the law gives to certain recognised practitioners, and to the equally protective arrangements of trades-unions. These rules are, as far as the favoured class is concerned, a means by which competition is checked and remuneration increased, though they are often said to be in the public interest, as securing the efficiency of the practitioner.

After these limitations and explanations we shall be better able to illustrate the effect of protection as it is generally understood; i. e. the assistance given to manufacture or agriculture by the levy of duties on foreign produce, these duties being intended, when they are moderate, to check imports, and when they are heavy to totally exclude them. Analogous to these productive duties are *bounties*, that is, sums of money paid out of the public income to exporters of certain goods, or occasionally to those who are engaged in particular industries, the continuity of whose produce is considered to be of public importance; as, for example, whale fisheries.

Protective enactments and bounties have both originated in the belief that it is expedient to give the direct assistance of law to particular industries. If every producer of every kind were protected, foreign trade might cease, and, as far as regards home trade, everybody would pay more, i.e. give more labour for what he gets, than he need have given if the trade were not protected. Such a system prevails, at least as far as manufactures go, in Munich, where every craftsman belongs to some guild or the other. As a consequence, all manufactures in this city are bad and dear. But it is hardly possible, and were it possible it would be certainly futile, to protect everybody, and to thoroughly regulate the employment of capital. All protection then, to be effectual, is partial; and, just as we saw before, when speaking of protected labour (p. 95), that those who combine in a trades-union may be said to mulct other labourers, so it has, with equal pithiness, been said that all protection means robbing somebody else; i.e. it constrains somebody to pay more for what he wants than he would have paid had his market been unrestricted.

It is clear that protection is unnecessary when capital flows of its own accord and fully into the protected industry. It is because, under particular circumstances, capital is not so advantageously employed in certain callings that the State attempts to divert capital from a more productive to a less productive channel. If protection is needed to sustain a manufacture, the very act implies that, without this assistance, the trade would be carried on at a loss; in other words, would ultimately not be carried on at all. Tea and coffee could perhaps be cultivated in hot-houses if the legislature of any country resolved on protecting such an industry by restraining foreign importation. Of course such an act would be madness, as the produce would probably cost fifty times as much on the adoption of such means. But there is only a difference in degree between such an expedient and that of a protective duty on corn, or iron, or silk, except that, in so far as the use of these latter articles is necessary, the loss and the mischief is the greater.

It will be clear also that protection cannot stimulate general industry. The State possesses no capital with which to aid labour; it must take capital from other employments in order to do so. In fact, whenever it protects particular kinds of labour, it diminishes capital by rendering some portion of it less productive. It aids one industry at the expense of others; it dwarfs what is thriving, in order to help what is weakly; it makes what is fertile less productive, in order to rear a scanty crop on sterile ground. What should we say of a farmer who starved his best land in order to try experiments on a rocky waste? A community which adopts such a course is only saved from bankruptcy by its inherent vitality. It clutches at an imaginary good, and gets a real loss. It inflicts actual suffering or inconvenience on the public in order to secure a delusive benefit to individuals. I say delusive, for unless the State were to go so far as to grant a monopoly of production to one, or a few individuals whom it protects, it could not prevent the operation of that economical law which reduces profits, other things being equal, to an equality. Manufacturers crowd into the protected occupation, and the benefit intended to be secured by the policy of the government is distributed and annihilated by competition.

It is sometimes alleged, that there are a set of circumstances under which protection is defensible. Protecting duties may, says Mr. Mill, be temporarily imposed with propriety, especially in a young and rising country, in hopes of naturalizing a foreign industry in itself perfectly suitable to the circumstances of the country. The limit which Mr. Mill allows to such protection is that of the time necessary for a fair trial.

Few statements made by any writer have, I am persuaded, been more extensively, though unintentionally, mischievous than this admission of Mr. Mill. The passage which I have referred to (Principles of Political Economy, vol. ii. p. 525, edit. 1862) has been quoted over and over again in the United States, and in the British colonies, as a justification of the financial system which these communities have adopted. The circumstances in which they are situated exactly square with the hypothesis of Mr. Mill. The countries are young and rising, industries, as yet nascent, are thoroughly suited to the natural capacity of the region and of the people; the latter being of the same stock with the mother country whose manufactures they prohibit or discourage. There is no reason, apparently, except that of priority in the market, why the industry of the old country should not be transplanted to the new. Hence, I repeat, Mr. Mill's concession is perpetually quoted, and is perpetually mischievous.

Every country enjoys a natural protection to its manufactures. When the article is cheap and bulky, the cost of carriage is equivalent to a prohibitive duty; when it is cheap and light, the same element of cost, amounting to a considerable percentage, is a protective impost. In the great majority of cases this charge, and similar incidents attached to foreign commerce, are abundantly sufficient to give a legitimate stimulus to home production. That 'trial under a new set of conditions,' if the expression mean anything at all in relation to manufactures, a notion which we may reasonably take the liberty to dispute, is best satisfied when the conditions are those of remoteness from the foreign market, and uncertainty of supply or cost.

Besides, the reasons which can be alleged against the diversion of capital from more profitable into less profitable channels, which is the necessary result of protective regulations, apply with overwhelming force to young and rising nations, that is to communities whose territory is imperfectly occupied. Such societies almost invariably suffer from a dearth of capital. The natural resources of the community are so vast, so undeveloped, so unappropriated, that most of those persons who constitute the community in question can employ every particle of capital productively, and are eager to obtain more. The rate of interest in young colonies is always high, for lenders are scarce, borrowers numerous. It is the height of folly then to starve such capital as does exist by wasting a portion of it in occupations or employments which are imperfectly productive, and which need, despite the natural advantages attached to home production, the artificial assistance of legislative protection in order that they may exist.

But again, who shall decide whether a particular industry should be developed in a country by protective regulations? Who shall determine the period at which the protection shall cease? Is it not manifest that the selection of favourite industries (of course I except those which may be conceived as absolutely necessary to the well-being of the country), and the prolongation of the term of protection, will be matter of perpetual intrigue; will be a powerful means for demoralising the administrative or legislative body which makes or extends these concessions? Why too should these indirect subventions to particular industries be confined to new and rising nations? Is it not possible to conceive new industries which may be developed among old and settled nations, under a 'new set of conditions,' under circumstances which are 'perfectly suitable?' And if so, who can resist the reflux of these protectionist fallacies which have done so much mischief already, and have been eliminated with so much difficulty?

There is a further argument constantly alleged in favour of a protective system, which is not so much economical, as political, or social. It is a favourite practice, especially with the protectionist orators and partisans of the United States, to insist that it is the duty of government to do its best to develope all industries; not so much in order that the country may be relieved from the necessity of depending on the foreign producer, as that the employments of the citizens should be as varied and the nation as self-contained as possible. We do not want, these people say, to have the whole community engaged in the production of raw materials; we want manufacturers as well as farmers, artisans as well as agriculturists. I have already said that they must have this variety from the natural protection afforded to all countries in consequence of their distance from the foreign market. If the importation of foreign goods into the United States were wholly free, or at least if no duty were imposed on foreign products in excess of excises at home, the Pennsylvanian or New England manufacturer would still enjoy great advantages over the British importer in the markets of Illinois, Missouri, and Ohio, because he is several thousand miles nearer to his customer, and can be much more easily informed of his customer's wants. But to strengthen a nation by impoverishing the purchaser, and by diverting the energies of the producer, is one of the strangest expedients which a mistaken view of public policy has ever recommended, or a narrow and suicidal selfishness ever insisted on.

It is hardly necessary to advert to those arguments once current among protectionists, which were derived from the fear of being dependent on foreign producers. If the British nation were left to the resources of the United Kingdom only, it would have to abandon most of its industries, and it would incur far more formidable risks of a deficient supply of food than it can incur at present. That nation is always most secure of a regular supply of food which draws its resources from the widest area. That nation is most near the contingency of scarcity or famine which depends absolutely on its home produce for the maintenance of its people. That nation can always get the most regular supplies of food at the cheapest rate which constitutes itself a free port for agricultural produce, and which, by manufacturing such articles as foreign countries desire and purchase, reaps a perpetual harvest from the whole surface of the globe. It is hardly possible to conceive ourselves at war with the whole world, it is equally impossible to conceive a universal dearth, a universal failure of crops.

There is one other argument which has been alleged in favour of protection. It is stated that the landowner in this country is subject to peculiar burdens, and that he should be compensated by such legislative arrangements as will raise the price of his produce. In the language of logicians, the antecedent and consequent of this argument are both false. It is not true that he is liable to peculiar burdens. It does not follow, even if he were made subject to special imposts, that he would be compensated by artificially raising the price of his produce. As a matter of fact the price of the produce in which he is interested has greatly risen in consequence of the abandonment of protective laws.

The position of a landowner in Great Britain may be favourably contrasted with that of the owner of any other kind of property. In the first place, his land, by the operation of natural causes, has risen and still rises in annual value. His direct liabilities are a small rent charge originally imposed on a valuation made one hundred and eighty years ago, and which cannot on economical principles be treated as a tax since it does not vary in amount according as income or consumption vary. He pays, it is true, certain local rates. Some of these rates, however, are the outlay of capital on the permanent improvement of the soil, in the construction and repair of roads. Some, again, are rates in aid of labour, the abolition of which would inevitably be followed by a rise in the rate of wages. In the two last-named cases, however, those persons who derive no benefit from the repair of the road, and who get no profit from hired labour, contribute towards the convenience of the former and the necessities of the latter, since these imposts are levied on the occupier. Rent, as we have seen, is all that remains over and above the cost of production from the soil. Anything which diminishes the cost of production, then, enhances rent. The farmer pays, unlike other men engaged in business and needing animal labour, no assessed tax on his horses. The landowner, unlike any other capitalist, can or could borrow money of the State at low and fixed rates, in order to make permanent improvements which return an interest far in excess of the outlay. He is liable to no probate duty, and only to a moderate succession duty. Nay, so tender is the legislature of his interest, that, a few years ago, when a murrain of uncommon severity and great deadliness raged among cattle, and it became necessary to check it by destroying infected herds, the compensation which, according to common justice, should have been paid by those whose cattle were saved by this expedient, was levied on the general body of ratepayers; who thus had to pay the tax twice over, once in the rise in the price of meat and dairy produce, next in providing the funds for insuring the losses of their neighbours. So far is land from suffering under peculiar burdens that it is really exceptionally favoured. Conveyance by sale or settlement involves, indeed, considerable cost, but these charges are, with the exception of the stamp duties, the necessary consequence of those large powers over the disposition of landed estates which their owners have acquired and defend, and are levied on other conveyances which are expressly denied the privileges of real estate.

Again, it does not follow that, were the landowner ever so burdened, the true compensation is to be found in an artificial enhancement of that which he produces. His real interest lies in exactly the reverse policy. A farm supplies not only corn, but meat and dairy produce. If the price of corn be raised, the price of other produce falls. Dear wheat means cheap meat. If the power of purchasing the first necessaries of life be crippled or limited, the power of purchasing the second necessaries, the familiar comforts of life, is much more crippled. I have adverted to this rule before, but its importance justifies a repetition, for the study of the laws which govern prices is every producer's business; a knowledge of these laws might become the most effectual check to over production and rash speculation. The general demand for different objects varies in intensity with the nature of the object, and its relevancy to the subsistence or the necessities of the public. The demand of a few consumers on a large scale does not raise prices so much as that of many consumers on a small scale does; just as the bulk of the public revenue is derived from the small contributions of the general public, the amount of this revenue being seriously affected by a decline in commercial or industrial activity. Farmers are beginning to understand these facts, and to look on a deficient, or merely average harvest, as a loss. Before long they will also see that any interruption in the supply of foreign corn, though it may appear as a transient advantage to them, is certain to be followed by a decline in the purchasing power of the general community, and by a fall in the value of that on which they depend for the net profits of agriculture.

CHAPTER XVIII.

Foreign Trade.

The various regions of the earth are variously favourable to the growth of vegetable and animal products. Different countries, too, have different geological characteristics. Thus, rice and cotton will grow in tropical or semi-tropical climates. Wool of the best quality, on the other hand, is produced only in warmer temperate regions. So, again, coal is found only in certain geological formations. It is remarkable that nearly all, if not quite all, the coal deposits which exist near the sea or great navigable rivers, are said to lie in Great Britain or in the British colonies. Gold is found only in primitive rocks, or in the detritus of such rocks. The produce of silver is characterised by similar limitations. These instances might be indefinitely multiplied, and might prove incontestably that the civilisation of mankind depends on reciprocity of trade. To buy these foreign commodities or utilities it is necessary to sell others; in order to be able to sell, a nation must labour; in order to labour, it must have the materials wherewith to work.

Particular commodities, however, though produced in particular districts or climates, are very seldom produced in so narrow a district as to be under the control of one government only. Again, there is scarcely any object which is in general demand but of restricted supply for which no substitute can be found. For example at the outbreak of the continental war the supply of saltpetre from

India, at that time the great source of this article, so essential for war purposes, was practically in the hands of the English. But the French contrived to obtain the salt from other and new sources. Again, the supply of colonial produce, especially sugar was, by reason of the naval supremacy of Great Britain during the same period, practically denied to the French consumer. The result of this exclusion from the supply of cane sugar, led to the manufacture of sugar from beet-root. It does not follow, therefore, that an export duty will be really paid by the purchaser of the exported article. It may be transferred to the seller by lowering the price, or by checking the production of the article in question.

As geological differences and differences of climate control the production of commodities or limit products to particular localities, so differences of race and habit may exercise a powerful influence on local or national industries. It is excessively difficult to determine the share which race has in modifying the economical position of a nation. The science of ethnology is in its infancy, and the inductions of those who study it are apparently often rash and unsatisfactory. In any case they are far too uncertain for practice or action, or even for the explanation of economical phenomena. Positive evidence appears to point to an identity in the early features of social life among races which are physiologically very different; for developments in the social system of particular countries are, it appears, due far more to the progress of social and political knowledge, and to certain accidents of government and tradition, than to any peculiarities in the stock from which the nation is, or is presumed to be, descended. For example, the village system of land tenure belonged to Hindostan, to Germany, to medieval England, to Ireland, and to Russia. Its abandonment in any of these regions is due, not to the influence of race, but to the habits induced by forms of government, rules of law, and similar social forces.

- It cannot be doubted, however, that different communities have different, and it appears permanently different, capacities for special industries, and that, therefore, as materials vary with climate and soil, so industries vary with national peculiarities. It cannot be by mere accident that, for a long time at least, the mechanical and chemical sciences, in so far as these sciences are relevant to mere economical objects, have been almost exclusively developed in Great Britain.

As climate is a condition for the production of certain raw materials, so it controls the exercise of certain industries. Bright dyes cannot be so well imparted to silk in England as they can in the south of France, where the sun is more powerful and the atmosphere more clear than with us. Again, the spinning of fine cotton, linen, and woollen yarns, is, it appears, much easier in a moist than in a dry atmosphere, and therefore more particularly an industry of Western England than of any other part of the world; this being a district in which the annual variation of the thermometer is, comparatively speaking, inconsiderable, and the air is always or nearly always moist. Similar peculiarities of climate determining industry will occur to my reader. In the same way (though here we are constrained to speak a little more doubtfully), it would seem that the influence of climate affects the muscular, nervous, or moral capacities of men or races so much as to develope or check their industrial powers. The inhabitants of tropical regions are, it is said, languid and indolent; those of such countries as suffer from long and severe winters are constrained to periodical inaction, while those who live in places where the climate is equable and mild are eminent for their industrial success. It is more certain that the inhabitants of warm countries, since they can more easily satisfy their natural wants, have less demand for the conveniences of life, and therefore exercise a less varied industry.

Plainly, then, natural science confirms the economical doctrine that civilisation is constituted by the interchange of services, and that the rule which the experience of one society affirms, is equally true of all societies. The best hope therefore which men can gather, as to the gradual and complete civilisation of the world, and the reclamation of nations, if it be possible, from barbarous customs, is gained from experience as to the humanising influences of honest trade. The missionaries of morality and religion have often failed to make any permanent impression upon uncivilised peoples, either because they have been indifferent to the value of those subordinate agencies; or because they have been unable to eliminate those persons who have generally intruded on such well-meant efforts. The slave-hunter, the buccaneer, the filibuster, and the trading adventurer have hindered the real progress of mankind and the wealth of nations far more effectually than the self-devotion of the moralist or missionary has helped them. It is very difficult to humanise a nation by conquest, it is impossible to civilise it by knavery.

Now in the earliest ages of economical history, even

long before any records which have survived to our time, or indeed have been written, trade between nations was familiar. There is indirect evidence of commercial intercourse between this country and the Tyrian colonies, in ages long antecedent to the knowledge of Britain by the Roman and Greek geographers. Fragments of very ancient porcelain, undoubtedly introduced from China, have been found in Ireland and the West of England, in situations which leave no doubt as to the distance of the time in which they were imported. Tin it appears was a regular article of traffic in the Homeric age, and it is probable that tin was in early times procurable only from Cornwall. In later times, and onwards to the early part of the middle ages, wine was imported into England from France, Spain, and Greece. Spices came from the East, either by the water route of the Red Sea and the Nile, or by the caravan road over Central Asia to the Black Sea and Mediterranean. So the policy of the Plantagenet kings was directed towards establishing close commercial relations between the East of England, then its richest and most prosperous region, and the thriving manufactures of Flanders.

Unfortunately, however, all men in those days were occupied by the notion that money was wealth. This fancy led the kings and statesmen of the age to encourage exports and prohibit imports, because this seemed to be the best way of increasing the stock of money. Indirectly they may have developed manufacturing industry, because they did everything in their power to induce a home growth of such products as, being exchanged for foreign goods, would bring about the result which they aimed at. But the policy induced the habit also of considering that trade could not flourish except under protection, and that the wisdom of government was best exercised in providing an artificial stimulus to industry.

Slowly, after many a hard struggle, and in the face of bitter hostility, the economical reformers of this country, long after the genius of Adam Smith had discovered the true theory of trade, induced the legislature of the United Kingdom to accept and act on the principle of free importation and exportation. It is true that the last relics of protection to domestic industry disappeared when the shilling duty on foreign corn was abolished, and Great Britain was made a free port for food. This duty while it lasted was equivalent to a tax levied on the public, of which about one-fourth went to the treasury and three-fourths to the landowners in the form of increased rent. Still, we have not yet acquired the right to say that we have adopted the principle of free trade. The discretionary exercise of labour in whatever direction the individual pleases, is by no means awarded; some classes of society being invested with special privileges, others burdened by special disabilities; many callings being closed except to particular persons; many branches of industry being hampered by such restrictive regulations as are not intended to promote the efficiency of the labour, but to check competition within the field of employment.

When a country, by dint of manufacturing or commercial activity, contrives to purchase largely in foreign markets, or to absorb great part of the carrying trade, so as to be constituted the port to which this foreign produce comes and from which it goes, this produce will be necessarily cheaper in the country which thus becomes a free port than it is in other countries which draw their supplies from its stores. If, as is very much the case, the precious metals are drawn to Great Britain from the countries in which they are mined in exchange for British goods, or for foreign goods exported in British ships, these metals will be cheaper in Great Britain than they will be in any other country, except that from which they are exported. It does not indeed follow that the prices of foreign produce will rise, for the same causes which tend to depress the value of the precious metals, will tend to depress the value of other articles, as corn, or cotton, or provisions. But such a trade will tend to raise the price of home produce, in so far as the imported stocks of precious metals bear upon the metallic currency of the country into which they are thus imported, the price of these metals being determined, other causes being considered and accounted for, by the amount which is employed in currency and manufactures.

Similarly the price of any kind of foreign produce is determined, not by its cost to the producer, but by the cost of that against which it is exchanged. For example, the chief imports of Spanish produce to the United Kingdom are wine, oil, and lead. The chief exports of British produce are iron, linen and cotton manufactures, and coal. On an average the value of Spanish produce in Spain will be relative to the cost of production, but its price to the British purchaser will be relative to the cost, not of producing it, but of producing that against which it is exchanged; not by the cost of wine, oil, and lead in Spain, but by the cost of the goods sent from Great Britain, and thence to the Spanish market, added to the carriage of Spanish goods to the home market. Thus it may even happen that the importing country may obtain foreign goods at an easier and cheaper rate, value for value, than they can be procured in the country which produces them.

The profit of foreign trade consists in the difference between the price at which the goods are bought and carried, and the price at which they are sold. A rough index of its amount is to be found in the difference between the money-value of the exports and imports of a country. The aggregate value of the latter is greatly in excess of that of the former. Thus, for example, in 1872 and 1873, the imports of the United Kingdom were represented by the figures 275 and 290; the exports by 249 and 240. At first sight it would seem that the people of this country bought more than they sold by 26 and 50, during these two years. In fact, the exports paying for the imports, they bought the greater sum by the less, the difference, some deductions being made, being the profit on the foreign trade. A century ago these proportions would have excited the liveliest alarm. It would have been supposed that the country was being drained of its treasure, that the balance of trade was against us, and that we were on the high road to commercial ruin instead of being in the enjoyment of considerable commercial prosperity. The real test of the efflux of specie, and of the evils, real or imaginary, which such an efflux involves, is supplied by the rate of the foreign exchanges referred to in Chapter xv.

The advantages of foreign trade do not consist so much in the gains of merchants, on which persons are accustomed to look with admiration, nor even in the fact that trade with another country implies productive industry at home, but in the material advantages which ensue from the distribution of conveniences or comforts, in the addition which this trade makes to the enjoyments of life, and much more in the moral benefits which ensue from the interchange of services and advantages by the machinery of trade. People are now disabused of the notion that the greatness or prosperity of any one country is to be measured by the poverty or depression of another; and have learned instead that the prosperity of one country is intimately connected with the moral and material progress of others. At one time, as Mr. Mill has justly observed, it was thought the duty of a patriot, if possible, to make other countries poor and weak, or at least to wish that such should be their condition. This miserable jealousy, as Adam Smith noticed, arose from the habit of estimating all foreign relations from a military point of view, and of believing that a foreigner was an enemy. It is impossible to over-estimate the moral value which ensues from the absolute reversal of this opinion. We have not yet indeed reached the true inference which can be derived from the rule, that the prosperity of one people is involved in the prosperity of others; for international law is in its infancy, and municipal jealousies, the offspring of long enmities, studiously fostered by ambition and selfishness, still exist. But every wise and prudent man knows that in the present day a war between civilised nations is more and more a folly and a public crime; and that as it is stripped of its old excuses and its false pleas, excuses and pleas which sprang from the erroneous commercial and political theories of a bygone age, it becomes less and less possible, because it is more and more irrational and mischievous.

CHAPTER XIX.
Colonial Trade.

THE British government has never founded a colony. It has appropriated colonies founded by other nations; it has assumed the conquests of the great mercantile company which gradually occupied the peninsula of India, and it has associated the so-called colonies, which were the result of private enterprise. It has never systematically colonised with anything but convicts. The so-called colonial empire may be divided into dependencies, military outposts, and colonies proper. India is a notable example of the first, Malta and Gibraltar of the second, Australia, Canada, and the Cape colony of the third. The last two, however, were more or less conquests.

The colonies of modern Europe, and especially those of Spain and Holland, were essentially the subjugation of regions occupied by communities whose political organisation had been considerably developed, but who were unable to resist the shock of European warfare. In accordance with the prevalent idea, that the precious metals constituted wealth, the Spanish conquerors of the New World busied themselves with the search after gold and silver. During the time of their sway, they looked on these dependencies as the sources of revenue, as tributaries; and in order to keep them more fully in hand, they deliberately disabled every native, whether of European, mixed, or native blood, from any share in the administration. The functions of government were confined to officials who were born in Spain, were sent out to its Transatlantic possessions for this very purpose, and were prohibited from forming connexions with the dependency.

The American plantations were of a different character, and stood in a different relation to the mother country. They were not military conquests, nor military colonies. The Eastern coast of North America has no considerable mines of the precious metals. The emigrants who settled on its shores, generally in order to escape religious or political persecution, disturbed no settled or civilised government. They found only a few hunting tribes. The savage character however of the native races became an excellent training-school for the settlers, who developed a strong civil government from the difficulties and dangers of their early career. The soil was barren, the climate rugged and inhospitable. The chief natural wealth of the region was timber and fish. The colonists were poor, and were rather protected than ruled. Their earliest charters allowed them municipal institutions and the privilege of self-government. The home government exacted no tribute from them, but merely imposed on them a system which, according to the ideas of the time, was one of fair and intelligible reciprocity.

By the colonial system the mother country restrained the colonists from manufacturing goods, or from purchasing manufactured articles from any but the mother country; and at the same time granted the raw produce of the colony either differential advantages, or the sole right of market. The arrangement, as we now see, was absurd; for in the pursuit after an imaginary gain, it inflicted an obvious and certain loss. Had the colonist been unable to procure manufactured goods at cheaper rates, or the mother country to get raw materials of better quality or at lower prices, the colonial system would have been wholly nugatory, and its regulations superfluous. As a matter of fact, both communities deliberately excluded themselves from the cheapest market, or, in the language of exchange, got the goods which each wanted at greater cost than they could have got them had the market been free. But, notwithstanding, the statesmen of the last century believed that the colonial system was a policy of the highest wisdom, and imagined that the commercial prosperity of Great Britain depended on its rigid retention. When the American plantations resented the attempt of the British parliament to tax them, and achieved their independence, it was generally feared that the mercantile supremacy of Great Britain would be totally and permanently annihilated. The only consolation which the statesmen of the age entertained, was the fact that Great Britain had still some colonies left, in which this beneficent system of reciprocity would still be maintained.

It is only a few years ago that the last relics of the colonial system, the differential duties in favour of colonial timber, were abolished. But for many a year the British people were condemned to use dear sugar and coffee, the familiar luxuries, or even necessaries of life, in order to keep up colonial interests, as well as dear and inferior timber, a raw material, the importance of which in house-building is of the greatest significance to a country in which the local supply is far inferior to the demand. At the present time, the whole of this policy is abandoned. The colonies put what charges they please on imported goods, and the home government affords them no advantage in the markets of the United Kingdom.

Most of the colonies have adopted a protective system. Occasionally they excuse this policy on the plea alleged by Mr. Mill—that it is expedient to develope possible or nascent industries. Sometimes, and with greater reason, they apologise for their tariffs on the ground that it is all but impossible to collect excises and direct taxes in a thinly-peopled country, and that customs' duties are the most obvious and the cheapest means by which a revenue may be raised. The proportion of taxation to every head of population is very high in the British colonies.

The value of these colonies to the British Empire is maintained by political and economical arguments. With the former we have nothing to do. The latter are mainly three. It is alleged that the connexion between the colonies and the United Kingdom secures a readier market to British goods, a more obvious field to British capital, a readier outlet for British emigration. It may be doubted, however, whether any of these ends are secured by the connexion. As I have said, the financial policy of most of the colonies has been strongly protectionist. No direct assistance is therefore given to the British manufactures. It may be questioned whether this assistance is even given indirectly. No doubt the emigrant from Great Britain carries with him a taste for British produce, or at least a preference for it, due to his familiarity with such produce at home. But these tastes need not be enduring, and are not necessarily associated with so slender a political connexion as that which subsists between Great Britain and a distant society, whose municipal institutions are not only independent of, but alien to, those of the mother country; whose association with an imperial policy is of the slightest kind, and which is chiefly concerned with the return of such emigrants as have accumulated wealth in the colony. With the majority of those settlers, who never could or would return, the conncxion between themselves and the mother country is a mere sentiment which would not bear the least strain, which is often nominal, however loudly expressed, while the real ties are often those between the colony and some near but alien state. No rational person can doubt that the commercial connexion between Canada and the United States is far closer than that between Canada and Great Britain, and that in the event of a dilemma, the colony would not be long in making up its mind as to the association which it would sacrifice. Men buy goods, i. e. enter into those commercial relations which constitute the ordinary and continuous routine of civilised life, for reasons of convenience and cheapness far more readily than they do on grounds of habit and sentiment. Prior to the civil war in America, the trade between this country and the United States was worth more than that of all the British possessions put together, even if we include India under the latter head. It is the accident, apparently, of that war, and the consequence of the fiscal system which followed it, that so much British trade was diverted into the Indian possessions. At present (1875) British trade with the American Union is greater than ever.

It is probable that the connexion between the mother country and the colony does facilitate the operations of borrowers, whether they be public or private, in the latter society. The connexion between the mother country and the colony suggests a political unity which does not, indeed, deceive astute investors, but can be utilized by speculators, and may be accepted by a less wary public. It is possible that had Canada been an independent State, the questionable enterprise known under the name of the Grand Trunk Railway would hardly have been accomplished. It is certain, we may believe, that the Indian railways would not have been constructed at all, or not have been constructed on such easy terms, had it not been for the guarantee implied in the maintenance of British supremacy in India. But one or two shocks given to colonial credit may put these colonial enterprises on the same footing with other foreign speculations. The colonial connexion may have been useful as a good-will, but the continuance of this good-will will be determined by the good faith of the borrowers. A colony may take liberties with its creditors, but it will cease to get fresh creditors, as assuredly as any defaulting foreign government does; since no legal process can issue, in the present state of international law, against a society whose municipal institutions render it independent. Nor will British capital continue to be available for private enterprise in these colonies, unless the borrowers put themselves in such a position as will give adequate security for their commercial integrity, either by the employment of responsible agents, or by subjecting themselves to an easy and efficient civil process.

Lastly, the economical argument which considers the colonies as an outlet for emigration appears to have no foundation. By far the largest part of the emigrants from the United Kingdom have settled and do settle in the United States. Out of 6,888,070 emigrants which have left the United Kingdom in the years 1840-73, 4,720,570, i.e. more than two-thirds, have gone to the United States, and many of those, it is said, whose apparent destination was the North American colonies, and who are about 1,000,000 in number, have merely taken these colonies on their way to the Union. Many reasons have contributed to this choice. The passage is shorter; labour has been in more regular demand, and employment more open to the emigrant on his landing. Moreover, the United States, though they have employed no artificial stimulants to emigration, have by their liberal grants of public land to bona fide settlers drawn away from Europe a large number of intelligent and enterprising labourers. The number of emigrants to the Australian colonies, though considerable, is far less than that which has gone to the United States. It amounted in the period referred to above, to 984,505. It would have been, however, much scantier had not these colonies adopted the system of assisted emigration, first suggested by Mr. Gibbon Wakefield.

It has been said that the British government has never colonised, and that the Anglo-Saxon settlements began with private enterprise, assisted subsequently by colonial legislation on the basis of Mr. Wakefield's scheme. This process was to sell public lands to settlers at fixed prices (prohibiting, of course, permanent settlement except on these terms), and to employ the funds acquired by these means in assisting emigration. The objections to the scheme are two. It takes away from the purchaser a portion of his capital at a time when this capital is of the greatest value to him; and it discourages settlers by fixing a high price on public lands. There is no doubt that the regulation price in Australia, viz. £1 an acre, was excessive, considering the fact that prairie land, naturally cleared and immediately available for farming purposes, can be had in the United States for less than one-fourth the amount. In practice, we are informed, the full price demanded by the Australian government was never paid. Besides, the Homestead Act of Congress gives free plots to settlers, the quantity of which is proportioned to the family of the settling emigrant. But, on the other hand, it is urged that there is no true competition between the United States and the Australian colonies; that the advantages which the former possesses are special, and will be specially attractive; that the growth of the Australian colonies had to be assisted; that the inveterate habit of voluntary colonists, that of scattering themselves, had to be arrested; that if the settler was mulcted in a portion of his capital under particular circumstances, he was compensated by the cheapness of the labour imported under the system; and that finally, all things considered, the plan had worked well. It is better, the advocates of the Gibbon Wakefield scheme allege, to adopt a process which draws capitalists as well as labourers, not only because it has an immediate bearing on the growth of the colony, but because it tends to constitute a permanent society which shall, as far as possible, contain every kind of social rank. It should be added, that the Wakefield scheme is only partially operative at present, the price of the settler's purchases being no longer devoted to the process of assisting the emigration of labour.

It is alleged, and with considerable reason, that it is the duty of the British government to provide some general and systematic scheme of colonisation. The custom of voluntary or spontaneous colonisation, however assisted by the Gibbon Wakefield scheme, draws away the best class of artisans and labourers, leaving the feeblest and least enterprising behind. The proof of this lies in the fact that years in which food is cheap give, as a rule, the lowest number of emigrants. Nor does it leaven the new colony with that social class whose culture and habit of life are of eminent service to society, though their use is only slowly appreciated, while their absence, when the want is felt, is filled up with difficulty. No one can fail to be painfully struck with the vulgarity, the noise, the coarse selfishness of some among the newer colonies, especially of those in which wealth has grown rapidly, and the commoner kinds of labour only have been attracted. But though in the abstract it may be asserted that the duty of systematic colonisation has been improperly neglected by the government, it is by no means easy to sketch the plan which it would have been wise to adopt, or to discover the means by which the plan could be carried out.

Though the government does not colonise, it watches over emigration. For obvious reasons, the discipline of an emigrant, or indeed of any other ship, must be nearly as strict as that of an army. Great discretionary power must be lodged in the hands of the master or captain; but this power is very likely to be abused, and has been very grossly abused. Seafaring men are apt to be rough and brutal; contractors and shippers, in the sharp competition of business, to be rapacious and fraudulent. Hence various regulations, intended to secure the health, the comfort, the decencies of life among emigrants, have been enacted by law on the principle alluded to so often before, that the object of law is to restrain the strong from aggression on the weak. But these regulations, highly necessary as they are, rather check than promote emigration, because they make the process more expensive. In course of time, perhaps, the transit of passengers will be further cheapened by the economy of the means of travel, and by shortening the time necessary for the conveyance of persons.

But though emigration is no remedy for over-population, except it be undertaken on a large scale and under an organised and inclusive system, the voluntary expatriation of those who have the energy or enterprise to leave the home of their birth, is developing and will develope results which are full of the most profound interest to the statesman and economist. Remote regions, hitherto occupied by a few savage tribes, are gradually being peopled by men who bring with them all the appliances and many of the tastes which have been accumulated by the highest civilisation. By the side of these gigantic settlements, the efforts of colonists in the early part of the world's recorded history are puny. Every year of this action is taking away from the risks of barbarism, is giving overwhelming strength to the power of intelligent labour and civil government, is testing the habits and traditions of the old world. The tide of empire may change, and the influence of Europe may, in a century or two, be lost in the vast and rapid progress of communities which, as yet, are in their infancy. But the course of this progress will be the gain of humanity.

There is indeed a reason why the British nation may congratulate itself on the relation in which her colonies stand to the mother country. The legal bonds by which both were once tied together have been nearly fretted away by the wear of interests which are necessarily diverse. The presumed economical advantages of that system of commercial reciprocity which once prevailed have been exploded by experience, as they were long ago repudiated by reason and argument. At present, the colonies are situated in so peculiar a financial position, that on merely trade principles, they have become worse customers to us than many nations of wholly alien origin. The political connexion between them and the United Kingdom would be, if it were complete, only mischievous; but as it is little more than a mere name, it is gradually being understood by both parties as a sentimental tradition, as a tie which will be ruptured by the first sharp experience. It is impossible that the colonies can long submit, except under manifest degradation, to the policy of Great Britain; it is equally impossible that the home government can continue the duty of their defence or superintendence. But the possession of that social system which this country has developed in the course of its political and economical history, the extension on our part, and the inheritance on theirs, of those memories, laws, municipal institutions, and with them those liberties which our race has won, all which it is bound to commend to its so-called dependencies, are a tie which is not the less powerful, because it is seldom recognised as the real bond between Great Britain and her distant children. It is, however, just as strong in the United States as it is in the so-called colonies.

CHAPTER XX.

On the Functions of Government.

A GOVERNMENT, whatever be its form, is always assumed to exist for the benefit of its people or subjects. The great Greek philosopher, Aristotle, when he treated of that form of government which was known as a tyranny, and which was always most odious to the experience or imagination of his fellow-countrymen, said that the tyrant aimed at three things:—to crush the spirit of his subjects; to sow mutual distrust among them; and to keep them poor. In our time, a government which deliberately preferred to impoverish and distress its subjects, or to prevent the growth of material prosperity among them, or to lower their motives for accumulating wealth, or to prohibit or discourage the development of their resources, would be justly deemed, however powerful it were, a reproach to humanity and civilisation.

We must always therefore, whatever the errors which it may commit, credit a civilised government with good intentions. Similarly, a government should always, and generally does, permit free criticism on its economy. To refuse this right of criticism is to assume infallibility as well as power, an assumption which has been often made, but which abundant experience has made ridiculous. We shall find however, that most of the errors which governments have committed in managing the economy of society have arisen from a wish to further the public good by interfering with the harmless exercise of the individual's discretion. But good intentions may lead to unwise practices, to mischievous laws, to intolerable oppression, to the destruction of public wealth, to the permanent hindrance of social progress.

It has been stated several times already, that the earliest and the most urgent duty of government is to protect the weak against the strong. On this plea government watches over contracts; forbids some, annuls others, interprets on equitable principles another set. It is not only justified in this protective action, but, in case it is certified of the propriety of taking such steps, it assumes the initiative of other acts. In our time no one doubts that a government may wisely and properly undertake such public works as confer great public benefit, but are too vast for private or corporate enterprise, or are not so immediately remunerative as to attract private capital. Such are, for example, the formation of roads and harbours, and the erection of light-houses. The extent to which a government will take these works on itself, is relevant to the deficiency of enterprise among its subjects. Thus, for example, railroads have been constructed by private enterprise throughout the United Kingdom, but have been assisted by the State in most foreign countries. Perhaps the most striking among these undertakings are the vast tanks whose ruins still exist in Ceylon, and which a native government constructed ages ago for the purpose of artificial irrigation.

Again, a government may take the initiative in acts which confer lasting benefits on the whole community by increasing the powers of some classes in it. At the present time no one disputes that a government may properly take upon itself the duty of insisting on the education of the whole community, of controlling the labour of the young so as to make this education as complete as possible, and of levying a tax or rate in aid, in order to supply such an education to children whose parents are unable or unwilling to incur the necessary charge of such instruction as may be required. Such action may be justified on political, on moral, and on economical grounds. Our business is with the last.

An educated community is more apt in doing what it knows, and in learning what it does not know, than one which is generally uninstructed. The German emigrants to the United States, most of whom are fairly possessed of primary education, are much more handy than those who come from states where equal care is not taken. Now it does not follow if a general education were given at the public charge that wages would rise; but it is almost certain that labour would be greatly lightened. It is also certain that the risk which every nation occupying a prominent place among industrial communities must incur, that of being outstripped in the race of wealth by other communities, is to a great extent provided against if the subjects of such a government are gifted with education. An educated nation is stronger and safer than one in which the advantages which ensue from such culture are not generally present. This is not the place in which to discuss the details of such a process, or to state, even in the most general terms, what is the outline of a primary public education.

Again, a government may properly take in hand specialities of education when the result of such public patronage is an increase in the productive powers, the economy of industrial undertakings, the moral progress of a people. Instruction in what is vaguely called technical education, that is, the acquisition of scientific method and a knowledge of the principles and practice of the applied sciences, is of indirect service to the community at large. But it is doubtful whether the funds necessary for such a training should be supplied from general taxation, for as the benefit of increased power in working and earning wages is not conferred on all, and the direct advantages of the training belong to the instructed student, it cannot be equitably argued that the cost should be borne by the general community. One obvious resource, however, for such a system of special training, is to be found in the fees of the patent-office. Fees are levied on patents in order to check useless applications of frivolous claims. The disposal of these fees in developing scientific training, in the case of persons who possess a peculiar aptitude for scientific method, would give a proper direction to this fund, and might compensate for some of the restrictions which the concession of patents involves.

The government may properly contribute towards the economy of industrial undertakings. Geological investigations, astronomical observations, meteorological research, the study of physical geography (especially the theory of winds and currents), the sciences of animal and vegetable physiology, are all proper objects for government assistance whenever private enterprise is unwilling or incompetent to carry out these researches. The value of the inductions gathered from the sciences adverted to is enormous, even when this value is interpreted on the lowest material grounds. The labour given to the development of this learning, rarely secures any advantage to those who expend it. Similarly, researches into the conditions of health, known generally as sanitary science, have a vast economical importance, for the saving of health is an economy of labour. Sickness, and the premature extinction of strength or vigorous life, when due to remediable causes, are loss and waste, and induce economical efforts on society, which differ only in their moral aspect from vice and crime. And among other sciences which have a direct bearing on the material progress of society, that which deals with the conditions of society itself, the interchange of services, and the distribution of the fruits of labour, and which is known as political economy, should take as important a position in public education as any which can be named, since it is the science of social life.

It is hardly necessary to say that a government cannot neglect to exercise a due supervision on everything which bears upon the moral progress of a people. But it is not possible to define the extent to which it may or should interfere. No one doubts that it ought to repress whatever is indecent or openly profligate. Every one is agreed that there should be a police over gross immorality and impudent vice. Occupations, in themselves harmless, are justly brought under the censorship of law when they may easily be turned to the purposes of crime or may debauch unwary or unguarded persons. Places of public resort, houses of public entertainment, theatres, and the performances exhibited in them, are fairly committed to the control of the police, and must be inspected with discretionary severity, because they may be turned to the worst purposes. The limits however of such government interference are, and perhaps always will be, contested, because it is always difficult to decide between the boundaries of that sense of personal responsibility which constitutes individual character, and a wise supervision or control. There is a border land, for the occupation of which the advocates of liberty and discipline perpetually contend. The contention is of no small advantage, because liberty and order only differ in details, the concession of the former and the action of the latter varying with circumstances and with individuals. And as the government may and should repress vice, so should it inculcate morality, not by direct rewards, but by the sanction of its example; for the intercourse of nations is the intercourse of individuals on a larger, a more striking, and a more instructive scale.

In the early economical history of this, as of other organised governments, the interference of executive or legislative authority was incessant and minute. The central power was perpetually attempting to exercise a supervision over the home and foreign trade; over the labour, the wages, the incomes, the expenditure of the people. The police of the parish or manor was exact and precise. I cannot contrast the difference between past and present theories of the function of government more clearly than by giving a short sketch of the policy of England five centuries ago.

The utmost efforts of government were directed towards preventing the exportation of the precious metals. To secure this measure of police the principal articles of export and import could be sold or purchased only at certain places, sometimes at one place only, under the supervision of the King's Exchequer. Again, to protect the community, officers were appointed whose duty it was to examine foreign imports, especially foreign cloth, and to secure that they rigidly fulfilled statutable conditions. Encouragement however was given to foreign artificers and merchants, who might be willing to settle in England, and the eastern counties grew wealthy by the imported industry of the Flemings. To obviate a fall in home produce, the exportation of wool and hides was occasionally forbidden, these being the articles by which foreign produce was chiefly purchased.

The domestic life of the people was carefully regulated. The civil rights of a large portion of the community were mutilated. A person who occupied the status of a villain could not change his calling without the leave of his lord, could not educate his son or marry his daughter without licence from his feudal superior. The legislature strove to tie him to his occupation by distinct enactments. The police of the manor, at whose courts every member was bound to appear thrice every year, was of the strictest character. A man without land, lord, or occupation was a vagabond, and, as such, was liable to outlawry and condign punishment. The residence of a stranger for more than three days in the house of any subject of the manor rendered his host, unless due and careful notice was given, or privilege pleaded, liable to a fine. Every child had to be registered when it reached the statutable age. Non-resident dependants were liable to an annual impost, or could be reclaimed by their lord.

Various occupations were placed under inspection. The keeper of an ale-house was fined, if he broached a cask without due notice given to certain officers, whose duty is implied in their name of ale-tasters. The assize of bread, that is the regulation of its price by the price of wheat, was carefully taken, frauds and over-charges being visited by severe penalties. The avarice of the miller, at whose mill the inhabitants were generally bound to grind their corn, was coerced by similar fines or mulcts. In order to facilitate the cause of justice, the initiative of informations against offenders was left to aggrieved parties, the lord of the manor receiving the fines inflicted as part of his income. Hence, the former were discouraged from any but *bonâ fide* prosecutions, the latter, not being able to commence proceedings, was also interested in not levying such penalties as would check informations.

The dress and other expenditure of the people was regulated by sumptuary laws. The kind of food, the number of dishes, the character and fineness of the clothing which might be used or worn by the various classes of the community were prescribed. The motive of these restrictions was not merely that of maintaining the distinctions of social rank, but, according to the judgment of the age, public economy. The resources of the community were few. As the food of the nation was derived from its soil only, and the climate was as capricious and uncertain as it now is, the people ran risk of dearth if not of famine. It is true that these sumptuary laws were unsupported by an example on the part of those who enacted them, and that prodigal expenditure and utter recklessness characterised the conduct of public affairs. But persons who are privileged to make laws are too apt to consider themselves privileged to break them.

The people of this country have slowly escaped from most of these restrictions, and have achieved complete social liberty with most of the benefits of free exchange.

In one direction only have these powers been restricted, this is, in the buying and selling of land, its settlement and accumulation, in which particulars the freedom of a past generation is markedly contrasted with the artificial restraints of the present.

In the time to which I have adverted the conveyance of land was completed by easy and simple symbols. The purchaser was taken to the spot, and the land was transferred to him in the presence of witnesses by the delivery of a clod or some other visible object, and by the utterance of a few formal words. But the theory that the feudal tenant had a permanent and indefeasible interest in the soil was by no means conceded. Resumptions of grants, especially when these grants were made by the Crown, were common. The real value of land was small. The law abhorred a perpetuity. Entails were looked on with much disfavour. Strict settlements were invented only after the restoration. Primogeniture conveyed certain rights, but as the value of stock on a well-tilled farm was, as I have said above, worth several times more than the fee-simple of the soil itself, and personal property was never liable to this custom, the privilege of the eldest son was very different from that which exists at present. Besides, the under tenant was, in accordance with feudal principles, able to control the sale of his lord's lands, by refusing to attorn to, that is acknowledge, the new purchaser. Without his assent the sale was voidable. The refusal of this assent was, we may believe, a considerable check upon the rapacity or oppression of the feudal superior. The free conveyance of land, therefore, was controlled only by the means which existed for enforcing the duties of the landowner.

It is contended that the custom of primogeniture stimulates the energies of the younger and dispossessed children. The fact may be doubted. I have never heard that the energies of the people in the United States, in the British colonies, in Holland and Belgium, have been enervated by the expectation which each child entertains, of taking a share in his parent's property. If the custom is defensible on public grounds of economy, it should be extended to personal estate as well. But if the people were divided into a few luxurious millionaires and a host of impoverished men, if there were a few hundred elder sons, and the other millions were all debarred from a share in their progenitors' estates, it is probable that the energies of the majority would be aroused, but first towards doing away with the custom. Primogeniture endures only because it affects one kind of property, not the whole of that, and even that which it does affect only rarely and partially. To extend it would be to secure its destruction, and that which is of greater significance, the strict settlement of estates.

It is said again that the development of the science of agriculture has been greatly assisted by the existence of vast landed wealth, and by the experimental farming of rich proprietors. I suspect that the science of agriculture is far in advance of its application, that much of this science has been the discovery of tenant-farmers, and I am sure that the beneficent influence of great landowners is rarely exhibited except when their estates are unencumbered. Human nature and parental affection are stronger than the passion for the custom of primogeniture, and hence, though the vanity of the head of a family is consulted by giving him the nominal possession of the ancestral estate, the estate is generally seriously burdened, and by implication the improving powers of the life-owner are seriously crippled by the encumbrances put upon it in order to make provision for the widow and children of the last proprietor. If this were not the case, why was it found expedient to allow landowners the privilege of obtaining grants of public money at low rates, when it is well known that land improved by aid of these grants will let to the full amount of the interest on the loan, plus the sum annually paid off by the borrower from the amount of the principal? If the landowner can borrow at three per cent. and get six or seven for his improvements, why was it necessary to appeal to the State in order to enable him to make so advantageous an outlay? We know very little about the mortgages which encumber real estate in Great Britain; but nobody doubts that they are very large.

There are moral, social, and political consequences which flow from the custom of primogeniture on which it is unnecessary for the political economist to enter. It is possible that a system which condemns the mass of the agricultural population to a condition of absolute helplessness and hopelessness, which encumbers the possession of land with debts, and burdens its conveyance by a host of artificial disabilities, which cannot be shown to improve and may be expected to lower the art of agriculture, or at least to prevent its full development, may have its compensations. It may supply a nation with a learned aristocracy, with a host of grandees whose lives are great and powerful examples of high and unstained morality. It may intercept the distribution of wealth only in order to supply conspicuous proofs of the way in which its accumulation may be beneficently employed. It may offer the leisure needed for the acquisition of political wisdom, and by giving abundant opportunity for the highest employments of the human mind, may be the means of imparting instruction to the world on the true duties of rulers and nations. But as the custom is opposed to natural morality, proof should be given of these benefits.

If, therefore, a government interferes with the liberty of its subjects it is bound to show cause for the interference. These causes may be summarised as two. I. The protection of the weak against the strong. II. The development of such national powers and resources as could not struggle into usefulness except under such patronage.

CHAPTER XXI.

On the General Principles of Taxation.

MOST students of Political Economy are familiar with those rules of taxation which have been laid down by Adam Smith and have become classical. Briefly stated, they are as follows:—I. 'That the subjects of a State ought to contribute towards the support of the government as nearly as possible in proportion to their respective abilities; that is in proportion to the revenue which they enjoy under the protection of the State.' Adam Smith compares this payment to the expense of managing the estate of a number of joint tenants; who pay to such charges in proportion to the amount of their interests. The illustration is perfectly accurate and is of great significance. II. The tax should be certain and not arbitrary. III. It should be levied at the time at which it is most convenient to pay it. IV. The process of collection should be as inexpensive as possible. This unnecessary expense may occur in four ways: 1. By the number of officials which must needs be employed to collect it. 2. By obstructing particular industries. 3. By ruining those who evade or fail to comply with the conditions of the law. 4. By the vexatious interference of tax-gatherers.

It is plain that this division is not strictly logical, that the first of these rules is the most important, and that it virtually contains all the others. An uncertain or arbitrary tax is unequal. So is an inconvenient tax. A tax which wastes more than it gathers must affect particular persons, i.e. be partial in its operation, for were all taxation of this kind, the ends for which the government imposes and levies a tax would remain unfulfilled. But though the statement is philosophically inexact, it has the advantage of showing the various methods in which an unequal tax becomes unequal, and thereby violates the fundamental principles on which government should be carried on.

A government does a service to its subjects. It protects them, their persons, and their property against fraud and violence at home, and against the aggression of foreign enemies. The defence of private rights cannot be conferred so safely or so cheaply on private persons as it is undertaken by governments. Individuals form exaggerated notions of their rights and their wrongs, and were they left to do themselves justice, would, in the vast majority of cases, do others wrong in the vindication of what they believe to be their rights. Civilised nations are not stirred to war lightly, for public wrongs are distributed, and do not affect all alike. But in the absence of any international police, or supreme court of arbitration, war is resorted to in order to vindicate imagined rights, or to restrain imagined wrongs. It is not easy, however, to prove that a single war which has been undertaken for the last two centuries is capable of a moral justification.

Again, the government of a country affords the protection of law and police, civil and military, much more cheaply than individuals can. The industrial arts of social life would be brought to an end, or at least seriously crippled, if the artisan or the husbandman were under the necessity of perpetually defending himself against aggression. Men rather abandon a calling than continue it under the condition of running the perpetual risk of violence or fraud, and of being constrained to defend themselves against these chances by extraordinary prudence or force. We have seen that the distribution of capital over the world is seriously hampered by the absence of any effectual protection to lenders, when they negotiate business with such countries as do not extend the benefits of civil process to the foreign creditor; and we must acknowledge that one of the greatest benefits which diplomacy could bestow, would be the establishment of an international commercial law.

So great are the advantages derived from the assistance which law gives to the fulfilment of contracts, that the members of civilised communities are willing, if need be, to make personal payment for the benefit by incurring the costs of civil process. They do not hesitate to sacrifice the recovery of their property, and submit to the loss of time involved in prosecuting criminals who are guilty of such offences as are indictable, and in which the wrong done to the individual is forgotten or merged in the greater wrong done to the well-being of the community. In the abstract, since private citizens contribute to the public revenue under the implied contract that the State will, as far as possible, protect them in the enjoyment of life and property, the forcible or fraudulent interruption of this enjoyment should be made good by the State. The defence of costliness in law proceedings, (sufficient precaution being taken against vexatious and frivolous prosecutions,) that were law cheap, lawsuits would be enormously multiplied, was well met by Bentham when he pointed out that the very fact of a citizen being constrained to remedy himself in a court of law is a proof that the organisation of civil society is incomplete for the purposes of protection, and that, therefore, the aggrieved person has a right to compensation. In some cases, as, for example, loss of property during such disturbances as constitute, in legal language, riot, compensation is sometimes awarded by law to the sufferers.

The collection of a revenue then, in other words, the legal abstraction from each individual, according to some proportion or other, of a part of that which he would otherwise enjoy at his own discretion, is justified on the principle of the division of labour. A government does a service more cheaply, more effectually, more justly than the individual could perform it for himself. It can do this only by claiming a portion of each person's resources. It perpetually defends the claim on the plea of the value which must be assigned to the service done. The policy of a government stands or falls as it substantiates its assertion that it has acted and is acting for the public good. If it fails to make this out, it may coerce criticism, but it has ceased to be a government. It is treating its subjects as an inheritance, as the property of the ruler, as the dupes of an adventurer, or as the slaves of a despot. When a people is in such a condition, it must either be content to become demoralised or it will reverse the policy of its rulers.

It is admitted on all hands that taxation should be equitable. It should be determined, says Adam Smith, according to the amount of revenue which each person enjoys under the protection of the State. If it were determined by the comparative protection accorded to individuals, it is plain that women and children should pay a higher rate than strong and healthy adults, since they have more need of assistance; and, if the law be effectual, get more. In fact such was the theory of medieval finance. The lord protected his vassal; the vassal assisted his lord by his service or by his purse. But minors under the English military tenures, and women under some forms of the feudal assize, were in the hands of guardians, who were enabled to take the rents or profits of their estates, without account, during legal incapacity. The reason given was, that there was no reciprocity of service in these cases, and the plea might be justified because, in an age of violence, weakness taxes the energies of defence more than it excites the sentiment of pity. A more generous and less utilitarian theory has gradually prevailed. It is held that for practical purposes, and under the conditions of organised society, the strongest is too much indebted to the security which a wise and just government gives, to allow any such comparison between his condition and the condition of the weakest, as shall tend to lay a heavier impost on the latter.

Taxation then, to be equitable, should be determined according to the amount of revenue which each person enjoys. What is this revenue, and to what extent is the revenue which a person receives available for his personal enjoyment?

A man's revenue is not his capital, but the profit on his capital. His gross wages are not his revenue, for, as we have seen above, part of the total sum receivable under the circumstances of competition for the supply of services, as compensation for these services, is paid for maintaining the instrument by which the service is rendered, i.e. the life and health of the agent; part is insurance against risk; part a payment of the nature of a sinking fund, replacing the capital which is invested in the agent, and is gradually being worn out. It is confiscation to levy a tax on that which a man cannot save. We have seen that these constituents must be satisfied in the case of those subordinate animal or mechanical forces by which man assists his own labour, and that no person would reckon the whole of the product of a steam-engine or the whole work of a horse as net profit, but would have to consider the above-named quantities as deductions from such profit. He cannot ignore them in his own case. The only profit which he can recognise in his wages, or whatever else be the name which he gives to the remuneration of his own services, is that portion of the sum receivable, which is due as interest on the capital originally invested in making him fit for his employment, or has been subsequently accumulated in his professional reputation or improved powers of labour. The profit contained in wages, in short, is interest or rent, on the outlay of capital.

Nor can we call that revenue which a man receives but cannot personally enjoy. If a man is liable to the maintenance of children, whom he brings up in such a position as to enable them to labour and take his place after him, he does not enjoy his revenue, but invests it productively in the education or training of life for the purpose of labour. He has, it is true, no lien on the capital which he has invested in the maintenance of his children, for the usages of modern society do not recognise any such property in a parent; but he has, when the case is considered in its economical bearings, and on the hypothesis that the labour which he has reared is in demand, as surely invested capital productively as if he had laid out a part of his earnings in a drove of cattle, in a workshop full of machinery, in draining an estate, or in any other form which implies an addition to the stock of useful objects or useful forces in existence. Of course, if it be taken for granted, that labour is already redundant, and that the adult population is excessive, the existence and the maintenance of children may be conceived to be at the best a matter of private interest, or even the calling into being of a number of persons for whom the world has neither need nor room; but as long as men can emigrate, and until the earth is occupied, the dread of over-population is a vague fear, and in any case, the maintenance and education of children is an investment of capital.

If we take revenue, therefore, in its strictest sense, and conceive that only to be a man's revenue which is devoted to his personal enjoyment, under the protection of the State; and further conclude that this revenue, when strictly limited in the sense which I have given it, is alone properly liable to taxation; it will be clear that the necessary maintenance of the labourer, his investments while they are being made but are as yet unproductive, and such payments as represent insurance against the risks of sickness and the certainty of death, are not legitimately liable to taxation, because they are not a productive employment of his capital or labour.

This theory of the object on which an impost may be levied, is to some extent recognised in the income-tax. Incomes below a certain sum are untouched, below another limit are only partially visited, and all who are liable may deduct a certain amount for life-insurances actually effected. The first of these exemptions recognises that the bare maintenance of the labourer is no part of the profit of labour, though even to be roughly equitable it should be extended to all industrial incomes alike; the second acknowledges that the capital sum expended for making the labourer fit for his work should be replaced. Of course however, if the investment destined to replace the wear and tear of labour be taxed when it is saved, and taxed while it is being invested, all appearance of equity passes away. Now, I repeat, that as far as the aggregate of public wealth is considered, such a replacement is equally effected, whether the recipient of income devotes some of his savings to insurance, or employs them more wisely and productively in educating his children.

These facts are not alleged with a view to inferring that a system of taxation which levies unequal imposts on equal revenues is essentially vicious; for such an evil may be inevitable, but to show what would be the true incidence of a tax which exactly fulfilled Adam Smith's condition, and also what should be, as far as possible, before the mind of a financier when he imposes or adjusts taxes. That which cannot be cured may be palliated.

All taxation either diminishes the enjoyments of those who pay it, or appropriates part of their savings. It cannot, in the long run, take away from that part of a man's income which is needed for his maintenance. In such a case, the source of the tax would be extinguished. There are persons who may be constrained to say, 'If we pay we starve.' Their existence may be so near the margin of bare subsistence, and the food they live on may be so cheap and scanty, that they may be wholly unable to contribute any portion of their income to fiscal purposes. I cannot quote any example of such a class of persons, but it is said that many millions of the inhabitants of the Indian peninsula are nearly in such a condition, and that the salt tax is the only impost which will reach them.

The margin, therefore, from which taxation can be procured, increases with the increase of a nation's enjoyments, and by the excess of these enjoyments over the necessaries of life. The rate of taxation per head levied on the inhabitants of Australia is much greater than that levied on the population of the United Kingdom. The public expenditure may be extravagant and unnecessary; but its incidence is much lighter, as food is cheap and wages are high. The same facts apply to taxation in the United States. It is possible, to judge from the present course of events it is probable, that the fiscal system of the Union is a violation of every one of the rules laid down by Adam Smith, and endorsed by almost all economists. But the mischief is not so ruinous as the adoption of similar expedients would be, in a country possessing a denser population, and therefore fewer unappropriated resources.

Again, taxation is borne much more easily when wealth is distributed. In India a few persons possess much wealth. The impression which the glitter of such wealth induced on the imagination of the first visitors of India was very slowly effaced. In time it was found out that the people was in the aggregate poor, that the mass of the population was sunk in squalid misery. The wealth of Great Britain, though some portions of it are accumulated in a few hands, and particular classes of the community are thereupon depressed, is fairly distributed; the fiscal reforms of the last twenty-five years having greatly contributed to such a result. As a consequence, that part of the public revenue is most buoyant which is derived from the consumption of the mass of the people. In the thirty-four years from 1840 to 1873, the reductions of taxation were computed at nearly £25,000,000 of annual impost. But the revenue raised in 1874 was £15,000,000 in excess of that raised in 1851. The explanation is to be found in the enormous increase of the customs, that is, in the taxes paid for the use of common comforts or luxuries, which a series of prudent changes has brought more and more within the reach of a great part of the community.

I have observed that taxes are generally levied on enjoyments. But they may be levied on capital, that is, they may take away part of an individual's savings. Yet it cannot be generally laid down that a tax has the former or the latter incidence, for the appropriation of any resources which an individual obtains is matter of private judgment and action. He may at his discretion spend or save what he gets.

It is generally assumed, if a tax is likely to be levied on capital, that it is a bad tax; and on this ground Mr. Ricardo objected to legacy duties. But apart from the impossibility of determining what will be the incidence of the tax in particular cases, it does not follow that a tax which appropriates part of private capital is a public evil. The resources of the individual are doubtlessly diminished; it does not follow that the resources of the community will be. The State may employ the proceeds of the tax in public works, and may add by these means far more to the public wealth, than the persons from whom the capital is taken could have possibly added. The State may consume the proceeds unproductively in the maintenance of soldiers. But the original possessor might have also employed it as unproductively in the manufacture of luxuries to be consumed at home. In the hands of the State, it has distributed greater benefits than it would have in the hands of its original owner, for it has increased the occupation of the commoner kinds of labour.

If therefore the people at large suffers in no degree, but rather benefits by such an appropriation of capital, the particular instance is one in which every condition of equitable taxation seems to be satisfied. It is only by municipal law that a person is able to dispose of his property by will. The heir or legatee enters upon that which he has never laboured for, in which he has no property, or at best only an expectation of property. The law which allows testamentary disposition, can justly claim something for its concession; the recipient of the legacy, who is entering upon increased resources, can easily bear the deduction from his new acquisition. The only limit of such an impost is suggested by the risk which this source of public income would run, if the tax were so high as to induce a general evasion of it by a *donatio inter vivos*, or the erection of a fictitious obligation, of which the legacy would be a quittance. The contingency of such a risk seems to have dictated that graduated scale of legacy duties, in which the impost varies with the proximity of relationship between the testator and the legatee. The risk of this evasion is not imaginary. Some years ago, a penurious nobleman granted all his personal estate to his son, reserving to himself an annuity, with the secret purpose of defeating the legacy duties. The expedient failed, for the son became a lunatic and died. The father therefore inherited his own estate, and had to pay legacy duty on it, besides the additional charges incurred for the administration of an intestate person's effects. Ultimately, on the nobleman's decease, the same estate paid legacy duty again.

Of all taxes the worst are those levied on raw materials; i.e. on such goods as are not available for consumption until they have undergone further manipulation, or those goods the consumption of which is necessary for some industrial process. Thus, for example, a tax levied on raw cotton is of the former kind, a tax levied on coal used for the purpose of putting machinery in motion is of the latter. A similar tax is that levied on food required for the maintenance of productive labour.

These taxes violate Adam Smith's fourth rule. They take out of the pocket of the consumer more than they put into the coffers of the State. They add to the cost of production in the first stage of the process, and by increasing the capital needed for supplying the object in question, accumulate a charge on the consumer. If a tax of two-pence a pound were levied on raw cotton, the increase in the price of a pound weight of cotton cloth would be much more than the amount of the tax. A tax on food, moreover, depresses the condition of the labourer. It creates, says Adam Smith, an artificial barrenness.

When a tax is imposed on any article which is imported from abroad, and is produced untaxed at home, the whole which is consumed will pay the tax. If the product is agricultural, the tax will be added to the rent of land. Thus, for example, foreign corn up to 1869 paid a shilling a quarter, on importation. If, in order to maintain the population of the United Kingdom, 25,000,000 quarters of wheat were needed, and 5,000,000 were imported, the government got £250,000 by the tax, the landowner £1,250,000. The same kind of gain was obtained from the importation of other kinds of grain. The whole however of this benefit would not accrue to the landowner in case the power possessed by the public of purchasing other kinds of agricultural produce be curtailed by the charge. But as the tax when distributed is very small, it is probable that the saving was effected in the consumption of luxuries, and that the landowner reaped the whole benefit of this fiscal operation. This incidence of an impost on corn or any similar product, can be obviated only by an equivalent excise, or by a land tax equal in amount to the average quantity of the produce, whose price has been thus exceptionally exalted. If the product is a manufacture, the price will equally rise by the imposition of the tax, but the benefit, if any, which results from the protective duty, will be distributed among all the manufacturers, and ultimately among all capitalists, by the competition of producers.

When a tax is imposed on an export, the tax may be paid by the consuming country; but only if it cannot dispense with the article, cannot get it from any other source, and cannot substitute anything else for it. When either of these ways of escape is open, the effect of the tax will be to diminish the quantity exported, and to visit with exclusion from the market those regions in the exporting country which were only just able to bring their produce to port before the tax was levied.

The power of transferring a tax from the person who actually pays it to some other person, varies with the object taxed. A tax on rents cannot be transferred. A tax on real profits cannot be transferred, though a tax on what is popularly called profits may be. A tax on commodities is always transferred to the consumer, and some such taxes, as I have said above, will be multiplied in the process of taxation, for the producer is merely an agent for the consumer. A tax on labour will generally be paid by the person who employs the labour. But it may, as we shall see, check or discourage the employment of labour. The incidence of a tax on the occupier varies with the nature of the occupation. If the occupation is economical or productive, i. e. if the occupier considers his rent as part of the capital engaged in his business, he reckons his outgoings, and making his bargain for occupation accordingly, transfers his tax to the landowner. If, however, his occupation is part of his expenditure only, he has by no means an equal opportunity of transferring his tax. Thus, for example, a farmer deducts poor rates, &c. from his rent. But the ordinary tenant of a house pays them himself. The same rule holds good in the case of local taxes for permanent improvements.

CHAPTER XXII.

Direct and Indirect Taxation.

THE greater part of the taxes raised in this and in most other civilised countries are known as indirect. They consist in the levy of imposts on articles of consumption, and in general, as good sense and public morality have reformed the fiscal system of the United Kingdom, the impost on such commodities as are not absolutely necessary for subsistence, and are therefore more or less of voluntary use. To this rule there are two notable exceptions, one of which has been several times alluded to,—the tax on imported corn. The personal contribution however which each member of the population makes to this tax is small. The other is the tax on sugar and saccharine matters, which is much more considerable. The rest of these indirect taxes are levied on articles of luxury, or on such comforts as may be used or relinquished at discretion.

The amount of indirect taxation which is now (1874) raised in the United Kingdom for imperial purposes, as compared with that which is direct, is as 47 to 30.

Direct taxes are either derived from income or property. Of the former kind are taxes on wages, rents, and profits, and some stamp duties, as those on insurance, bills, notes, and drafts. Of the latter are stamps on deeds, on probates of wills, on legacies and successions.

In most countries, a tax on the rent of land forms a notable item in the revenue receipts. In the United Kingdom it is included in the income-tax, the so-called land-tax being a rent issuing from the land, invariable, redeemable, and wholly disproportionate to the present value of the property from which it is derived.

In addition to those taxes which form the imperial revenue, and are annually voted and appropriated in parliament, a considerable sum is raised by local authority, and for local purposes. Most of these taxes however are either directly productive, as those which are devoted to the formation and repair of roads, bridges, and drains, or operate as a rate in aid of wages, as for example the poor-rate. Some, as the payments made on behalf of the county constabulary and lunatic-asylums, are contributions to the general purposes of police and protection.

The systems of direct and indirect taxation have each their advocates. Under the latter kind of method, a large revenue is easily collected. When the tax applies only to a few objects, all of which are largely consumed, the machinery for gathering the tax is comparatively simple and inexpensive, amounting to about four per cent. of the total sum raised. The tax being for the most part levied on objects of voluntary use, no one can complain that the tax is oppressive, though the incidence is unequal; as persons who should contribute to that revenue which is expended for the benefit of all, may as far as indirect taxation goes, avoid this duty by omitting the use of the taxed article.

Again, an indirect tax takes as little as possible out of the pockets of the people, over and above that which is paid into the exchequer. When the tax was paid at the moment of importation, the consumer paid much more than the government received, because the dealer, reckoning the tax as part of his capital, and as included in the charge, would, as in the case of taxes on raw material, add interest to the amount of the tax, when he sold the taxed article to the consumer. This liability is obviated to a very great extent by the establishment of bonded warehouses, in which duty-paying goods, whether liable to customs or excise, are stored till they are needed for sale. The result of this provision is that the article pays the tax for as short a time as possible before it is sold for consumption.

The same difficulty however which affects all taxation of revenue, and which has been commented on in the last chapter applies in some degree to these taxes on consumption. Two persons whose revenue is very different in point of continuity may be taxed in equal quantities, but contribute in a very unequal degree. Two persons, who invest the same amount of revenue in very different objects, may be taxed in very different quantities. Most of these unequal charges have been obviated by the general limitation of customs and excise duties to the luxuries of life, and the exemption of its necessaries from any fiscal visitation. But until this system is complete, the tax is unequal. If a labourer, his wife and his three children consume five quarters of wheat annually, they formerly contributed five shillings in indirect taxation, some to the State, most to the landowner. If they consumed twenty pounds of sugar, they paid about fifteen pence more. Another labourer with a wife and five children pays a larger sum in taxation, from equal gross revenue, if we follow the same proportion. The case is still stronger if a portion of one man's revenue is derived from permanent and indestructible sources, the whole of another man's from precarious and terminable sources. Again, when excise duties were levied on bricks and tiles, tile drainage, as an investment of capital, was burdened by a considerable additional cost; brick buildings, where stone was scanty or not to be obtained, were exceptionally chargeable. The consequence in some kinds of trade and manufacture, is to banish them entirely from the country. Thus the manufacture of transparent soap, for which alcohol is requisite, is said to be commercially impossible in the United Kingdom in consequence of the heavy excise-duties on spirits, these duties amounting to ten times the value of the untaxed article.

Another plea for indirect taxation is, that being levied generally on articles of voluntary use, the abuse of which is mischievous or immoral, the process of taxation is conducive to public morality. The argument is quoted to be immediately refuted. The State can hardly teach morality; still less can the tax-gatherer. Expenditure should not be the subject of legislation. The private conduct of men, in so far as it does not reflect on the general good, or on the interests of other persons, must not be matter of censorship. Besides, it is open to grave doubt, whether fiscal regulations, by putting obstacles in the way of enjoyments, do not create the very craving which the interference of law is intended to check. The

Gin Act of the last century, by which a prohibitive tax was imposed on this beverage, led to far greater immorality than a freer system; just as the usury laws, which were intended to check rapacious money-lenders, in reality assisted their machinations. The excuse for any tax at all is, the exigencies of the revenue; the defence for any particular tax is, the lightness of its incidence, or the fact that it does not interfere with the productive energies or the economical tendencies of society.

On the other hand it is asserted, though with no great show of reason, that the existence of a customs' law hinders a country like our own from becoming a free port. The tax on imported corn did doubtlessly hinder this country from being the entrepôt for grain; but only because it was paid even when the corn is re-exported. Now that this tax, for which there was no defence, and to which there was every economical objection, has been repealed, Great Britain will be as much the entrepôt for grain, as it is for the precious metals and for cotton. In all commodities which can be re-exported from bonded warehouses, without the payment of anything but rent for storage, the conditions of a free port are virtually present. The customs and excise system of the United Kingdom, though not theoretically perfect, is nearer the maximum of productiveness to the revenue, and the minimum of loss to producer and consumer, than any similar system adopted by any other nation.

An excise on manufactures is invariably a hindrance to the process. Before the reforms in our fiscal system, excises were levied on every conceivable object. Those on glass, leather, and soap were among the most objectionable. An excise involves constant supervision on the part of the government officer, a right of entry on all occasions, and a right of effectual protest against any process which may possibly be construed into an evasion of the tax. Hence manufactures liable to such visitations, unless the process be exceedingly simple, are with difficulty improved, as is evidenced by the extraordinary activity and success which follow on the remission of such imposts. The duty on glass was repealed in 1844. The price of crown glass, according to Mr. Chance, an eminent glass manufacturer, has fallen to one-seventh of the price at which it was sold before the repeal of the duty; that of plate glass to one-fifth. My reader will see in this example the counterpart of the law of prices mentioned above (p. 194). When the tax was repealed, the greatest fall took place in the cheapest article.

Among these excises, one has been perpetually the subject of attack. This is the tax on malt. The tax is considerable, amounting on an average to rather more than one-half of the value of the raw material. The object of the tax is to levy an impost upon an article used for the manufacture of an alcoholic drink. In proportion to the value of the article manufactured, the tax is far higher than that on wine; very much less than that on spirits. In proportion to the quantity of spirit which is developed by fermentation, the tax on malt is the lightest levied on any alcoholic fluid. It is not however on malt as a fermentable substance that these objections to the excise are mainly founded, but on its use in the economy of agriculture.

The process of malting (that is of partial germination, which is suddenly arrested), changes a portion of the starch contained in the grain into sugar, and when the malt is infused, facilitates the conversion of the rest. The sugar of malt has, it is said, great merits for bringing stock into condition; and it is averred that much of the economy of agriculture is hampered by the excise. In the absence of the tax, it is said that more land would be cropped with barley, and more cattle would be fed on malt.

A series of experiments were instituted by the Board of Trade in the year 1866, with a view to verifying or refuting this notion as to the superior economical value of malt over barley. If we can rely on the report, the result was universally unfavourable, the experiment establishing the fact, that malt was much less valuable than barley for the purposes referred to. It may be added, that from the very nature of rent, no benefit would ensue to the tenant-farmer, if any advantage accrued from the use of malt in place of barley, for everything over and above the cost of production is invariably resolved into rent.

The advocates of direct taxation assert that the system is more just and more cheap; that it is more nearly in accordance with the canon alluded to above, of levying equal rates from equal resources, of closing up the door against any escape which a parsimonious consumer may find, and that it has the advantage of calling the attention of the community to the expenses of government, and thereby of suggesting thrift in the management of public money. There is perhaps but little weight in the latter of these recommendations. Since the time that a larger quantity of the public revenue has been obtained by direct taxation, there is no reason to think that the public has grown more impatient of taxation, or the public service less costly.

An income-tax, to be just, must be a tax on real profits. If it be taken on gross profits, it is, for reasons given before, unequal. The possessor of a permanent income, who gives no labour to the production of his revenue, is in possession of real, or net profits; the possessor of a precarious income, for earning which continual labour or supervision is necessary, is in possession of a sum of gross profits, in which, as I have said, are included the maintenance of labour, and the replacement or insurance of capital. To tax both these incomes at equal rates, is to tax profit only in the former, to tax profit and capital in the latter case. And if the two persons devote a portion of their income to the education of their children, the taxation of this part, is to tax unproductive capital, to tax an investment on which no profit is yet realised. It is to a conviction that an equal tax on permanent and precarious incomes is unjust, that much of the unpopularity of the income-tax is due. I have already shown where the injustice lies. An income-tax cannot be just, except it be a tax on the profits of capital; in the case of a labourer, if it be on the capitalised value of himself as an industrial agent, as he earns net profit; in the case of those who receive fixed incomes, as the recipients of net profit. A little reflection however will show how hard it would be to levy a tax on such net profits when they are held in small quantities, and constitute the sole means of subsistence possessed by the recipients.

In the case of common labour a poll-tax is a form of income-tax. It is unfair, when great part of the earnings of the labourer are devoted to the maintenance of his children; for in this case, there is little left after the sustenance of the labourer and the outlay of capital in the support of his children are supplied. But it could be easily collected. It is imposed in many states of the American Union. It was adopted in a graduated form in the early ages of English financial history, but was dropped after the insurrection of Tyler. In the first poll-tax of Richard the Second, the minimum levied on persons of sixteen years old and upwards was a groat, the maximum, that imposed on the king's uncles, was £8 13s. 4d.

The most convenient form in which a just income-tax could be levied, would be a property-tax, which should include capital invested in productive labourers, i.e. such as work for income, as well as on visibly productive property, allowance being made in the estimate of such property for necessary depreciation. A property-tax has long been familiar in the American Union; and though the assessments to the tax are generally voluntary, the obligation is said to be honourably and fully met. In the United Kingdom, where assessments of real estate are made for the purpose of local or imperial taxation, it is reported that the return is scandalously below the mark. Great mansions are said to be valued at nominal sums, on the plea that they would not let for more, in consequence of the expense entailed on keeping them up. It is impossible to speak too strongly of a concession, which condones vanity and ostentation at the expense of the public purse.

It is a question whether in such assessments to property-tax, furniture, plate, books, pictures, and the like are subjects for valuation. At first sight they do not seem to be productive investments. But they may be and frequently are. A judicious purchaser of pictures, painted by rising artists, will constantly realise, on selling these works of art, many times the amount of his first purchase-money. A gallery of Turner's early paintings might have been once made at small cost, and would now fetch a very large sum. The same fact applies to paintings of the early masters, and to the best specimens of the English school. A similar rise in value is effected by collectors of rare books, of peculiar furniture, of bijouterie, antiquities, and scarce wine. The taxation of such articles, if they increase in value, is manifestly just, for they derive their value from the skill of the purchaser, a skill which brings a profit, and is, economically speaking, capital. The taxation of articles which do not improve, but merely minister to luxury, may be just, but only on the same ground that the taxation of consumption is.

There are one or two peculiar forms of direct taxation, on which a few words may be said. First then for a house-tax. To many persons this seems one of the most obvious kinds of direct taxation, and withal the most just. A house they allege, though necessary, is still, as a rule, proportionate to the income of the occupier, and is thus a means by which he practically assesses himself. I have already observed that the cost of some houses is not considered to be an index of their taxable value. But even in the case of such persons as would not or could not evade the tax, the house is by no means an index of the occupier's income. The premises may be inhabited for business purposes. In some such cases, the house-tax already recognises a difference of liability, though the rule is decided in the wrong way, since the occupation of a shop, as it is a productive outlay of capital, enables the trader to put the tax on his customer, as he does his rent in a fashionable thoroughfare or locality. But the scheme is otherwise imperfect. A physician or lawyer must needs occupy a house in a more prominent position, or a more expensive locality, than an ordinary individual does. To deal between these parties justly, it is necessary that an allowance should be made in the former case, the most obvious method being a deduction of the ground-rent from the annual valuation. Again, it is probable that the outgoings of no business represent so high a percentage on the receipts as school-keeping, particularly of a middle or cheap kind does. A house-tax on such occupiers levied at the same rate as that put on ordinary occupiers, would be, indeed is, exceedingly unfair. In the general competition of occupations, it is possible that the extraordinary charges to which such persons are put, may narrow the field of employment, and so secure a higher average of earnings. But it is certain that a house-tax presses with peculiar severity upon certain callings.

In the case of the poor, a house-tax has special disadvantages. It leads to crowding, to defective sanitary arrangements, and is finally a serious hindrance to an important branch of industry. The old hearth-tax was not only said to be inquisitorial (that is, subjected the occupier to frequent and offensive visits, an objection on which too much stress may be laid), but hindered proper ventilation in chambers. The window-tax, which was a kind of house-tax, involved similar evils or inconveniences. But there can be no reason why, as all classes of the community are protected by the expenditure which government incurs, any considerable class should evade its contribution to a common fund; though there is every reason for imposing such taxes only as can be levied without seriously compromising the moral and material interests of society at large.

Let us take another form of direct taxation, that namely on male servants. When this is a tax on a luxury, it has no other effect than that of checking a particular employment for adult males. A direct tax on luxuries is by no means objectionable. Much, indeed most, of such expenditure is mere ostentation, and the tax-gatherer is really furthering the ends of those who incur the expenditure, and becomes their truest friend and ally, by confining the outlay to a narrower and more select class in society. But such an incidence of certain taxes, suggested at first I believe by Sismondi, is accidental, and if it be turned into an apology for the tax, is misleading. A vast number of persons who use or would use the service of adult males, do so on grounds of economy or necessity. No man's character or reputation would be injured if he blacked his own shoes, brushed his own clothes, groomed his own horse, cleaned his own carriage and harness. Some of these practices are necessary to the discharge of ordinary business in certain professions or trades, some of them are requisites of ordinary decency in civilised life. They are delegated from employers to servants, not because they are necessarily derogatory, but because it would be a waste of time to do them one's-self. If one man's time is worth, one day with another, £5 to him, why should he do that for himself which he can get another man to do for him at a cost of 5s.? The division of labour cannot be carried out satisfactorily, if the law handicaps one kind of labour, and so hinders its employment. That the domestic service of adult males is hindered by the imposition of a considerable assessed-tax on its employment is, I believe, uncontested. But apart from the limitation which the tax puts on a particular branch of industry, certain social inconveniences attend the discouragement of such relations as are implied in the employment of male domestic labour. There is nothing, I believe, which more fully tends to bring about a proper and right understanding between persons in very different ranks of life, than the relative duties of master and servant do, when they are fulfilled on both sides with honesty, consideration, and good manners. The daily intercourse of persons whose early bringing up represents very different degrees of refinement and culture, is sure, if it be properly conducted, to be of great service in developing habits of decorum, order, and the inestimable virtue of self-respect. To some extent a training in the army brings about these results, though the material, in the great majority of cases, is the most unfavourable that could be selected. Nor is it necessary that the relations of domestic service should lead to any sacrifice of honourable independence. On the contrary, it could be constantly made the means by which the poorer classes might learn to attempt a higher standard of life and comfort, and to develope those prudential motives in which they are confessedly so deficient at present.

When a tax is levied on some employments which cannot be dispensed with in the economy of society, the tax is ultimately paid by those who employ the service, or use the commodity on whose production the service is exercised. Thus licences on special trades are paid by customers. The case would be different if all employments without distinction were liable to proportionate licence duties. No person will, under the ordinary conditions which reduce the rate of profit to an equality, enter into a calling which is weighted with a heavy licence duty, unless he makes those who use his services, pay him to the full for the service which he renders. One of the heaviest licences is that levied on the London pawnbrokers. The persons with whom these traders deal are the poorest classes in London, and we may be sure that the tax which government levies, is paid, notwithstanding the regulations which fix the rates of interest payable on pledges, over and over again by those who employ these functionaries. It would be far better for the general public, and even for the revenue, if so wasteful a tax were repealed, and the impost replaced by an *ad valorem* stamp-duty on the pawnbroker's ticket. In short, the existing licence-duties offend against the fourth of Adam Smith's celebrated rules. They either check employment, and deprive the public of a convenient service, or they visit the community at large with an impost, which is far in excess of the amount which the exchequer collects.

To sum up the question. If a system of indirect taxation is to be defended and maintained, it is difficult to find any process by which a larger revenue can be obtained in so legitimate, and with a few exceptions, in so little wasteful a fashion as that which prevails among ourselves. By far the largest part of this revenue is derived from articles of voluntary consumption. From one point of view this fact constitutes the chief merit of the system. From another it is its chief blemish; since persons may evade payment to the revenue by evading the use of the article. But I repeat, it does not, except slightly, affect the use of the necessaries of life, or that investment of capital on which I have several times insisted so strongly, the maintenance and education of the young. On the other hand, direct taxation is never just, unless it be limited to profits on·capital, unless all productive investments of capital are visited by the tax, and therefore, unless the tax extends to all callings and occupations from which a revenue can be derived, the basis of the calculation in the case of income being taken from the capital which an industrial agent may be fairly taken to represent, and the tax levied on the ordinary rate of interest procurable from such an amount. The basis of such an assessment will be found in the income of the labourer.

CHAPTER XXIII.

On Public Debts.

IT is a saying of Macaulay, that monarchs and governments have often got into debt, but that in England at least, the government of the Revolution was the first to acknowledge and pay its obligations. The statement is historically true. The debts of Edward III. were for the time enormous, his creditors being certain Italian houses. The later Plantagenet kings raised loans, under the strange name of benevolences.. These were forbidden by a statute of Richard III. Henry VIII. got deeply into debt, but his complaisant parliaments gave him a formal release from his obligations. James I.

was frequently involved in difficulties. Charles I. robbed the merchants of their specie, Charles II. the goldsmiths. A portion of the latter debt was acknowledged some time after the Revolution, and forms the oldest item in the public debt of Great Britain. This country, however, was not the first to contract a funded debt. The Dutch borrowed sums during their long contests with Spain. These amounted in 1650 to 153,000,000 guilders. In fact, most of the fiscal expedients, which governments have from time to time adopted, were copied from the early financial policy of Holland, as most of the political liberties which nations have obtained were suggested by the heroism of that illustrious commonwealth.

The English public debt grew with great rapidity, whenever this country was involved in foreign war. By the conclusion of William III.'s reign it was £15,730,000. By that of Anne £54,145,000. In the third year of the reign of George III. it reached £138,385,000. On February 1st, 1817, it was £840,850,000. In 1874 it was about £779,000,000. Since the war of 1870, the debt of France has become greater, than that of this country.

The greater part, if not the whole of the British debt has been contracted for purposes which are technically called unproductive. To use familiar language, there is nothing to show for the expenditure. Governments have sometimes, especially in our own day, borrowed money for the purpose of accomplishing important public works, particularly railways. Such loans are productive, that is, are sources of annual revenue or advantage. The outlay on such objects, provided they are remunerative, does not differ practically from any other investment of capital; the sole difference being that they are due to public instead of to private enterprise.

When we say, however, that the whole, or nearly the whole, of the public debt of Great Britain has been expended on unproductive objects, the term is not used with any intention of adverse criticism. The costs incurred by the several wars, part of the expenditure of which is comprised in the several additions to the public debts, may have been necessary to the security of the national existence. It is better to consume some part of the public wealth unproductively, than to lose all. A nation cannot be indifferent to its defence, its reputation, its honour. The best sacrifice which it can make, even if we take the harshest economical estimate of such sacrifices, is that which it makes in order to secure its integrity. Just as an honourable merchant must put up with loss, in order to keep his credit unimpeached, so must a nation be jealous in the defence of its public character. Whether or no the wars into which this nation has entered have been necessary or even expedient, is another question, which we need not discuss.

It is necessary to advert to the fact, because even if the cost of war in past generations could be shown, not only to have been unnecessary, on the plainest grounds of public morality and justice, but to have been, to take the strongest case, unwarrantable attempts at unsuccessful aggrandisement, and if we could add that they were entered on with a full knowledge on the part of those who engaged in them, that they were capable neither of justification nor apology; we should not be relieved from the obligation involved in the creation of debt. In the language of lawyers, an heir is liable to the debts of his ancestor, if the assets of the inheritance are sufficient to defray the debts. The ancestor may have created these obligations by reckless or immoral expenditure. If the debts exceed the assets, no such over-burdened inheritance would be accepted. It is true that we have accepted a great debt, a debt the liquidation of which is as yet an unattainable aim, but we should take care in calculating the liabilities which our ancestry have put upon us, to make an estimate of the estate which they have bequeathed us. Nay more, the fact that the nation or the great part of the nation did not formally enter into the obligation is no quittance. We can escape from the liability, only if we can show that we have no share in the inheritance, and the only way in which we can prove that we have no share, is by removing ourselves from the political institutions under which these liabilities were contracted. As long as we reside in the country, we tacitly, but effectually acknowledge our personal and proportionate liability to the public engagements of the nation.

It would not be difficult to enumerate some items of that great inheritance which the accumulated industry and intelligence of past generations have conferred on the present occupants of the soil, the constitution, the traditions, the history of Great Britain, and which are shared, though in very varying proportions, by those who inhabit these islands.

The British nation has never committed a breach of public faith. But it has been once very near the offence, an offence which, I have already said, is never forgiven. For a certain period of the present century, the Bank of England, whose notes were a legal tender, was empowered to refuse cash for its notes. For some years, the issues of the Bank were managed so prudently that the note was not depreciated. In course of time however the Bank made excessive issues, and for intelligible and inevitable causes, the note was depreciated. In April 1815, the one pound bank note was worth only 14s. 5d., i.e. a person who offered gold, weighing a sovereign, got a bank note and 5s. 7d. in silver for it. It is almost unnecessary to say, that prices rose proportionately, and that persons became gradually habituated to the difference between the nominal and real prices of articles. They bought and sold in notes, reckoned values by notes, and made bargains, some of them of a permanent character, in this depreciated paper.

Now when a general and permanent rise in prices has been effected, in consequence of an artificial depreciation of the currency, it is exceedingly difficult to restore that currency, and thereupon to reduce prices to their proper level. It is easy enough for the merchant or wholesale dealer to do so, for these people never value a currency at more than its worth. But it is very difficult to accommodate the alteration or restoration to retail trade, to contracts already entered into, and above all to labour prices; because all these matters are settled to a great extent by custom and to a far less extent by competition; contracts of course bring special arrangements. A rise in the value of money would then disturb prices, would make labour very much dearer, unless early advantage could be taken of the change, and would put the debtor in a contract in a position of serious disadvantage as regards the lender. The difficulty of dealing with such a condition of things is so enormous, that hardly any government has had the courage to make the restoration fully and peacefully, though sometimes the discredited paper, and the obligations it has expressed, have been violently swept away, as was done with the *assignats* and *mandats* of the French revolution. Generally however the differences between paper and money have been permanently established, as is the case in many European states.

Difficulties like those which affected the restoration of the paper currency which was issued by the Bank of England during the great Continental war, to its real as well to its nominal value in specie, exist at the present time, but in an exaggerated form, in the United States. The issues of the Bank of England were those of a private corporation; those of the United States are treasury notes, and are the liabilities of the nation. If the honour of the United States be saved, and its notes be redeemed at par, a contingency which public opinion has (1875) lately rendered probable, this honour will be saved by the righteous and just fulfilment of public duties to the public creditor. If the republican government maintains its promise to pay the interest on its public debt in gold, it will be possible to reduce, and ultimately extinguish, the discount on its paper; if it breaks faith with the public creditor, it will, whenever it resumes cash payments and issues strictly convertible paper, be strongly, perhaps irresistibly tempted to reduce the amount of bullion in its unit of currency. It can have no motive in disturbing the arrangements under which home trade is carried on and home prices have been settled, if it once takes the step of repudiating any part of its obligations towards those who have lent it money. The former step is easy, and if prices are accommodated to the depreciated paper currency, the process by which nominal values in paper are replaced by equivalent values in specie, is simple, obvious, and convenient. If a number of persons are accustomed to pay in paper, which as compared with gold is at a discount of twenty-five per cent.; all that is meant by such a discount, when the paper is used for purposes of internal trade, is that fifteen shillings in gold is worth as much as twenty shillings in paper. Supposing the discount is an invariable quantity, the simplest resumption of cash payments would be to issue pieces of money, called dollars, as before, and to take care that they contained exactly three-fourths in quantity of the old unit of currency. Such a process would be nothing more than a general ratification of the existing state of things, and would affect adversely neither home nor foreign trade. It would do neither good nor harm to any creditors or debtors, who have entered into contracts which are strictly relevant to the depreciated paper. Of course, however, it would reduce the public debt by exactly the same amount as the discount on paper, and the subsequent issue of coins corresponding to this discount, signify. But, a matter which is perhaps worth considering, it would render the negotiation of fresh loans almost impossible in the home or foreign market; for the public creditor, though powerless against violence, bears a long memory, and inextinguishable malice against those who have defrauded him, a malice which no moralist would condemn.

The expedient of an issue of government notes bearing interest, to be subsequently capitalised into a funded debt, has been customary with the financiers of the United States, whenever the country has been engaged in war.

It has its advantages, for it is a ready means of distributing the debt, without employing the services of loanmongers, especially when, as was the case during the late war, the notes issued by the government were made legal tender, and gold was accumulated in the government treasury. With these notes, the government paid wages, bought stores, and provided munitions of war, the notes flowing back through the banks, and being, as occasion arose, capitalised into a permanent debt, much of which was exported in the shape of securities to Europe. But it has greater disadvantages. The depreciated currency is issued in small parcels, and in indefinite quantities. It seriously affects prices, wages, and, subsequently, production; the latter because the fluctuations of the notes are part of the risks of the producer, and like all risks, must be provided against; the former, because both accommodate themselves to the altered currency. But worst of all, the longer such a currency is in circulation, the more difficult it is to contract it, for its restoration involves inevitable loss and confusion to some persons. Hence the attempt to gradually contract the paper currency was restrained by act of Congress in the year 1868, though later acts of the American parliament had indicated a resolution to maintain that character for public integrity which the Union has always possessed. But the effect of a paper currency on rates of wages in the United States was indicated by the report on wages furnished by Mr. Young in 1869.

During the suspension of cash payments by the Bank of England, the legislature had regularly provided, as it prolonged the suspension, that cash payments should be resumed within six months after a definite treaty of peace was signed. Shortly after the battle of Waterloo, such a treaty was signed, and the Bank, though the time was again prolonged, prepared to meet its obligations. Circumstances, however, prevented the completion of this plan, and the resumption of cash payments was postponed till 1821.

But the resumption of cash payments was effected in the face of serious difficulties. The whole business of the country had accommodated itself to the altered currency. Leases had been signed, in which rents were calculated in paper. The prudent proviso of Lord King, by which rents were reserved in gold, or in notes at the rate of exchange with gold, had been nullified by the foolish resolutions of Lord Stanhope and Mr. Vansittart, resolutions which were accepted by the Houses of Parliament, the purport of which was, that although the note was at a discount, the currency was not depreciated, or in the jargon of the time, that paper was not cheaper, but gold was dearer. General prices also had accommodated themselves to the depreciated paper. The debt too, interest on which had been paid in paper during the suspension, was enormous, and many persons thought that it would be a perfectly just and legitimate operation, considering that so large a part of this debt had been contracted in paper, if it were to be hereafter treated at its paper, and not at its nominal amount. Had this scheme been adopted, the public debt of the United Kingdom would have stood at £600,000,000 instead of £800,000,000 or thereabouts. It would still have been reckoned at the latter sum, but it would have required the weight of only the former sum in sovereigns in order to redeem the latter sum; or, in other words, taking the whole debt as consols, the weight of gold contained in £18,000,000 sovereigns, would have sufficed to pay £24,000,000 of annual interest.

The country was hardly saved the disgrace of repudiation, with those consequences which are sure to ensue from such dishonesty. It was answered, that what might be said of that part of the public debt, which had been created in a depreciated paper, was an argument, whatever might be its worth, which could have no relevancy to that portion which had been lent in gold, or in paper at par, and that this was the largest portion of the debt. If it were said that the purchasers of old stocks had been habituated to a tax of twenty-five per cent. on their dividends, and that the value of the stock had accommodated itself to this impost, it was answered, that stocks were created and transferred, on the distinct understanding, that cash payments should be resumed within six months after a definitive treaty of peace had been signed, and that a delay in doing justice is no plea for permanent robbery. During the period in which the rate was depreciated, the holders of public securities were losers. Was it just, then, that they who had been mulcted, because it was inconvenient or impossible for the State to discuss or adjust their claims, should, in the face of repeated protestations and assurances, be defrauded of their due when it became possible to consider the position?

I have dwelt at length on these financial operations, partly because they form an illustration of the consequences which ensue when a government paper is issued on securities, and becomes, in the inevitable course of events, depreciated; partly because the perils which beset the British fund-holder between 1815–20, reappeared in the United States after the wars of 1860-65. There is indeed no danger that any rational English economist will now endorse the arguments which, fifty years ago, nearly made shipwreck of British integrity. It is probable that at the present time, the cautious inferences of experience and forethought are developing that joint system of a metallic and subsidiary currency which secures the maximum of convenience with the minimum of risk. But the theories of 1815-20 are not extinct, and there always will be a class of enthusiasts or adventurers, who, taking advantage of the fact, that an enlarged subsidiary currency, whatever be its basis, supplies at first a great stimulus to mercantile and manufacturing enterprise, will invite the adoption of a plan which assuredly ends in commercial bankruptcy, and may involve a national repudiation.

Here it will be desirable to point out the process by which the greater part of the public debt of Great Britain was created. It must not be supposed that the sum (£779,000,000) at which it is now computed was received for the public service. It has been calculated by Mr. Macculloch that the amount actually received was £200,000,000 less than the sum to which the fund-holder is credited. If the operation of the old sinking fund be also taken into account, the sum, according to the same authority, will be found to represent £300,000,000 more than the money really borrowed. (Macculloch on Taxation and the Funding System, p. 445.)

There are two ways in which a perpetual debt may be created. The borrower may raise the sum needed, either by varying the amount of interest, or by varying the amount of the principal. Thus if a government wishes to get a sum of money, it may fix the sum and invite tenders for the lowest amount of interest at which borrowers will be willing to make the loan. Or it may fix the rate of interest, and invite borrowers to subscribe for stock at the highest amount which they may be willing to pay for the stock. Both these methods of borrowing have been adopted at various periods of English financial history. The latter however, which was begun as early as the reign of Anne, became general after the war which ended with the peace of Aix-la-Chapelle, and has been all but universal ever since.

There is a manifest disadvantage in the customary system. When it is adopted on a large scale, it is all but impossible to reduce the amount of interest by any subsequent financial operation; and when permanent annuities are dealt with, a reduction of the rate of interest is equivalent to a reduction of the public debt. Some of the old stocks were created at ten per cent., and others at sums varying from this high rate to the ordinary rate of consols. In course of time, the government has been able to take advantage of accumulations of capital seeking investment, and to lower these high rates to the lowest sums which will be taken, the option of receiving the principal being of course offered to the public creditor. When however the rate of interest is set so low as to be, except under very rare circumstances, the minimum at which persons will lend, the possibility of reducing the tax is exceedingly improbable. The improbability amounts to an impossibility when the gross amount of the fund is very large.

Of the whole sum known familiarly as consols, only a very small portion is ordinarily in the market. What this portion is, can only be guessed, for we have no statistics, as far as I am aware, of the actual transfers of public stock. But it is clear that while the saleable value of consols at any given time is relevant to the amount ordinarily in the market, and the average value in any year to the average amount of sellers and buyers; a far larger amount of the fund would be affected by any great financial operation; and the resistance to or dissent from a diminution in the rate of interest would involve a far larger number of persons than are buying or selling from day to day, or from year to year.

But on the other hand, the system is said to have its advantages. It is averred that the government, at the time of making the loan, when of course, by the very fact that a loan is negotiated, it is admitted that the resources of the ordinary revenue are insufficient for the emergency, borrows on better terms than it would if it attempted to borrow a fixed sum at a varying rate of interest. Some persons have gone so far as to assert that large loans upon the latter plan would not be negotiated at all, or at least would have been negotiated on such unsatisfactory terms, that the aggregate loss in interest would be fully equal to the permanent excess of the lower rate, when taken over a space of years; and that in short the best course was adopted, not only for the immediate exigency, but for posterity. It is possible, exaggerated as this view appears, that had the creation of a series of small funds, all bearing different rates of interest, been adopted, the risk of a reduction in the rate, when such sums reached or exceeded par, would have hindered the possibility of reducing the rate of interest to a greater extent than persons who argue in favour of the creation of such stocks believe. The market value of small stocks is always less, the security being otherwise equal, than that of larger masses of public debt. It is also alleged that the larger fund is better and more strongly held by such persons or corporations as invest habitually in public securities, than any less fund would be.

I have observed that the only way in which debt could be extinguished was by a surplus of revenue over expenditure. But for many years financiers imagined that it was possible to extinguish the debt, by borrowing money annually, by putting it into the hands of commissioners appointed for the purpose, and by 'adding annually the interest received on this portion, so as, it was hoped, to make, under the beneficent operation of compound interest, the sinking fund finally absorb the debt. The author of this scheme, an arithmetician named Price (who intended that the fund should be derived from an excess of income over expenditure, and is therefore not answerable for the loans which constituted the fund in later times), induced the younger Pitt to adopt and continue such a plan. To enforce his reasonings, Mr. Price gave the results of certain calculations, the effect of which was to prove, that a penny put out at compound interest, at the commencement of our era, would amount after eighteen centuries to several globes' bigness of gold. A surplus of revenue may be employed in the purchase of public debt. This purchase may be retained in the hands of a body of trustees, and the interest added to it, so as in course of time to absorb a large amount of the debt. But such a process necessitates the continuous maintenance of revenue over expenditure; the only way in which, as I have said already, debts can be extinguished. The annual purchases of stock, the annual interest on stock, must be derived from the proceeds of taxation. But to retain stock in the hands of a body of trustees, in place of extinguishing debt by purchasing stock, as a surplus can be employed for the purpose, is to saddle the operation of extinction with the costs of an office.

But it is desirable to extinguish the public debt for various reasons. As I have already said, taxation is either a burden on the capital of those who pay it, or a curtailment of their enjoyments. If it be the former, they who are liable to such an impost are likely, in the production of comparative wealth, to fall behind other countries, behind such at least as are less weighted in the race. If it be the latter, the emigration of labour and capital to regions where it can escape from such diminutions of its resources, is a mere question of time. Men save to spend, and even if they save for profit, they contemplate subsistence or enjoyment on that profit. The day in which this impulse will stimulate emigration to seek places in which taxation is less oppressive seems nearer. It is apparently farther off than it was, when at the close of the great Continental war, the load of debt was enormous, and the distress which it caused was general. But on the other hand, though the resources of the nation, and by implication its power of bearing taxation, have greatly increased, it must be remembered that the power of transferring capital and labour from heavily to lightly taxed regions, has increased in greater proportion; the intelligence which understands the escape from financial burdens is more general. As the conditions under which society is constituted, and wealth is distributed, become more and more plain, the distribution of society itself will be effected with increasing rapidity.

Again, it has been alleged, and with great show of reason, that the industrial powers of this country are the chief source of its wealth, and that these industrial powers depend upon the continued supply of a particular mineral, the quantity of which is limited. It does not indeed follow that the wealth of the United Kingdom would be seriously or at least fatally compromised, if it were to fall behind other nations in consequence of the increasing dearness of this raw material of motion. At present, it is true, heat is the most familiar motive power, but it does not follow that other forces may not be discovered. The cheapness of any object is constantly a bar to the substitution of any equivalent, and it has happened more than once that extraordinary scarcity or dearness has been a spur to very active discovery or invention. Even if Great Britain lost her manufacturing supremacy, she might compensate these losses by increasing mercantile activity.

In effect however, even if Great Britain depended absolutely on her coal supplies for her economical position, it is easy to anticipate the steps by which much saving would be made in consumption. Already the economy of fuel has been carried to great lengths, in certain branches of industry. It is said, for example, that it does not take one tenth part of the amount of coal once used in the process, in order to smelt cast iron, and we may be quite sure, that as coal gets dearer, every effort will be made to diminish the cost of production, and that ultimately, as the scarcity increases, some of those coarser operations, which consume great quantities of coal, as the smelting of the common metals, will be transferred to other regions where coal is cheaper. The conditions of holding a place in the market of the world are so closely related to the costs of production and the competition of purchasers, that due warning must needs be given before the dearness of coal affects British industry, by making it impossible to satisfy demand more cheaply than other nations can.

It is another question whether an artificial dearness should not be put upon the supply of the mineral, either by prohibiting its exportation, and limiting the quantity which is extracted from the earth, or by taxing the rents of mines; the proceeds of such taxation being employed in liquidating portions of the public debt. Where corporations hold mines, it is a rule of law, that a certain portion of the rent derivable from such mines must be saved from annual income, because the income itself is terminable. It may be urged, that the nation should check the exhaustion of its resources; not by denying the usufruct of the soil to the private owner, but by providing that a part of these limited and separable properties of land should be devoted to extinguishing that, on whose behalf all the land is pledged; that the capital value of the soil should not be exhausted, nor in the language of law, waste committed, except compensation be made in some shape or other, for the depreciation of the national resources. The question however, whether such a tax should be levied in order to cover permanent loss, lies more in the province of the jurist than in that of the economist.

There yet remains a question. What is the security of national debts? What is the real pledge which a government gives when it borrows? Unless it placed an embargo on the exportation of capital, an expedient which no one would dream of, at least in these days, it has not pledged any portion of that wealth which can be carried out of the country. Unless it similarly prohibited emigration, it could not pledge the labour of the country to the liquidation of permanent obligations. It may put upon the profits of capital and the wages of labour the condition of contributing towards the satisfaction of the public faith, as long as capital and labour reside in the country, just as fairly as it may levy a tax for those working expenses of government, the benefit of which reverts, or is supposed to revert, immediately to the taxpayer. It remains then that the ultimate pledge given as a security for public debts is land, and capital fixed upon land, and that the repayment of the principal of the public debt would be the release of land from an obligation, to which it is none the less liable, because the annual incidence of the obligation has been shifted to other kinds of property.

INDEX.

A.

Agricultural labourers, trades-union of, would affect rent, p. 91; causes why they find it hard to combine to raise wages, 93.

Agriculture, labour in, superseded by machinery, 131; growth of, in the 14th century, 158; what kinds of, best effected by small cultivation, 174.

Alcohol, needed to manufacture transparent soap, 290.

Ale-taster, functions of, 268.

Allowance, system of, its effects, 124.

Antiquity, trade of, unrecorded, 246.

Appropriation, necessary condition of value, 6.

Archimedes, story of, 32.

Aristophanes, objections to interest, in his 'Clouds,' 140.

Aristotle, his objections to the levy of interest, 140; his definition of a tyranny, 262.

Army, British, cost of training, 118.

Art, education in, its value, 116.

Association, of employers and operatives, 109.

Australia, rate of interest in, 144; its temporary adoption of the Wakefield scheme, 257; rate of taxation in, 281.

B.

Bacon, error of, in relation to voluntary contracts, 4.

Bank, proportion of assets reserved, 206.

Banker, his relations to the depositor's capital, 40; to his own, 41.

Bankers, their habit of encouraging deposits, 44; the conditions of their trade, 44; obliged to keep their capital in hand, 149.

'Banking, free,' checked by government, 226.

Bankruptcy law, inadequacy of, 215; lax, evil effects of, 217.

Banks, Credit, German system of, 108.

Bargains, hard, in what they consist, 3.

Barley, relative value of, to wheat and oats, 19.

Bastiat, refers to socialist views about interest, 140.

Bavaria, restraints on marriage in, and consequences, 69.

Beddgelert, rent of land near, what it is, 168.

Beethoven, his love of music, 9.

Belgium, potato famine in, 72; price of land in, 145.

Benevolences, 301.

Bentham, his defence of usury, 141; his criticism on costs of law, 276.

Board of Trade, its experiments on malt, 293.

Books, old, price of, 191.

Borrowers, colonial empire an advantage to, 255.

Bounties, nature of, 232.

Bread, loaf of, distribution of price of, 48.
Bricks, effect of tax on, 290.
Briggs, Mr. H., his experience with colliers, 110.
Building trades, trades-unions in, 95.
Burdens, peculiar, meaning of phrase, 99.

C.

Canada, relations of, to U. S., closer than to England, 255.
Capital, rude forms of, origin of, 50; loosely defined, 50; must be replaced, 51; derivation of name, 54; origin of, *ib.*; employment of, 55; its relations to labour, 56; its profits, 57; accumulations of, 58; illustrations of its growth or diminution, 62; under what conditions employed, 197; distribution of, 215; profits of, on equal conditions equal, *ib.*; destination of wealth as, determined by the owner, 283.
Carriage, cost of, element in price, 17.
Carrying trade, effects of, 247.
Cash payments in 1821, resumption of, 309.
Celtic, ancient rule in Ireland, 177.
Ceylon, tanks in, 263.
Chalmers, Dr., his apparent paradox, 221.
Chance, Mr., his testimony to the effect of the repeal of the glass duty, 292.
Charteris, Col., story of, 137.
Cheques, use of, 204.
Children, education of, an investment of capital, 279.
China, custom of, in matters of currency, 33.
Civilisation, conditions of, Union and Association, 1.
Civil process, costs of, levied on litigants, 275.

Civil war in America, effects of, on price of cotton, 195.
Clearances through bankers, 148.
Clearing-house, operations of, 202.
Clergymen, low earnings of, 114.
Climate, effects of, on rent, 154; influences of, 244-5.
Clothing, demand for, 187.
Coal, should Government check its consumption? 227; distribution of, 242; supplies of, and their relation to public debt, 310.
Coins, origin of, 33.
Collier, wages of, why high, 66.
Colonial system, character of, 252.
Colonies, supposed value of, 254; social tone of, 259; ultimate effects of, on Old World, 260.
Colonies, English, origin of, 251.
Colonies, modern, of Spain and Holland, 251.
Colonisation, mistaken views of its value, 102.
Combination of labourers, laws against, abolished, 88.
Commerce, international, mistakes about, 4.
'Commercial distress,' its incidence, 214.
Commercial law, necessity of an international, 217.
Commodities, price of, affected by division of labour, 15; how far Government may check consumption of, 227; however local their origin, very little under the control of Government, 242.
Common sense, what it is, 116.
Companies, grants to, 81; joint stock, dishonesty of, 215.
Company, East India, character of its trade, 82.
Competition, settles price of some things absolutely, 191; effects of checks on, 200.
'Connexion,' economical interpretation of, 134.

INDEX. 321

Consols, quantity of, in market, is probably small, 312.
Consumer, his relations to a trades-union, 97.
Contracts, cases in which the law ineffectually tries to annul them, 3; control of law over, 182; superintended and controlled by Government, 225.
Co-operation, of labour, its uses, 10; among labourers, kinds of, 105; Continental, kinds of, 106.
Co-operators, Rochdale, their plan, 136.
Copper, currencies of, 26.
Copyright, grounds on which allowed, 226.
Corn, duty on, effects of, 285.
Corn-dealer, use of, 193.
Corn-laws, folly of, 162.
Corporations, effect of tenure of land by, 199.
Cost, involved in the production of labour, 63; real and nominal, distinguished, 194.
Cottages, demolition of, in close parishes, 125.
Cottier tenancy, peculiar to Ireland, 175.
Cottiers, competition for land by, 179.
Cotton, price of, and inferences from, 195.
Cotton cloth, analysis of production of, 11; currency of, 26.
Cotton plant, wide area for its production, 197.
Coventry, trade of, 94.
Cowrie, currency of, 26.
Credit, only metaphorically capital, 62; mercantile and government, compared, 142.
Creditor, public, his powers, 307.
Crown, its grant of monopolies, 81.
Cultivation, small, when most advisable, 174.

Cumberland, labourers of, their prudence, 102.
Currency, must be indestructible by atmosphere, 31; must be divisible, and capable of re-union, *ib.*; contraction of, 207.
Currency, double, inconveniences of, 30.
Currency, English, nature of, 30.
Currency, inconvertible, causes which determine value of, 46; effects of, on prices, 305.
Currency quacks, expedients of, 311.
Customers, indolence of, a cause of 'connexion' and 'good-will,' 138.

D.

Davis, Sir J., his abstract of the great Irish Gavelkind case, 177.
Dearness of labour, machinery an escape from, 129.
Debt, obligation of, like that of a charge burdening an estate, 303; incidence of, on capital, or revenue, 315.
Debt, English, growth of, and chiefly for unproductive purposes, 302; nominal and real, amount raised, 309.
Debt, public, should it be extinguished? 314.
Debts, national, security of, 317.
Deceased persons, power of controlling the living by, mere creations of law, 230.
Decimal system, convenience of, 118.
Defence, could not be undertaken by private individuals, 274.
Delitzsch, M. Schultze, his expedients, 106.
Demand, must be effectual, 21; its relation to wages, 51; origin of, 186.

Y

Deposit, Banks of, 42.
De Quincey, Mr., his theory of demand, 188.
Dexterity in labour, origin of, 12.
Diamond, cause of value of, 17.
Direct taxation, chief kinds of, 287; arguments of its advocates, 293.
Discipline, border land between, and liberty, 267.
Discount, rise in rate of, will generally check exportations of specie, 211; how exceptionally high rates may be checked, 212; ordinarily lower than rate of interest, and why, 212.
Discounts, cause in the variation of, 149.
Distribution, into three classes of persons, 48; of profit, wages, and rent may not take place, but all may be united, 53.
Domestic life, regulated by feudal system, 268.
Donatio inter vivos, risk of, 284.
Drill, time it takes to learn, 118.

E.

Earth, distribution of products over the, 242.
Economy in production, and in exchange, 38.
Economy, Political, its harmony with morals, deals with services on which a price is put, 2.
Education, what it is, 115; a proper function of Government, 264; special, no justification of, when the skill it confers is in demand, 117; general, reasons why State should provide, 118; technical, source of funds for, suggested, 265.
Edward III, debts of, 301.
Edward VI, his base money, 34.
Effectual, demand must be, 188.

Emanuel, Mr., his estimate of diamonds, 17.
Emigration, progress of, 101; colonies no value for, 256; voluntary, takes away the best of the people,—more active in cheap years, 258.
Employers, do not pay poor-rates, 127.
Employment of capital, twofold, 55.
Employments, division of, Mr. Wakefield's correction, 10.
Endowments, effect of, on the aggregate earnings of those who enjoy them, 114; use of, 115.
England, custom of paying by weight in, 33; food of labourer in, 64; like a vast city, 163; distribution of soil in, six centuries ago, 170; ownership of land in, 228.
Equilibrium of demand and supply in labour, conditions of, 68.
Estates, great, supposed benefits of, 271.
Europe, food of labourer in parts of, 65.
Exchange, acts of, basis of economical inquiries, must represent mutual benefits, 3; money in, like thought to language, 23; motives for, 36; rate of, between London and Edinburgh in Adam Smith's time, 203; arbitrated, 209; free, admitted to be naturally right,—the counterpart of personal liberty, 224.
Exchange, bills of, their origin, 38; their operation, 209; bill of, what it purports, 150.
Exchequer bills, nature of, 214.
Excise, disadvantages of, 291.
Expenditure, by Government, gives an appearance of prosperity, 219; war, the reaction from, 221.

Export duty, incidence of, 243.
Export duties, why objectionable, 227.
Exports, effects of taxes on, 285.
Exports and imports, policy of dealing with, 25.

F.

Famine, Irish, effects of, 72; last, in England, 73.
Farmer, disadvantage of corn-laws to, 193.
Farmers' rents, almost peculiar to England, 168.
Farms, large and small, 111.
Fashion, fickleness of, 78.
Female costume, changes in, and their effects on labour, 78.
Fertility of soil, not always followed by high rent, and why, 164.
Food, character of, affects wages, 65; effects of customary, on wages, 71; raw material of labour, 74; supplies of, increasing, 75; price of, in a seige, 180; demand for, 186, 188; importation of, will not be checked by rise in rate of discount, 211; supplies of, most secure, when drawn from the largest area, 238.
Foreign trade, necessity for bills of exchange in, 208.
France, base money in, 34; established companies in, 82; price of land in, 145.
Frauds, effects of, on profit, 216.
Freedom of labour, restrictions on, 100.
Free port, advantages of a, 291.
Funding, two methods of, 311.

G.

Gavelkind, Irish, extinction of, 176.
Genius, definition, of, 12.
Gin Act, effects of, 291.

Glass, duties on, the effect of their repeal, 292.
Gold, relative value of, to silver, 18; currencies of, 26; disturbances of price of, in its relations to silver, 29.
Gold and silver, distribution of, in mines, 242.
'Good-will,' its economical interpretation, 134.
Government, duty of, to certify money, 32; credit of, 142; competition of, with other borrowers, 219; rightly protects the weak against the strong, 226; does not colonise, but watches over emigration, 259; supposed to have good intentions, should permit criticism, should protect weak against strong, 263; summary of duties of, 273; does a service to its subjects, 274.
Government, British, has never founded a colony, 251.
Grain, proportionate value of, 65.
Grass land, high rent of, why, 165.
Guilds, their purpose, 81.

H.

Hand to month, practice of living by, weakness of labourers, 104.
Hangman, the, highly paid, 77.
Hanse Towns, their decline, 58.
Hatto, Bishop, story of, 180.
Hearses, demand for, 188.
Henry VIII, his base money, 34, 123; his savage laws, 122; debts of, 301.
Hides, currency of, 26.
Higgling of the market, limited in its effect, 187.
Hindostan, empire in, its consequences, 82.
Hoards, why made, and when unwise, 24, 25; motives for, 37.
Holland, established companies, 82; rates of interest in, 144; debts

of, 302; its precedents of political liberty, *ib*.
Homestead Act, its effects on colonisation, 258.
House-room, demand for, 187.
House-tax, defended and criticised, 296.
Houses, how affected by accumulation of land in few hands, 199.
Hypothesis, objection to, in Political Economy, 97.

I.

Illegitimacy, consequent on legal restraint of marriage, 70.
Importation of commodities, also produced at home, its relation to trades-unions, 94.
Imports, proportionate value of, to specie ordinarily retained, 213; taxes on, when the article is produced, untaxed at home, effects of, 286.
Imports and exports, policy of dealing with, 25.
Income-tax, recognises certain exemptions, 280; when just, 295.
India, famines in, 73; land tenures in 169; ownership of land in, 228; incidence of salt-tax in, 281; poverty of, 283.
Indirect taxation, chief kinds of, 287.
Industrial undertakings, how far Government can assist, 265.
Industry, general, not stimulated by Protection, 234.
'Inferior lands,' theory of, in interpreting rent, 156.
Inheritance, public, particulars of, 304.
Insecurity, hindrance to distribution of capital, 215.
Instrument, land considered as, 146.
Instrument of agriculture, land con- considered as, 173.
Instruments, economy of, 129.

Insurance, effect of, on wages, 113.
Intelligence, remuneration of, a form of wages, 91.
Interest, forbidden anciently, 140; high rates of, generally because the security is insufficient, 142; rate of, determined by amount of capital, 143.
Interloping, attempts of the East India Company to stop, 82.
Intermediaries in trade, origin of, 13.
International law, as yet imperfect, 250.
Investment, land considered as, 146.
Ireland, food of labourer in, 65; its disaffection, 112; poor law in, 127; ancient tenancies in, 175; population of, in agriculture generally, 178; scarcity price of land in, 180.
Irish disaffection, remedy for, 183.
Iron, relative value of, to lead, 19.
Issue of notes, in excess of specie, why, 41; cannot be a fixed quantity, 43.
Italy, gold currencies of, in 13th century, 18; republics of, their decline, 58.

J.

Jews, maintenance of poor among, 120; forbidden to take interest, and why, 140.
Julius Cæsar, his reduction in the value of gold, 28.

K.

King, Lord, his attempts to reserve rents in gold, 309.

L.

Labour, kinds of, 7; not all kinds of, economical; need not be dis-

INDEX. 325

agreeable, 8; economy of, why desirable, 9; division of, 10; division of, how originated, 12; must be judiciously exercised, 17; must devote a portion of its earnings towards maintenance of future labour, 49; what constitutes its productiveness, 60; production of, involves cost, 63; in what sense to be understood, 67; cheap and dear, 119; maintenance of, by poor-rates, effects of, *ib.*; division of, exemplified in the collection of a public revenue, 276.

Labour and capital, not antagonistic, 56; their functions rarely understood, 60.

Labour fund, value of, 103.

Labourer, capital invested in, must be replaced, 66.

Labourers, statute of, 86.

Land, in settled countries, possesses value, apart from labour, 7; bank on security of, in 1696, 45; desire to possess, how arises, 145; as an investment, and instrument, 146; similar to an invariable quantity of capital, 160; permanent property in, why allowed, 166; progressive growth in value of, 173; scarcity price of, 179; objections to any hindrance put in the way of its distribution, 198; no legislature allows absolute ownership in, 228; 'free trade in,' used inaccurately, 229; subdivision of, objections to, 230; conveyance of, 231; ancient conveyance of, 270.

Landowner, increase of his natural rent, not due to his own labour, 167; his claims to protection considered, 238; his position in Great Britain advantageous, 239.

Landowners, policy of, in legislature, 161.

Language to thought, like money to exchange, 23.

Law, practice of, in England, 14; etiquette of, 84; Anglo-Norman, in Ireland, 175.

Law, Mr., his scheme, 45.

Laws, policy of, to keep money in the country, 25; effect of, endure long after their repeal, 128.

Laws, bad, effect of, 99.

Lead, relative value of, to iron, 19.

Leclaire, M., his relations with his work-people, 110.

Legacies, tax on, 283; why a tax on, just, and how far prudent, 284.

Lenders, competition of, 150.

Liberty, individual, is properly curtailed, 225; border-land between, and discipline, 267.

Licences, by whom paid, 299.

Life, human, analysis of, 49.

Lloyd Jones and Ludlow, Messrs., their 'Progress of the Working Classes' quoted, 135.

Loans, Government, mode and effects of, 217; difference between them and a tax, 222.

Lock-out, an expedient of masters, 89.

Lollards, the, their objects, 87.

Lombards, practised usury, 141.

Ludlow and Lloyd Jones, Messrs., quotation from their 'Progress of the Working Classes,' 135.

M.

Macaulay, saying of, 301.

Macculloch, Mr., on funded debt, 311.

Machinery, uses of, 15; use of, in agriculture, 93; effect of, on wages, 129; introduction of heightens rent, 167; not easily employed in small cultivation, 174.

Maintenance of labour, a matter of habit or tradition, 65.
Male servants, tax on, 298.
Malt, duty on, its amount in proportion to value, and spirit, 292; tax on, objections to, *ib.*
Malthus, Mr., his theory of population, 68; his illustration of the growth of population, 73; circumstances of the time in which he wrote, 75.
Manor court, procedure of, 268.
Mansions, great, assessed at nominal sums, 295.
Market, width of, 16.
Marriage, legal restraint of, its effects, 70; social checks to, in our own country, *ib.*
Marriages checked in dear years, 71.
Material, raw, effect of deficiency in, 79.
Materials, raw, taxes on, indefensible, 284.
Measure of value, necessity of, in civilised life, 22; necessary, even if money did not exist, 23.
Mechanism, excellence of, 40.
Medicine, etiquette of, 84.
Mental labour, the most important kind of, 8.
Mercantile bills, character of, 149.
Mercantile credit, generally higher than that of Government, 142.
Merchant, object of, 208.
Metals, precious, causes which have determined their use, 27; their value determined by what conditions, 201; how distributed, 203.
Métayer tenancy, characteristics of, prevailed once in England, 169.
Mill, Mr., his praise of Bavarian institutions, 70; his quotation from De Quincey, 188; his defence of Protection, 235; criticism of this view, 235; just observation of, in relation to foreign policy, 250; his protective theory adopted by colonies, 254.
Misery, effects of, on population, 69.
Monasteries, suppression of, its effects, 87.
Money, mistaken notions about, 4; use of, 22; machinery of trade, costly, and always got rid of, except when used as a hoard, 24; a pledge, 26; base, effects of, issue of, by Government, 34; when unemployed, no service or profit in, 36, 37; functions of, in exchange, 139, 186; loanable, excess or deficiency of, 151; ambiguous word, 201; as merchandise, 201; as currency, 202; economy in use of, 204; delusion that this was wealth, 246.
Monopoly, trading, defence alleged for, 82.
Moral qualities, in what sense capital, 62; may have an economical value, 135.
Morality, cannot be taught by the State, 290.
Morier, Mr., his report on German co-operation, 107.
Mortgages incurred by peasant proprietors, 172.
Munich, rate of illegitimacy in, 70; trade in, 233.

N.

Nations, young and rising, commit the gravest error in adopting Protection, 236.
Natural powers must exist in land, 154.
Necessaries, primary and secondary, law of price in, 190-191.
Needle-grinder, wages of, high, 66.
Norway, prudent marriages in, 70.

INDEX. 327

Notes, power of bank to issue, 207.
Notes, bank, origin of, 39; conditions under which they can be circulated, 45; small, the dangers of, when depreciated, 47.
Notes, Bank of England, a legal tender, 304.

O.

Oats, relative value of, to wheat and barley, 19.
Overend and Gurney, house of, their policy, 148.

P.

Panic, commercial, its origin, 313.
Paper circulation, what it professes to do, 205.
Par, of exchange, its meaning, 209.
Parishes, open and close, 124.
Parliament, granted monopolies, 82.
Patents, grounds on which they are granted, 226; fees for, might be employed in technical education, 265.
Pawnbrokers, licence duties of, bad, 300.
Peasant, his isolation, 111; Irish, peculiar position of, 184.
Peasant holdings, real disadvantages of, 173.
Peasant proprietors, universality of, 171.
Petroleum, in United States, its importance, 220.
Physician, income of, why such and such an amount, 17.
Pictures, old, price of, 191.
Pitt, Mr., adopted Price's sinking-fund scheme, 314.
Plague, Great, of 1348, effects of, 86; its effects on the occupation of land, 171.
Police, medieval, character of, 267.
Policy, public, may justify an interference with free trade, 226.

Poll-tax, character of,—examples in England, 294.
Poor-law, origin of, 87; old, effects of, on rent, 92.
Poor-laws, origin of, religious, 120; history of, 121.
Poor-rates, effects of, on wages, on the character of labourers, 126.
Population, Mr. Malthus' theory of, 68; of England and Wales, in middle ages, 73; excessive, alarms about, 74; may make urgent demands, without rent being forthcoming, 155.
Porcelain, ancient, found in Ireland 246.
Potato, effects of using, in Ireland, 178.
Precious, why metals called so, 26.
Price, may generally rise or fall, 20; what constitutes it, 21; law of, as interpreted by demand, 189; depends on cost, in the long run, 190; of imported goods, what determined by, 248.
Price, Mr., his sinking fund scheme, 314.
Prices, fluctuations of, 15; law of, 196; effect on, by scarcity, by general or enlarged demand, 241; in an inconvertible currency, 306-7.
Primogeniture, custom of, and defence of, 270.
Production, cost of, the aggregate of labour expended, 7; co-operation of, 106.
Professions, liberal, remuneration in, 77; bye-laws of, 84.
Profit, a term used loosely, 52; synonymous with interest, *ib.*; used vaguely, 57; rate of, not affected by prices, 90; to be identified with rate of interest, 132.
Property, rights of, respected under conditions, 180.
Property-tax, just, 295.

INDEX.

Proprietorship, passion of, 145.
Protection, origin of, 25; ground on which claimed, 99; origin of, 232; when manifestly unnecessary, *ib.*; a natural, in all societies, 237; comparative, not the basis of taxation, 277.
Public cost, education by, its effect on wages, 113.

R.

Race, influences of, exaggerated, 242.
Recognizances, entered into, when a non-settled servant was hired, 123.
Reformation, after the, interest made lawful, 141.
Rent, rise in value of, 19; when does it arise? 52; not a part of capital, 56; how affected by a trades-union, 91; definition of, *ib.*; varieties of, 92; importance of, with English economists, 152; definitions of, 153; common theory of, hypothetical, 155; received theory of, how it originated, 157; true definition of, 161; paid last, 165.
Rents, house, in London, what composed of, 163; Irish, enormous, 181.
Republic, French, the, and its rule fixing relative value of gold and silver, 30.
Repudiation, common among European Governments, 143; risks of, in England, in 1815, 309.
Reserve, wealth not employed, but which might be, 56; of capital, and its relation to loans, 219.
Restraint, effects of, on population, 69.
Revenue, private, what it is, 278; taxation of, necessarily unequal, 289.

Revolution, French, its assignats and mandats, 306.
Ricardo, Mr., his objection to taxes on capital, 283.
Richard II, poll-tax of, 295.
Rights, natural, disputes about the origin of, a contemptible quibble, 225.
Risk, its effects on the capitalist, 60; followed by increase of apparent profit, 90; effect of, on wages, 113.
Risks attending labour, paid for, 66.
Rochdale Pioneers, movement of, 135.
Rock-salt, a currency, 26.
Routes, commercial, in middle ages, 246.
Russia, foreign trade of, 210.
Rutland, statute of, 176.

S.

Salt, tax on, the solitary tax which some Hindoos can pay, 281.
Saltpetre, produce of India, 242.
Saving, antecedent to capital, 54.
Scarcity, effects of, on labour, 79; effects of, on prices, 194.
Scotland, food of labourer in, 65; poor-law in, 127.
Security necessary, before loans are made, 141.
Securities, export of, may balance an adverse exchange, 210.
Senior, Mr., his definition of interest, 90, 140.
Serfage, extinction of, 87.
Service, benefits of, socially considered, 299.
Services, some not economical, 2.
Settlement, parochial law of, 123.
Sheep-farming in the 16th century, 87.
Silk, manufacture of, how affected by trades-unions, 94.
Silver, relative value of, to gold,

18; currencies of, 26; disturbances in its relations to gold, 29.
Sismondi, his defence for taxes on articles of luxury, 298.
Slavery, existence of, proves that labour is an investment of capital, 51; parents prohibited from selling their sons into, generally, 225.
Slaves, their commercial value, 64.
Sliding scale, effects of, 192.
Smith, Adam, his two sources of value, 7; his illustration of the division of labour, 11; his views of Political Economy, 16; recognises expenditure of capital in labour, 64; his illustration of a hangman's wages, 77; his explanation of the low earnings of clergymen, 113; speaks of English farmers making great outlay on their land, 185; his view about the higgling of the market, 187; his 'natural price,' 193; mentions a rate of exchange between London and Edinburgh, 203; the value of his demonstrations, 247; his criticism of the theory that we ought to wish our neighbours poor, 250; his rules of taxation, 273; his explanation of equitable taxation, 277; the fulfilment of his condition perhaps impossible, 281; recognises that taxes on raw materials induce artificial barrenness, 285.
Smith, Sydney, his view on diligence, 12.
Smuggling, difficulty of checking, 25.
Soap, transparent, needs alcohol to manufacture it, 290.
Society, civilised, the benefits which it confers, 2; affords remedies against force and fraud, 3; civil conditions of, 100; not existent for production only, 112.

Soil, constituents of wheat-growing, 154.
Somerset, his base money, issued in the name of Edward VI, 34.
Spain, its conquests in the New World, 28.
Specie, efflux of, test of, 149; causes of efflux of, 208; efflux of, will continue if the imports are of food, 211.
Speculation, what it does, 5-6.
Speke, Mr., his travels, 26.
Stanhope, Lord, his resolutions, 309.
State, unable to teach morality, 290.
Stock on land, proportionate value of, to land, 176.
Stocks, market value of different, 312.
Strike, when adopted, 89; risks of, and effects on capital, 216.
Success, chance of, generally overestimated, 6.
Sugar, cane, produce of British colonies, 243.
Sumptuary laws, rules of, 269.
Supply, co-operation of, 105; to be effectual, what conditions required, 197.
Sycee, meaning of, 33.
System, feudal, the, its theory of taxation, 277.

T.

Taille in France, 181.
Tanistry, Irish, extinction of, 176.
Tax, difference between a, and loans, 222; excuse and defence of a particular, 290.
Tax, income, is seldom fairly levied, 223.
Tax, war, difficult to apportion fairly, 222.
Taxation, Adam Smith's rules of, 273; should be equitable, 277; cannot be collected from what a man cannot save, 278; what

is legitimately exempt from it, 280; incidence of, when capable of being transferred, 287.
Taxation, direct and indirect, their respective merits, 288.
Taxation, local, kinds of, 288.
Tenancy, ancient Irish, 175.
Tenant-right, claim of, 185.
Thrift, value of, to labourers, 102.
Tools, economy of, 9.
Trade, foreign, in the United Kingdom, its amount, 38; profit of, 249.
Trade, honest, humanising effects of, 245.
Trade-profit is made up of interest and wages, 133.
Trader, speculative, his position, 5.
Traders, devices of, to attract customers, 138.
Trades and occupations, what, may be under the control of Government, 266.
Trades-unions, origin of, 87; if universally possible, effects of, 97; good effects of, 100.
Turner, Mr., his love of painting, 9.
Tyler, Wat, his insurrection, 87, 295.
Tyranny, Greek, idea of, in time of Aristotle, 262.

U.

Uncertainty, mischievous to commerce, 193.
Union rating, effects of, 125.
United States, accumulation of capital in, 59; value of land in, 153; arguments alleged in favour of Protection in, 237; chief emigration to, 256; reason why they can endure a vicious fiscal system, 281; paper currency of, 306.
Unproductive, not necessarily a term of reproach, 218; not a phrase of adverse criticism, 303.
Use, what it is in political economy, 21.

V.

Value in exchange, depends on labour expended, 7.
Values, relative to each other; no general rise or fall in possible, 20.
Van der Weyer, M., his testimony to the economy of the Belgian peasantry, 72.
Vansittart, Mr., his resolutions, 309.
Vice, effects of, on population, 69.
Village system, places in which it exists, 244.

W.

Wages, economical nature of, 5; variation in rate of, 13; means for maintaining labour, 51; to be used in a wide sense, ib.; what determines the ordinary rate of, 63; of all labour, determined by similar causes, 67; rate of, raised by general education, 119; high rates of, go with high rates of interest, 144.
Wakefield, Mr. Gibbon, his theory of labour, 10; his colonial system, 257.
War, justification of, 222.
Warehouses, bonded, use of, 289.
Wealth, inheritance of, in what it consists, 8; of one people, and of nations, 16; origin of impression that money is, 24; greater than capital, 56.
Weight, payments by, in England, 34.
Westmoreland, labourers of, their prudence, 102.

Wheat, estimate of price of, 17; relative value of, to barley and oats, 19; best land for, 154; constituents of a soil which grows, *ib.*; only one of the series of farm products, 162.
Whittlesea Mere, rent of, what it is, 168.
Window-tax, bad house-tax, 297.
Wool, best places for producing, 242.
Works, what may be done by Government, 263.

Workshops, Parisian, of 1848, 106.

Y.

Year 1867, character of the trade of the, 214.
Yeomanry, rise of, 87.
Young, Arthur, his opinion as to improvement under precarious tenancies, 185.
Young, Mr., his observations on the effect of United States currency on wages, 308.

January, 1886.

The Clarendon Press, Oxford,
LIST OF SCHOOL BOOKS,

PUBLISHED FOR THE UNIVERSITY BY

HENRY FROWDE,

AT THE OXFORD·UNIVERSITY PRESS WAREHOUSE,
AMEN CORNER, LONDON.

⁎⁎⁎ All Books are bound in Cloth, unless otherwise described.

LATIN.

Allen. *An Elementary Latin Grammar.* By J. BARROW ALLEN, M.A.
Forty-second Thousand . . . . Extra fcap. 8vo. 2s. 6d.

Allen. *Rudimenta Latina.* By the same Author. Extra fcap. 8vo. 2s.

Allen. *A First Latin Exercise Book.* By the same Author. *Fourth Edition.* . . . . Extra fcap. 8vo. 2s. 6d.

Allen. *A Second Latin Exercise Book.* By the same Author.
Extra fcap. 8vo. 3s. 6d.

Jerram. *Anglice Reddenda; or, Easy Extracts, Latin and Greek, for Unseen Translation.* By C. S. JERRAM, M.A. *Fourth Edition.*
Extra fcap. 8vo. 2s. 6d.

Jerram. *Reddenda Minora; or, Easy Passages, Latin and Greek, for Unseen Translation.* For the use of Lower Forms. Composed and selected by C. S. JERRAM, M.A. . . . . . Extra fcap. 8vo. 1s. 6d.

Lee-Warner. *Hints and Helps for Latin Elegiacs.*
Extra fcap. 8vo. 3s. 6d.

Lewis and Short. *A Latin Dictionary,* founded on Andrews' Edition of Freund's Latin Dictionary. By CHARLTON T. LEWIS, Ph.D., and CHARLES SHORT, LL.D. . . . . 4to. 25s.

Nunns. *First Latin Reader.* By T. J. NUNNS, M.A. *Third Edition.*
Extra fcap. 8vo. 2s.

Papillon. *A Manual of Comparative Philology* as applied to the Illustration of Greek and Latin Inflections. By T. L. PAPILLON, M.A. *Third Edition.*
. . . Crown 8vo. 6s.

[1]

Ramsay. *Exercises in Latin Prose Composition.* With Introduction, Notes, and Passages of graduated difficulty for Translation into Latin. By G. G. RAMSAY, M.A., Professor of Humanity, Glasgow. *Second Edition.*
Extra fcap. 8vo. 4s. 6d.

Sargent. *Passages for Translation into Latin.* By J. Y. SARGENT, M.A. . . . . Extra fcap. 8vo. 2s. 6d.

Caesar. *The Commentaries* (for Schools). With Notes and Maps. By CHARLES E. MOBERLY, M.A.
   Part I. *The Gallic War. Second Edition.* . . Extra fcap. 8vo. 4s. 6d.
   Part II. *The Civil War.* . . . . . . Extra fcap. 8vo. 3s. 6d.
   The Civil War. Book I. *Second Edition.* . . Extra fcap. 8vo. 2s.

Catulli Veronensis *Carmina Selecta*, secundum recognitionem ROBINSON ELLIS, A M. . . . . Extra fcap. 8vo. 3s. 6d.

Cicero. *Selection of interesting and descriptive passages.* With Notes. By HENRY WALFORD, M.A. In three Parts. *Third Edition.*
Extra fcap. 8vo. 4s. 6d.
   Part I. *Anecdotes from Grecian and Roman History.* . *limp*, 1s. 6d.
   Part II. *Omens and Dreams; Beauties of Nature.* . . *limp*, 1s. 6d.
   Part III. *Rome's Rule of her Provinces.* . . . *limp*, 1s. 6d.

Cicero. *Pro Cluentio.* With Introduction and Notes. By W. RAMSAY, M.A. Edited by G. G. RAMSAY, M.A. *Second Edition.* Extra fcap. 8vo. 3s. 6d.

Cicero. *Selected Letters* (for Schools). With Notes. By the late C. E. PRICHARD, M.A., and E. R. BERNARD, M.A. *Second Edition.*
Extra fcap. 8vo. 3s.

Cicero. *Select Orations* (for Schools). *First Action against Verres; Oration concerning the command of Gnaeus Pompeius; Oration on behalf of Archias; Ninth Philippic Oration.* With Introduction and Notes. By J. R. KING, M.A. *Second Edition.* . . . . Extra fcap. 8vo. 2s. 6d.

Cicero. *Philippic Orations.* With Notes, &c. by J. R. KING, M.A. *Second Edition.* . . . . 8vo. 10s. 6d.

Cicero. *Select Letters.* With English Introductions, Notes, and Appendices. By ALBERT WATSON, M.A. *Third Edition.* . . . 8vo. 18s.

Cornelius Nepos. With Notes. By OSCAR BROWNING, M.A. *Second Edition.* . . . . Extra fcap. 8vo. 2s. 6d.

Horace. With a Commentary. Volume I. *The Odes, Carmen Seculare,* and *Epodes.* By EDWARD C. WICKHAM, M.A., Head Master of Wellington College. *Second Edition.* . . Extra fcap. 8vo. 5s. 6d.

Livy. *Selections* (for Schools). With Notes and Maps. By H. LEE-WARNER, M.A. . . . . Extra fcap. 8vo.
   Part I. *The Caudine Disaster.* . . . . . *limp*, 1s. 6d.
   Part II. *Hannibal's Campaign in Italy.* . . *limp*, 1s. 6d.
   Part III. *The Macedonian War.* . . . . *limp*, 1s. 6d.

Livy. *Book I.* With Introduction, Historical Examination, and Notes. By J. R. SEELEY, M.A. *Second Edition.* . . . . 8vo. 6s.

Livy. *Books V—VII.* With Introduction and Notes. By A. R. CLUER, B.A. . . . . Extra fcap. 8vo. 3s. 6d.

LIST OF SCHOOL BOOKS. 3

Livy. *Books XXI—XXIII.* With Introduction and Notes. By M. T. TATHAM, M.A. . . . . . Extra fcap. 8vo. *Nearly ready.*

Ovid. *Selections* (for the use of Schools). With Introductions and Notes, and an Appendix on the Roman Calendar. By W. RAMSAY, M.A. Edited by G. G. RAMSAY, M.A. *Second Edition.* . Extra fcap. 8vo. 5s. 6d.

Ovid. *Tristia,* Book I. Edited by S. G. OWEN, B.A.
Extra fcap. 8vo. 3s. 6d.

Persius. *The Satires.* With Translation and Commentary by J. CONINGTON, M.A., edited by H. NETTLESHIP, M.A. *Second Edition.*
8vo. 7s. 6d.

Plautus. *The Trinummus.* With Notes and Introductions. By C. E. FREEMAN, M.A., Assistant Master of Westminster, and A. SLOMAN, M.A., Master of the Queen's Scholars of Westminster. . . . Extra fcap. 8vo. 3s.

Pliny. *Selected Letters* (for Schools). With Notes. By the late C. E. PRICHARD, M.A., and E. R. BERNARD, M.A. *Second Edition.*
Extra fcap. 8vo. 3s.

Sallust. *Bellum Catilinarium* and *Jugurthinum.* With Introduction and Notes, by W. W. CAPES, M.A. . . . Extra fcap. 8vo. 4s. 6d.

Tacitus. *The Annals.* Books I—IV. Edited, with Introduction and Notes for the use of Schools and Junior Students, by H. FURNEAUX, M.A.
Extra fcap. 8vo. 5s.

Terence. *Andria.* With Notes and Introductions. By C. E. FREEMAN, M.A., and A. SLOMAN, M.A. . . . . . Extra fcap. 8vo. 3s.

Virgil. With Introduction and Notes, by T. L. PAPILLON, M.A. In Two Volumes. . . . Crown 8vo. 10s. 6d.; Text separately, 4s. 6d.

GREEK.

Chandler. *The Elements of Greek Accentuation* (for Schools). By H. W. CHANDLER, M.A. *Second Edition.* . Extra fcap. 8vo. 2s. 6d.

Liddell and Scott. *A Greek-English Lexicon,* by HENRY GEORGE LIDDELL, D.D., and ROBERT SCOTT, D.D. *Seventh Edition.* . 4to. 36s.

Liddell and Scott. *A Greek-English Lexicon,* abridged from LIDDELL and SCOTT's 4to. edition, chiefly for the use of Schools. *Twenty-first Edition.*
Square 12mo. 7s. 6d.

Veitch. *Greek Verbs, Irregular and Defective:* their forms, meaning, and quantity; embracing all the Tenses used by Greek writers, with references to the passages in which they are found. By W. VEITCH, LL.D. *Fourth Edition.*
Crown 8vo. 10s. 6d.

Wordsworth. *Graecae Grammaticae Rudimenta in usum Scholarum.* Auctore CAROLO WORDSWORTH, D.C.L. *Nineteenth Edition.* . 12mo. 4s.

Wordsworth. *A Greek Primer, for the use of beginners in that Language.* By the Right Rev. CHARLES WORDSWORTH, D.C.L., Bishop of St. Andrew's. *Seventh Edition.* . . . . Extra fcap. 8vo. 1s. 6d.

Wright. *The Golden Treasury of Ancient Greek Poetry;* being a Collection of the finest passages in the Greek Classic Poets, with Introductory Notices and Notes. By R. S. WRIGHT, M.A. . . Extra fcap. 8vo. 8s. 6d.

Wright and Shadwell. *A Golden Treasury of Greek Prose;* being a Collection of the finest passages in the principal Greek Prose Writers, with Introductory Notices and Notes. By R. S. WRIGHT, M.A., and J. E. L. SHADWELL, M.A. . . . . Extra fcap. 8vo. 4s. 6d.

A SERIES OF GRADUATED READERS.—

First Greek Reader. By W. G. RUSHBROOKE, M.L., Second Classical Master at the City of London School. *Second Edition.*
Extra fcap. 8vo. 2s. 6d.

Second Greek Reader. By A. M. BELL, M.A.
Extra fcap. 8vo. 3s. 6d.

Third Greek Reader. In Preparation.

Fourth Greek Reader; being Specimens of Greek Dialects. With Introductions and Notes. By W. W. MERRY, M.A., Rector of Lincoln College. . . . . Extra fcap. 8vo. 4s. 6d.

Fifth Greek Reader. Selections from Greek Epic and Dramatic Poetry, with Introductions and Notes. By EVELYN ABBOTT, M.A.
Extra fcap. 8vo. 4s. 6d.

THE GREEK TESTAMENT.—

Evangelia Sacra Graece. . . . Fcap. 8vo. *limp,* 1s. 6d.

The Greek Testament, with the Readings adopted by the Revisers of the Authorised Version.
Fcap. 8vo. 4s. 6d.; or on writing paper, with wide margin, 15s.

Novum Testamentum Graece juxta Exemplar Millianum.
18mo. 2s. 6d.; or on writing paper, with large margin, 9s.

Novum Testamentum Graece. Accedunt parallela S. Scripturae loca, necnon vetus capitulorum notatio et canones Eusebii. Edidit CAROLUS LLOYD, S.T.P.R., necnon Episcopus Oxoniensis.
18mo. 3s.; or on writing paper, with large margin, 10s. 6d.

The New Testament in Greek and English. Edited by E. CARDWELL, D.D. . . . . 2 vols. crown 8vo. 6s.

Outlines of Textual Criticism applied to the New Testament. By C. E. HAMMOND, M.A. *Fourth Edition.* . . Extra fcap. 8vo. 3s. 6d.

Aeschylus. *Agamemnon.* With Introduction and Notes, by ARTHUR SIDGWICK, M.A. *Second Edition.* . . . . Extra fcap. 8vo. 3s.

Aeschylus. *The Choephoroi.* With Introduction and Notes, by the same Editor. . . . . Extra fcap. 8vo. 3s.

Aeschylus. *Prometheus Bound.* With Introduction and Notes, by A. O. PRICKARD, M.A. *Second Edition.* . . . Extra fcap. 8vo. 2s.

LIST OF SCHOOL BOOKS. 5

Aristophanes. *The Clouds.* With Introduction and Notes, by W. W. MERRY, M.A. *Second Edition.* . . . . . Extra fcap. 8vo. 2s.

Aristophanes. *The Acharnians.* By the same Editor. *Second Edition.* Extra fcap. 8vo. 2s.

Aristophanes. *The Frogs.* By the same Editor. Extra fcap. 8vo. 2s.

Cebes. *Tabula.* With Introduction and Notes, by C. S. JERRAM, M.A. Extra fcap. 8vo. 2s. 6d.

Demosthenes and Aeschines. *The Orations of Demosthenes and Æschines on the Crown.* With Introductory Essays and Notes. By G. A. SIMCOX, M.A., and W. H. SIMCOX, M.A. . . . . . . 8vo. 12s.

Euripides. *Alcestis.* By C. S. JERRAM, M.A. Extra fcap. 8vo. 2s. 6d.

Euripides. *Helena.* For Upper and Middle Forms. By the same Editor. . . . . Extra fcap. 8vo. 3s.

Euripides. *Iphigenia in Tauris.* With Introduction and Notes. By the same Editor. . . . . Extra fcap. 8vo. 3s.

Herodotus. *Selections,* edited, with Introduction, Notes, and a Map, by W. W. MERRY, M.A. . . . . . . Extra fcap. 8vo. 2s. 6d.

Homer. *Iliad,* Books I-XII. With an Introduction, a brief Homeric Grammar, and Notes. By D. B. MONRO, M.A. Extra fcap. 8vo. 6s.

Homer. *Iliad,* Book I. By the same Editor. *Third Edition.* Extra fcap. 8vo. 2s.

Homer. *Iliad,* Books VI and XXI. With Notes, &c. By HERBERT HAILSTONE, M.A. . . . . . . Extra fcap. 8vo. 1s. 6d. each.

Homer. *Odyssey,* Books I-XII. By W. W. MERRY, M.A. *Thirty-second Thousand.* . . . . Extra fcap. 8vo. 4s. 6d.

Homer. *Odyssey,* Books XIII-XXIV. By the same Editor. *Second Edition.* . . . . Extra fcap. 8vo. 5s.

Homer. *Odyssey,* Book II. By the same Editor. Extra fcap. 8vo. 1s. 6d.

Lucian. *Vera Historia.* By C. S. JERRAM, M.A. *Second Edition.* Extra fcap. 8vo. 1s. 6d.

Plato. *The Apology.* With a revised Text and English Notes, and a Digest of Platonic Idioms, by JAMES RIDDELL, M.A. . . 8vo. 8s. 6d.

Plato. *Selections* (including the whole of the *Apology* and *Crito*). With Introductions and Notes by J. PURVES, M.A., and a Preface by B. JOWETT, M.A. Extra fcap. 8vo. 6s. 6d.

Sophocles. (For the use of Schools.) Edited with Introductions and English Notes by LEWIS CAMPBELL, M.A., and EVELYN ABBOTT, M.A. New and Revised Edition. In two Volumes. Vol. I. Text. Vol. II. Notes. Extra fcap. 8vo. 10s. 6d. *Just Published.*

☞ *Also in single Plays. Extra fcap. 8vo. limp,*
Oedipus Tyrannus, Philoctetes. New and Revised Edition, 2s. each.
Oedipus Coloneus, Antigone. 1s. 9d. each.
Ajax, Electra, Trachiniae. 2s. each.

Sophocles. *Oedipus Rex:* Dindorf's Text, with Notes by W. BASIL
JONES, D.D., Lord Bishop of S. David's. . Extra fcap. 8vo. *limp,* 1s. 6d.

Theocritus. Edited, with Notes, by H. KYNASTON, D.D. (late
SNOW), Head Master of Cheltenham College. *Third Edition.*
Extra fcap. 8vo. 4s. 6d.

Xenophon. *Easy Selections* (for Junior Classes). With a Vocabulary,
Notes, and Map. By J. S. PHILLPOTTS, B.C.L., Head Master of Bedford
School, and C. S. JERRAM, M.A. *Third Edition.* . Extra fcap. 8vo. 3s. 6d.

Xenophon. *Selections* (for Schools). With Notes and Maps. By
J. S. PHILLPOTTS, B.C.L. *Fourth Edition.* . . Extra fcap. 8vo. 3s. 6d.

Xenophon. *Anabasis,* Book I. With Notes and Map. By J. MARSHALL,
M.A., Rector of the High School, Edinburgh. . . Extra fcap. 8vo. 2s. 6d.

Xenophon. *Anabasis,* Book II. With Notes and Map. By C. S.
JERRAM, M.A. . . . . Extra fcap. 8vo. 2s.

Xenophon. *Cyropaedia,* Books IV, V. With Introduction and Notes,
by C. BIGG, D.D. . . . . Extra fcap. 8vo. 2s. 6d.

ENGLISH.

Reading Books.

—— *A First Reading Book.* By MARIE EICHENS of Berlin; edited
by ANNE J. CLOUGH. . . . . . Extra fcap. 8vo. *stiff covers,* 4d.

—— *Oxford Reading Book,* Part I. For Little Children.
Extra fcap. 8vo. *stiff covers,* 6d.

—— *Oxford Reading Book,* Part II. For Junior Classes.
Extra fcap. 8vo. *stiff covers,* 6d.

Tancock. *An Elementary English Grammar and Exercise Book.*
By O. W. TANCOCK, M.A., Head Master of King Edward VI's School, Norwich.
Second Edition. . . . . Extra fcap. 8vo. 1s. 6d.

Tancock. *An English Grammar and Reading Book,* for Lower
Forms in Classical Schools. By O. W. TANCOCK, M.A. *Fourth Edition.*
Extra fcap. 8vo. 3s. 6d.

Earle. *The Philology of the English Tongue.* By J. EARLE, M.A.,
Professor of Anglo-Saxon. *Third Edition.* . . Extra fcap. 8vo. 7s. 6d.

Earle. *A Book for the Beginner in Anglo-Saxon.* By the same Author.
Third Edition. . . . . Extra fcap. 8vo. 2s. 6d.

Sweet. *An Anglo-Saxon Primer, with Grammar, Notes, and Glossary.*
By HENRY SWEET, M.A. *Third Edition.* . . Extra fcap. 8vo. 2s. 6d.

Sweet. *An Anglo-Saxon Reader.* In Prose and Verse. With Grammatical Introduction, Notes, and Glossary. By the same Author. *Fourth Edition, Revised and Enlarged.* . . . Extra fcap. 8vo. 8s. 6d.

LIST OF SCHOOL BOOKS. 7

Sweet. *Anglo-Saxon Reading Primers.*
  I. *Selected Homilies of Ælfric.*   Extra fcap. 8vo. *stiff covers,* 1s. 6d.
  II. *Extracts from Alfred's Orosius.*   Extra fcap. 8vo. *stiff covers,* 1s. 6d.

Sweet. *First Middle English Primer, with Grammar and Glossary.*
By the same Author. . . . . Extra fcap. 8vo. 2s.

Morris and Skeat. *Specimens of Early English.* A New and Revised Edition. With Introduction, Notes, and Glossarial Index. By R. MORRIS, LL.D., and W. W. SKEAT, M.A.
  Part I. From Old English Homilies to King Horn (A.D. 1150 to A.D. 1300).
  Second Edition. . . . . Extra fcap. 8vo. 9s.
  Part II. From Robert of Gloucester to Gower (A.D. 1298 to A.D. 1393). *Second Edition.* . . . . Extra fcap. 8vo. 7s. 6d.

Skeat. *Specimens of English Literature,* from the 'Ploughmans Crede' to the 'Shepheardes Calender' (A.D. 1394 to A.D. 1579). With Introduction, Notes, and Glossarial Index. By W. W. SKEAT, M.A.
  Extra fcap. 8vo. 7s. 6d.

Typical Selections from the best English Writers, with Introductory Notices. *Second Edition.* In Two Volumes. Vol. I. Latimer to Berkeley. Vol. II. Pope to Macaulay. . . Extra fcap. 8vo. 3s. 6d. each.

A SERIES OF ENGLISH CLASSICS.—

Langland. *The Vision of William concerning Piers the Plowman,* by WILLIAM LANGLAND. Edited by W. W. SKEAT, M.A. *Third Edition.*
  Extra fcap. 8vo. 4s. 6d.

Chaucer. I. *The Prologue to the Canterbury Tales; The Knightes Tale; The Nonne Prestes Tale.* Edited by R. MORRIS, LL.D. *Fifty-first Thousand.* . . . . Extra fcap. 8vo. 2s. 6d.

Chaucer. II. *The Prioresses Tale; Sir Thopas; The Monkes Tale; The Clerkes Tale; The Squieres Tale, &c.* Edited by W. W. SKEAT, M.A. *Second Edition.* . . . . Extra fcap. 8vo. 4s. 6d.

Chaucer. III. *The Tale of the Man of Lawe; The Pardoneres Tale; The Second Nonnes Tale; The Chanouns Yemannes Tale.* By the same Editor. *Second Edition.* . . . . . Extra fcap. 8vo. 4s. 6d.

Gamelyn, The Tale of. Edited by W. W. SKEAT, M.A.
  Extra fcap. 8vo. *stiff covers,* 1s. 6d.

Wycliffe. *The New Testament in English,* according to the Version by JOHN WYCLIFFE, about A.D. 1380, and Revised by JOHN PURVEY, about A.D. 1388. With Introduction and Glossary by W. W. SKEAT, M.A.
  Extra fcap. 8vo. 6s.

Wycliffe. *The Books of Job, Psalms, Proverbs, Ecclesiastes, and the Song of Solomon*: according to the Wycliffite Version made by NICHOLAS DE HEREFORD, about A.D. 1381, and Revised by JOHN PURVEY, about A.D. 1388. With Introduction and Glossary by W. W. SKEAT, M.A. Extra fcap. 8vo. 3s. 6d.

Spenser. *The Faery Queene.* Books I and II. Edited by G. W. KITCHIN, D.D.
  Book I. *Tenth Edition.* . . . . . Extra fcap. 8vo. 2s. 6d.
  Book II. *Sixth Edition.* . . . . . Extra fcap. 8vo. 2s. 6d.

Hooker. *Ecclesiastical Polity.* Book I. Edited by R. W. Church, M.A., Dean of St. Paul's. *Second Edition.* . . . Extra fcap. 8vo. 2s.

Marlowe and Greene.—Marlowe's *Tragical History of Dr. Faustus,* and Greene's *Honourable History of Friar Bacon and Friar Bungay.* Edited by A. W. Ward, M.A. . . . . . Extra fcap. 8vo. 5s. 6d.

Marlowe. *Edward II.* Edited by O. W. Tancock, M.A.
Extra fcap. 8vo. 3s.

Shakespeare. Select Plays. Edited by W. G. Clark, M.A., and W. Aldis Wright, M.A. . . . . . Extra fcap. 8vo. *stiff covers.*

The Merchant of Venice. 1s.   *Macbeth.* 1s. 6d.
Richard the Second. 1s. 6d.   *Hamlet.* 2s.

Edited by W. Aldis Wright, M.A.

The Tempest. 1s. 6d.   *Coriolanus.* 2s. 6d.
As You Like It. 1s. 6d.   *Richard the Third.* 2s. 6d.
A Midsummer Night's Dream. 1s. 6d.   *Henry the Fifth.* 2s.
Twelfth Night. 1s. 6d.   *King John.* 1s. 6d. *Just Published.*
Julius Cæsar. 2s.   *King Lear.* 1s. 6d.

Shakespeare as a Dramatic Artist; *a popular Illustration of the Principles of Scientific Criticism.* By Richard G. Moulton, M.A.
Crown 8vo. 5s.

Bacon. I. *Advancement of Learning.* Edited by W. Aldis Wright, M.A. *Second Edition.* . . . . . . Extra fcap. 8vo. 4s. 6d.

Bacon. II. *The Essays.* With Introduction and Notes. *In Preparation.*

Milton. I. *Areopagitica.* With Introduction and Notes. By John W. Hales, M.A. *Third Edition.* . . . . Extra fcap. 8vo. 3s.

Milton. II. *Poems.* Edited by R. C. Browne, M.A. 2 vols. *Fifth Edition.* . . Extra fcap. 8vo. 6s. 6d. Sold separately, Vol. I. 4s.; Vol. II. 3s.

In paper covers:—
Lycidas, 3d.   *L'Allegro*, 3d.   *Il Penseroso*, 4d.   *Comus*, 6d.
Samson Agonistes, 6d.

Milton. III. *Samson Agonistes.* Edited with Introduction and Notes by John Churton Collins. . . . Extra fcap. 8vo. *stiff covers*, 1s.

Bunyan. I. *The Pilgrim's Progress, Grace Abounding, Relation of the Imprisonment of Mr. John Bunyan.* Edited, with Biographical Introduction and Notes, by E. Venables, M.A. . . . Extra fcap. 8vo. 5s.

Bunyan. II. *Holy War, &c.* By the same Editor. *In the Press.*

Dryden. *Select Poems.*—*Stanzas on the Death of Oliver Cromwell; Astræa Redux; Annus Mirabilis; Absalom and Achitophel; Religio Laici; The Hind and the Panther.* Edited by W. D. Christie, M.A.
Extra fcap. 8vo. 3s. 6d.

LIST OF SCHOOL BOOKS. 9

Locke's *Conduct of the Understanding.* Edited, with Introduction, Notes, &c. by T. FOWLER, M.A. *Second Edition.* . . Extra fcap. 8vo. 2s.

Addison. *Selections from Papers in the 'Spectator.'* With Notes. By T. ARNOLD, M.A. . . . . Extra fcap. 8vo. 4s. 6d.

Steele. *Selected Essays from the Tatler, Spectator, and Guardian.* By AUSTIN DOBSON. . . Extra fcap. 8vo. 5s. *In white Parchment,* 7s. 6d.

Berkeley. *Select Works of Bishop Berkeley,* with an Introduction and Notes, by A. C. FRASER, LL.D. *Third Edition.* . . Crown 8vo. 7s. 6d.

Pope. I. *Essay on Man.* Edited by MARK PATTISON, B.D. *Sixth Edition.* . . . . Extra fcap. 8vo. 1s. 6d.

Pope. II. *Satires and Epistles.* By the same Editor. *Second Edition.* Extra fcap. 8vo. 2s.

Parnell. *The Hermit.* . . . . . . *Paper covers,* 2d.

Johnson. I. *Rasselas; Lives of Dryden and Pope.* Edited by ALFRED MILNES, M.A. . . . . . Extra fcap. 8vo. 4s. 6d. *Lives of Pope and Dryden.* . . . . . . *Stiff covers,* 2s. 6d.

Johnson. II. *Vanity of Human Wishes.* With Notes, by E. J. PAYNE, M.A. . . . . *Paper covers,* 4d.

Gray. *Selected Poems.* Edited by EDMUND GOSSE. Extra fcap. 8vo. *Stiff covers,* 1s. 6d. *In white Parchment,* 3s.

Gray. *Elegy, and Ode on Eton College.* . . *Paper covers,* 2d.

Goldsmith. *The Deserted Village.* . . . *Paper covers,* 2d.

Cowper. I. *The Didactic Poems of* 1782, with Selections from the Minor Pieces, A.D. 1779-1783. Edited by H. T. GRIFFITH, B.A. Extra fcap. 8vo. 3s.

Cowper. II. *The Task, with Tirocinium,* and Selections from the Minor Poems, A.D. 1784-1799. By the same Editor. *Second Edition.* Extra fcap. 8vo. 3s.

Burke. I. *Thoughts on the Present Discontents; the two Speeches on America.* Edited by E. J. PAYNE, M.A. *Second Edition.* Extra fcap. 8vo. 4s. 6d.

Burke. II. *Reflections on the French Revolution.* By the same Editor. *Second Edition.* . . . . . Extra fcap. 8vo. 5s.

Burke. III. *Four Letters on the Proposals for Peace with the Regicide Directory of France.* By the same Editor. *Second Edition.* Extra fcap. 8vo. 5s.

Keats. *Hyperion,* Book I. With Notes, by W. T. ARNOLD, B.A. *Paper covers,* 4d.

Byron. *Childe Harold.* With Introduction and Notes, by H. F. TOZER, M.A. Extra fcap. 8vo. Cloth, 3s. 6d. In White Parchment, 5s. *Just Published.*

Scott. *Lay of the Last Minstrel.* Introduction and Canto I, with Preface and Notes by W. MINTO, M.A. . . . . *Paper covers,* 6d.

FRENCH AND ITALIAN.

Brachet. *Etymological Dictionary of the French Language,* with a Preface on the Principles of French Etymology. Translated into English by G. W. KITCHIN, D.D., Dean of Winchester. *Third Edition.*
Crown 8vo. 7s. 6d.

Brachet. *Historical Grammar of the French Language.* Translated into English by G. W. KITCHIN, D.D. *Fourth Edition.*
Extra fcap. 8vo. 3s. 6d.

Saintsbury. *Primer of French Literature.* By GEORGE SAINTSBURY, M.A. *Second Edition.* . . . . . Extra fcap. 8vo. 2s.

Saintsbury. *Short History of French Literature.* By the same Author. . . . . Crown 8vo. 10s. 6d.

Saintsbury. *Specimens of French Literature.* Crown 8vo. 9s.

Beaumarchais. *Le Barbier de Séville.* With Introduction and Notes by AUSTIN DOBSON. . . . . . Extra fcap. 8vo. 2s. 6d.

Blouët. *L'Éloquence de la Chaire et de la Tribune Françaises.* Edited by PAUL BLOUËT, B.A. (Univ. Gallic.). Vol. I. *French Sacred Oratory.*
Extra fcap. 8vo. 2s. 6d.

Corneille. *Horace.* With Introduction and Notes by GEORGE SAINTSBURY, M.A. . . . . . . Extra fcap. 8vo. 2s. 6d.

Corneille. *Cinna.* } In one volume, with Introduction and
Molière. *Les Femmes Savantes.* } Notes by GUSTAVE MASSON, B.A.
Extra fcap. 8vo. 2s. 6d.

Masson. *Louis XIV and his Contemporaries;* as described in Extracts from the best Memoirs of the Seventeenth Century. With English Notes, Genealogical Tables, &c. By GUSTAVE MASSON, B.A. Extra fcap. 8vo. 2s. 6d.

Molière. *Les Précieuses Ridicules.* With Introduction and Notes by ANDREW LANG, M.A. . . . . . Extra fcap. 8vo. 1s. 6d.

Molière. *Les Fourberies de Scapin.* { With Voltaire's Life of Molière. By
Racine. *Athalie.* { GUSTAVE MASSON, B.A.
Extra fcap. 8vo. 2s. 6d.

Molière. *Les Fourberies de Scapin.* With Voltaire's Life of Molière. By GUSTAVE MASSON, B.A. . . Extra fcap. 8vo. *stiff covers,* 1s. 6d.

Musset. *On ne badine pas avec l'Amour,* and *Fantasio.* With Introduction, Notes, etc., by WALTER HERRIES POLLOCK. Extra fcap. 8vo. 2s.

LIST OF SCHOOL BOOKS.

NOVELETTES :—

Xavier de Maistre.	*Voyage autour de ma Chambre.*	⎫ By Gustave
Madame de Duras.	*Ourika.*	⎪ Masson, B.A.
Piévée.	*La Dot de Suzette.*	⎬ 2nd Edition.
Edmond About.	*Les Jumeaux de l' Hôtel Corneille.*	⎪ Ext. fcap. 8vo.
Rodolphe Töpffer.	*Mésaventures d'un Écolier.*	⎭ 2s. 6d.

Quinet. *Lettres à sa Mère.* Edited by G. SAINTSBURY, M.A.
Extra fcap. 8vo. 2s.

Racine. *Andromaque.* ⎱ With Louis Racine's Life of his Father. By
Corneille. *Le Menteur.* ⎰ GUSTAVE MASSON, B.A.
Extra fcap. 8vo. 2s. 6d.

Regnard. . . . *Le Joueur.* ⎱ By GUSTAVE MASSON, B.A.
Brueys and Palaprat. *Le Grondeur.* ⎰ *Extra fcap. 8vo. 2s. 6d.*

Sainte-Beuve. *Selections from the Causeries du Lundi.* Edited by
G. SAINTSBURY, M.A. . . . . *Extra fcap. 8vo. 2s.*

Sévigné. *Selections from the Correspondence of* **Madame de Sévigné**
and her chief Contemporaries. Intended more especially for Girls' Schools. By
GUSTAVE MASSON, B.A. . . . . . . *Extra fcap. 8vo. 3s.*

Voltaire. *Mérope.* Edited by G. SAINTSBURY, M.A. *Extra fcap. 8vo. 2s.*

Dante. *Selections from the 'Inferno.'* With Introduction and Notes,
by H. B. COTTERILL, B.A. . . . . . *Extra fcap. 8vo. 4s. 6d.*

Tasso. *La Gerusalemme Liberata.* Cantos i, ii. With Introduction
and Notes, by the same Editor. . . . . *Extra fcap. 8vo. 2s. 6d.*

GERMAN, &c.

Buchheim. *Modern German Reader.* A Graduated Collection of
Extracts in Prose and Poetry from Modern German writers. Edited by C. A.
BUCHHEIM, Phil. Doc.
  Part I. With English Notes, a Grammatical Appendix, and a complete
  Vocabulary. *Fourth Edition.* . . . *Extra fcap. 8vo. 2s. 6d.*
  Part II. With English Notes and an Index. Extra fcap. 8vo. 2s. 6d. *Just Published.*
  Part III. In preparation.

Lange. *The Germans at Home*; a Practical Introduction to German
Conversation, with an Appendix containing the Essentials of German Grammar.
By HERMANN LANGE. *Second Edition.* . . . . . 8vo. 2s. 6d.

Lange. *The German Manual*; a German Grammar, a Reading
Book, and a Handbook of German Conversation. By the same Author.
8vo. 7s. 6d.

Lange. *A Grammar of the German Language,* being a reprint of the
Grammar contained in *The German Manual.* By the same Author. 8vo. 3s. 6d.

Lange. *German Composition*; a Theoretical and Practical Guide to
the Art of Translating English Prose into German. By the same Author.
8vo. 4s. 6d.

Goethe. *Egmont.* With a Life of Goethe, etc. Edited by C. A. BUCHHEIM, Phil. Doc. *Third Edition.* . . . Extra fcap. 8vo. 3s.

Goethe. *Iphigenie auf Tauris.* A Drama. With a Critical Introduction and Notes. Edited by C. A. BÜCHHEIM, Phil. Doc. *Second Edition.* Extra fcap. 8vo. 3s.

Heine's *Prosa,* being Selections from his Prose Works. Edited with English Notes, etc., by C. A. BUCHHEIM, Phil. Doc. Extra fcap. 8vo. 4s. 6d.

Lessing. *Laokoon.* With Introduction, Notes, etc. By A. HAMANN, Phil. Doc., M.A. . . . . Extra fcap. 8vo. 4s. 6d.

Lessing. *Minna von Barnhelm.* A Comedy. With a Life of Lessing, Critical Analysis, Complete Commentary, etc. Edited by C. A. BUCHHEIM, Phil. Doc. *Fourth Edition.* . . Extra fcap. 8vo. 3s. 6d.

Lessing. *Nathan der Weise.* With English Notes, etc. Edited by C. A. BUCHHEIM, Phil. Doc. . . . . . . Extra fcap. 8vo. 4s. 6d.

Schiller's *Historische Skizzen:—Egmonts Leben und Tod,* and *Belagerung von Antwerpen.* Edited by C. A. BUCHHEIM, Phil. Doc. *Third Edition, Revised and Enlarged, with a Map.* . Extra fcap. 8vo. 2s. 6d.

Schiller. *Wilhelm Tell.* With a Life of Schiller; an Historical and Critical Introduction, Arguments, a Complete Commentary, and Map. Edited by C. A. BUCHHEIM, Phil. Doc. *Sixth Edition.* . Extra fcap. 8vo. 3s. 6d.

Schiller. *Wilhelm Tell.* Edited by C. A. BUCHHEIM, Phil. Doc. *School Edition.* With Map. . . . . Extra fcap. 8vo. 2s.

Schiller. *Wilhelm Tell.* Translated into English Verse by E. MASSIE, M.A. . . . . Extra fcap. 8vo. 5s.

GOTHIC AND ICELANDIC.

Skeat. *The Gospel of St. Mark in Gothic.* Edited by W. W. SKEAT, M.A. . . . . Extra fcap. 8vo. 4s.

Vigfusson and Powell. *An Icelandic Prose Reader,* with Notes, Grammar, and Glossary. By GUDBRAND VIGFUSSON, M.A., and F. YORK POWELL, M.A. . . . . . . Extra fcap. 8vo. 10s. 6d.

MATHEMATICS AND PHYSICAL SCIENCE.

Hamilton and Ball. *Book-keeping.* By Sir R. G. C. HAMILTON, K.C.B., Under-Secretary for Ireland, and JOHN BALL (of the firm of Quilter, Ball, & Co.). *New and Enlarged Edition* . . . Extra fcap. 8vo. 2s.

Hensley. *Figures made Easy: a first Arithmetic Book.* By LEWIS HENSLEY, M.A. . . . . Crown 8vo. 6d.

Hensley. *Answers to the Examples in Figures made Easy,* together with 2000 additional Examples formed from the Tables in the same, with Answers. By the same Author. . . . . . Crown 8vo. 1s.

LIST OF SCHOOL BOOKS. 13

Hensley. *The Scholar's Arithmetic;* with Answers to the Examples.
By the same Author. . . . . Crown 8vo. 4s. 6d.

Hensley. *The Scholar's Algebra.* An Introductory work on Algebra.
By the same Author. . . . . Crown 8vo. 4s. 6d.

Baynes. *Lessons on Thermodynamics.* By R. E. BAYNES, M.A.,
Lee's Reader in Physics. . . . . Crown 8vo. 7s. 6d.

Donkin. *Acoustics.* By W. F. DONKIN, M.A., F.R.S. *Second Edition.*
Crown 8vo. 7s. 6d.

Euclid Revised. Containing the essentials of the Elements of Plane
Geometry as given by Euclid in his First Six Books. Edited by R. C. J. NIXON,
M.A., Formerly Scholar of St. Peter's College, Cambridge.
Crown 8vo. *Nearly ready.*

Harcourt and Madan. *Exercises in Practical Chemistry.* Vol. I.
Elementary Exercises. By A. G. VERNON HARCOURT, M.A.: and H. G.
MADAN, M.A. *Third Edition.* Revised by H. G. Madan, M.A.
Crown 8vo. 9s.

Madan. *Tables of Qualitative Analysis.* Arranged by H. G. MADAN,
M.A. . . . . Large 4to. 4s. 6d.

Maxwell. *An Elementary Treatise on Electricity.* By J. CLERK
MAXWELL, M.A., F.R.S. Edited by W. GARNETT, M.A. Demy 8vo. 7s. 6d.

Stewart. *A Treatise on Heat,* with numerous Woodcuts and Diagrams. By BALFOUR STEWART, LL.D., F.R.S., Professor of Natural Philosophy
in Owens College, Manchester. *Fourth Edition.* . Extra fcap. 8vo. 7s. 6d.

Vernon-Harcourt. *A Treatise on Rivers and Canals,* relating to
the Control and Improvement of Rivers, and the Design, Construction, and
Development of Canals. By LEVESON FRANCIS VERNON-HARCOURT, M.A.,
M.I.C.E. 2 vols. (Vol. I, Text. Vol. II, Plates.) . . . 8vo. 21s.

Vernon-Harcourt. *Harbours and Docks;* their Physical Features,
History, Construction, Equipment, and Maintenance. By the same Author.
2 vols. (Vol. I, Text. Vol. II Plates.) . . . . . 8vo. 25s.

Williamson. *Chemistry for Students.* By A. W. WILLIAMSON,
Phil. Doc., F.R.S., Professor of Chemistry, University College London. *A new
Edition with Solutions.* . . . . Extra fcap. 8vo. 8s. 6d.

HISTORY, &c.

Freeman. *A Short History of the Norman Conquest of England.*
By E. A. FREEMAN, M.A. *Second Edition.* . Extra fcap. 8vo. 2s. 6d.

George. *Genealogical Tables illustrative of Modern History.* By
H. B. GEORGE, M.A. *Second Edition, Revised and Enlarged.* Small 4to. 12s.

Kitchin. *A History of France.* With Numerous Maps, Plans, and
Tables. By G. W. KITCHIN. D.D., Dean of Winchester. *Second Edition.*
Vol. 1. To the Year 1453. . . . . . . 10s. 6d.
Vol. 2. From 1453 to 1624. . . . . . . 10s. 6d.
Vol. 3. From 1624 to 1793. . . . . . . 10s. 6d.

Rawlinson. *A Manual of Ancient History.* By GEORGE RAWLINSON, M.A., Camden Professor of Ancient History. *Second Edition.*
Demy 8vo. 14s.

Rogers. *A Manual of Political Economy,* for the use of Schools. By J. E. THOROLD ROGERS, M.P. *Third Edition.* Extra fcap. 8vo. 4s. 6d.

Stubbs. *The Constitutional History of England, in its Origin and Development.* By WILLIAM STUBBS, D.D., Lord Bishop of Chester. Three vols. . . . . Crown 8vo. each 12s.

Stubbs. *Select Charters and other Illustrations of English Constitutional History,* from the Earliest Times to the Reign of Edward I. Arranged and edited by W. STUBBS, D.D. *Fourth Edition.* Crown 8vo. 8s. 6d.

Stubbs. *Magna Carta*: a careful reprint. . . . 4to. *stitched,* 1s.

ART.

Hullah. *The Cultivation of the Speaking Voice.* By JOHN HULLAH.
Extra fcap. 8vo. 2s. 6d.

Maclaren. *A System of Physical Education: Theoretical and Practical.* With 346 Illustrations drawn by A. MACDONALD, of the Oxford School of Art. By ARCHIBALD MACLAREN, the Gymnasium, Oxford. *Second Edition.*
Extra fcap. 8vo. 7s. 6d.

Troutbeck and Dale. *A Music Primer for Schools.* By J. TROUTBECK, M.A., Music Master in Westminster School, (and R. F. DALE, M.A., B. Mus., Assistant Master in Westminster School. . Crown 8vo. 1s. 6d.

Tyrwhitt. *A Handbook of Pictorial Art.* By R. St. J. TYRWHITT, M.A. With coloured Illustrations, Photographs, and a chapter on Perspective by A. MACDONALD. *Second Edition.* . . . 8vo. *half morocco,* 18s.

Student's Handbook to the University and Colleges of Oxford. *Eighth Edition.* . . . . Extra fcap. 8vo. 2s. 6d.

Helps to the Study of the Bible, taken from the *Oxford Bible for Teachers,* comprising Summaries of the several Books, with copious Explanatory Notes and Tables illustrative of Scripture History and the Characteristics of Bible Lands; with a complete Index of Subjects, a Concordance, a Dictionary of Proper Names, and a series of Maps. . . . . Crown 8vo. 3s. 6d.

☞ *All communications relating to Books included in this List, and offers of new Books and new Editions, should be addressed to*

THE SECRETARY TO THE DELEGATES,
CLARENDON PRESS,
OXFORD.

BOOKS FOR SCHOOL LIBRARIES.

An Etymological Dictionary of the English Language, arranged on an Historical Basis. By W. W. SKEAT, M.A. Second Edition. 2*l*. 4*s*.

Shakespeare as a Dramatic Artist. By R. G. MOULTON, M.A. 5*s*.

English Plant Names, from the tenth to the fifteenth Century. By J. EARLE, M.A. 5*s*.

Baedae Historia Ecclesiastica. Edited by G. H. MOBERLY, M.A. 10*s*. 6*d*.

Chapters of Early English Church History. By W. BRIGHT, D.D. 12*s*.

History of the Norman Conquest of England: its Causes and Results. By E. A. FREEMAN, D.C.L. In 6 vols. 5*l*. 9*s*. 6*d*.

The Reign of William Rufus and the Accession of Henry the First. By E. A. FREEMAN, D.C.L. In 2 vols. 1*l*. 16*s*.

Fuller's Church History of Britain. Edited by J. S. BREWER, M.A. In 6 vols. 1*l*. 19*s*.

Burnet's History of the Reformation of the Church of England. New Edition, revised by N. POCOCK, M.A. In 7 vols. 1*l*. 10*s*.

Clarendon's History of the Rebellion and Civil Wars in England, together with his Life, including a Continuation of his History. 1*l*. 2*s*.

A History of England, principally in the Seventeenth Century. Translation edited by G. W. KITCHIN, D.D., and C. W. BOASE, M.A. In 6 vols. 3*l*. 3*s*.

A History of Greece, B.C. 146 to A.D. 1864. By GEORGE FINLAY, LL.D. New Edition, by H. F. TOZER, M.A. In 7 vols. 3*l*. 10*s*.

Italy and her Invaders. By T. HODGKIN, M.A. Vols. I-IV. 3*l*. 8*s*.

Some Account of the Church in the Apostolic Age. By W. W. SHIRLEY, D.D. Second Edition. 3*s*. 6*d*.

Hooker's Works: the text as arranged by JOHN KEBLE, M.A. In 2 vols. 11*s*.

Bacon's Novum Organum. Edited by T. FOWLER, M.A. 14*s*.

Scherer. A History of German Literature. Translated from the Third German Edition by Mrs. F. CONYBEARE. Edited by F. MAX MÜLLER. 2 vols. 21*s*. *Just Published.*

A Course of Lectures on Art. By J. RUSKIN, M.A. 6*s*.

Aspects of Poetry. By J. C. SHAIRP, M.A. 10*s*. 6*d*.

Geology: Chemical, Physical, and Stratigraphical. By JOSEPH PRESTWICH, M.A., F.R.S., F.G.S. In 2 vols. Vol. I. *Chemical and Physical.* Royal 8vo. With Maps and Illustrations. 25*s*.

Geology of Oxford and the Valley of the Thames. By JOHN PHILLIPS, M.A., F.R.S. 1*l*. 1*s*.

A Handbook of Descriptive Astronomy. By G. F. CHAMBERS, F.R.A.S. Third Edition. 1*l.* 8*s.*

A Cycle of Celestial Objects. By Admiral W. H. SMYTH, R.N. Revised, etc. by G. F. CHAMBERS, F.R.A.S. 12*s.*

British Barrows: a Record of the Examination of Sepulchral Mounds in various Parts of England. By W. GREENWELL, M.A., F.S.A. With Appendix, &c. by G. ROLLESTON, M.D., F.R.S. 25*s.*

A Treatise on Rivers and Canals. By L. F. VERNON-HARCOURT, M.A. 2 vols. 21*s.*

Harbours and Docks. By L. F. VERNON-HARCOURT, M.A. 2 vols. 25*s.*

Fragments and Specimens of Early Latin. By J. WORDSWORTH, M.A. 18*s.*

The Roman Poets of the Republic. By W. Y. SELLAR, M.A. 14*s.*

The Roman Poets of the Augustan Age. Virgil. By W. Y. SELLAR, M.A. 9*s.*

Lectures and Essays on Subjects connected with Latin Literature and Scholarship. By H. NETTLESHIP, M.A. 7*s.* 6*d.*

Catullus, a Commentary on. By ROBINSON ELLIS, M.A. 16*s.*

Selections from the less known Latin Poets. By NORTH PINDER, M.A. 15*s.*

A Grammar of the Homeric Dialect. By D. B. MONRO, M.A. 10*s.* 6*d.*

A Manual of Greek Historical Inscriptions. By E. L. HICKS, M.A. 10*s.* 6*d.*

Plato: The Dialogues. Translated into English, with an Analysis and Introduction, by B. JOWETT, M.A. 3*l.* 10*s.*

Thucydides. Translated into English, with Introduction, Marginal Analysis, Notes, and Indices, by B. JOWETT, M.A. 1*l.* 12*s.*

A New English Dictionary on Historical Principles. Founded mainly on the materials collected by the Philological Society. Edited by JAMES A. H. MURRAY, LL.D. Part I. A—ANT. Part II. ANT—BATTEN. 12*s.* 6*d.* each.

𝕷𝖔𝖓𝖉𝖔𝖓: HENRY FROWDE,

OXFORD UNIVERSITY PRESS WAREHOUSE, AMEN CORNER.

𝕰𝖉𝖎𝖓𝖇𝖚𝖗𝖌𝖍: 6, QUEEN STREET.

𝕺𝖝𝖋𝖔𝖗𝖉: CLARENDON PRESS DEPOSITORY,

116, HIGH STREET.

www.ingramcontent.com/pod-product-compliance
Lightning Source LLC
Chambersburg PA
CBHW021623250426
43672CB00037B/378